RADICAL EYE
FOR THE
THE INFIDEL GUY

RADICAL EYE
FOR THE INFIDEL GUY
Inside the Strange World of Militant Islam

KEVIN J. RYAN

 Prometheus Books

59 John Glenn Drive
Amherst, New York 14228–2197

Published 2007 by Prometheus Books

Inquiries should be addressed to
Prometheus Books
59 John Glenn Drive
Amherst, New York 14228–2197
VOICE: 716–691–0133, ext. 207
FAX: 716–564–2711
WWW.PROMETHEUSBOOKS.COM

11 10 09 08 07   5 4 3 2 1

Library of Congress Cataloging-in-Publication Data

Ryan, Kevin J.
    Radical eye for the infidel guy : inside the strange world of militant Islam / by
Kevin J. Ryan.
        p. cm.
    Includes bibliographical references and index.
    ISBN 978–1–59102–507–8 (alk. paper)
    1. Islam—Controversial literature. 2. Islamic fundamentalism. I. Title.

BP169.R93 2007
297.2'7—dc22
                                                                        2007000021

Printed in the United States of America on acid-free paper

CONTENTS

DEVELOPING A RADICAL EYE

If you know that fifteen out of the nineteen Sept. 11 terrorists are from one country and you happen to notice that, it's not profiling, that's minimally observant.[1]

—Comedian Dennis Miller

In 2006, we saw the fifth anniversary of 9/11 and President George W. Bush's formal declaration of a War on Terror. Since the destruction of the World Trade Center there have been some remarkable changes in the world.

In the first five years of the war, the regimes in two nations that were major sponsors of terrorism, Afghanistan and Iraq, have fallen. Both countries have held successful elections and are on their way to becoming—if not Club Meds of liberalism and democracy—reasonably stable constitutional governments where there is a passing nod to human rights, plastic shredders are now used primarily on plastics, and women can go to school.

Though the different factions in Iraq are killing each other at an astonishing rate, the fact is that the average Iraqi is still much safer today than he or she was under Saddam Hussein, who—according to human rights groups—was responsible for the deaths of more than 5,000 of his own people per month.[2] Despite the ongoing violence, more than fifty million people are now better off than they were before and have hope for the future.

In the first five years of the war, Libya saw which way the wind was blowing and *voluntarily* gave up its various weapons of mass destruction programs.

In the first five years of the war, Saudi Arabia took some time off from oppressing its women and from supporting and funding international terrorism to begin fighting terrorists within its own borders. Okay, actually the Saudis still put a high priority on oppressing women and providing ideological support for terrorism, but they did shoot a few terrorists and arrest a few more. It may not seem like much, but for Saudi Arabia, it's great progress. And there's always the possibility that they may eventually kill or arrest terrorists faster than they produce new ones.

In the first five years of the war, Lebanon threw out the terrorist-supporting Syrians who had been occupying the country for decades. Meanwhile, in Iran, student demonstrations and unrest suggest that the nation's theocratic regime's days are numbered, even as President Mahmoud Ahmadinejad rants and blusters on the world stage.

It does seem that we have made significant progress in the War on Terror and are starting to change things for the better in a part of the world that is not known for positive developments.

And yet . . .

Anti-Americanism in the Muslim world and in Europe is at an all-time high. Osama bin Laden still eludes us; terrorists in Iraq continue to exact a toll on civilians and coalition forces. In 2005, terrorists were able to launch the July 7 mass transit attacks in London and the October 1 restaurant bombings in Bali, Indonesia. And in 2006, Islamists killed more than two hundred people in the mass transit attack in Mumbai, India.

So, why is the War on Terror taking so long?

It's a fair question, especially considering that the War on Fascism (better known as World War II) took just under four years from the day that the United States joined the fight until the unconditional surrender of Japan.

And yet we are now entering the fifth year of the War on Terror. What gives?

Part of the problem is in the name we've given this conflict: the *War on Terror*. The fact is that terrorism is a tactic, and you can't fight a war against a tactic because a tactic has no borders, no soldiers, and no political or religious affiliation. Fighting a War on Terror makes no more sense than fighting a *War on Air Support for Ground Troops*.

Thus, the War on Terror is the most inaccurately named war since the Hundred Years' War (which everyone knows lasted 116 years) because, like World War II, the War on Terror is really a war on an ideology.

In World War II, we fought to eradicate and discredit an ideology: fascism. The war united virtually all citizens of the Allied nations in a massive military, industrial, and cultural effort. Today, fascism is thoroughly discredited and nearly extinct—and will be completely finished when the final, remaining fascist regime in Syria finally kicks the bucket.

However, in the War on Terror, people in the United States and other coalition countries are curiously divided on the war, with little agreement on the identity of the enemy. In the War on Terror, we resist even naming the ideology we're fighting.

Yet, on 9/11 Osama bin Laden and al Qaeda were fighting for this unnamed ideology. The bombers in Madrid were fighting for this ideology. The killers of children in Beslan, Russia, were fighting for this ideology. The subway and bus bombers in London were fighting for this ideology. The beheaders in Iraq are still fighting for this ideology.

Some have called it fundamentalist Islam, but that's also an inaccurate term since a majority of Muslims could legitimately be called fundamentalists. In fact, the term I use for nonfundamentalist Muslims is *Not-Muslims*. A better description of the ideology we're fighting would be militant Islam or radical Islam.

This radical belief system is centuries old. In modern times it has fed decades of acts of international violence—from the terrorist attack at the Munich Olympics in 1972, to the bombing of the Marine barracks in Lebanon in 1983, to the hijacking of the *Achille Lauro* cruise ship in 1985, to the crash of Pan Am Flight 103 in Lockerbie, Scotland, in 1988, to the first attack on the World Trade Center in 1993, to the 1998 attacks on two American embassies in Africa, to the attack on the USS *Cole* in 2000, and finally to 9/11, the suicide bombings in Iraq today, and dozens killed in riots and other violence related to the publication of the Danish cartoons of the Prophet Muhammad.

And the fact is that the overwhelming majority of terrorists—from Saudi Arabia to Indonesia to Chechnya—have one thing in common: their religion. As the Muslim journalist Abdel Rahman al-Rashed said, "It is a certain fact that not all Muslims are terrorists, but it is equally certain, and exceptionally painful, that almost all terrorists are Muslims."[3]

An inconvenient fact.

No one wants to make war on a religion, but there do seem to be a lot of irate people who share a faith and want to bring about the destruction of Western civilization. But who exactly are these radicals? This question is one of the biggest challenges in the War on Terror, and it shows that there is some value in learning about the history, culture, and—most importantly—location of these radicals, because without this information it's more difficult to program the right coordinates into a smart bomb.

The process of determining what makes a radical begins with his belief system, which contains a holy law handed down directly by Allah—a holy law that radicals want to spread over the entire globe. They have a term for the propagation of their ideology. They call it *jihad*, which, according to ranking Middle Eastern scholar Bernard Lewis, is an unlimited religious obligation that "would continue until all the world had either adopted the Muslim faith or submitted to Muslim rule."

Now we are getting somewhere.

In some cases, the radicals are a relatively small part of the landscape in more or less secular countries like Turkey. In other cases, they run the whole show like the Wahhabists of Saudi Arabia, the Taliban who formerly ruled Afghanistan, and the current Shiite rulers of Iran. In any case, the extremists are not that hard to spot if you know what to look for.

In a way, radicals are like water towers. I will explain . . .

Back in the early 1980s, I did a college internship in New York City at One Liberty Plaza, a fifty-four-story black tower that was located half a block east of the south tower of the World Trade Center. While I was there, my boss took me aside one day and pointed out a window, from which I could see the tops of many smaller buildings. "Look on the roofs, see the water towers?" he asked. I looked and, sure enough, there was a water tower on the roof of just about every building more than a few stories tall.

"They're invisible until someone points them out to you, but from now on you won't be able to look at the city without noticing them." It was true. Once you see the water towers, you can't *un-see* them.

Radicals are like that. Once you learn to recognize the signs—their beliefs, their behavior, their patterns, their code words, and the masks they wear—it's impossible to watch or read a news report about the Middle East without seeing radicals at work, even if it's a story about the most recent "peace" proposal. It's also impossible to look at much of a thousand years of European history—even the parts that you didn't think had anything to do with Islam—quite the same way. And finally, you won't be able to listen to innocuous statements about "interfaith dialogue" or "tolerance" or "Islamic outreach programs" without seeing the water towers lurking in the background.

My wife has a friend in England who half-seriously suggested that the problems of Islamic terrorism and interreligious conflict would go away if "we all just converted to Islam."

Radical Eye for the Infidel Guy will take a look at what that might be like. We'll survey several different aspects of life under radical and moderate Islamic regimes—from criminal justice and the rights and roles of women in society to military history, diversity, education, economics, and Islamic family values.

TOP TEN THINGS YOU PROBABLY DIDN'T KNOW ABOUT ISLAM THAT THE EXPERTS ARE IN NO RUSH TO TELL YOU

1. The Prophet Muhammad, the founder of the Religion of Peace, was a military leader and virtually all of his battles were acts of aggression against his neighbors.
2. The worldwide jihad launched by the Religion of Peace has involved more territory and a higher percentage of the world's population than either World War I or World War II.
3. The Crusades were not wars of aggression against the Islamic world but defensive wars waged by a Europe under siege from Muslim jihadists. This fact calls into question decades of historical misinformation and, perhaps even more disturbingly, the accuracy of the recent big-budget Ridley Scott film *Kingdom of Heaven*.
4. Islamic holy law and the possibility of the death penalty for religious "thought crimes" recently made inroads into North America—in Canada of all places.
5. "Honor killing" or murder at the hands of a father or a brother for crimes as innocent as suspicion of kissing a boy is a leading cause of death for young women in a number of Muslim nations.
6. The moderate Muslim organization, the Council on American-Islamic Relations, or CAIR, is, according to its own Web site, a fundamentalist group that believes the Qur'an is the

A study of the radical world is heartbreaking, infuriating, tragic, and almost comical in its extremism and contradictions. Theirs is a world ruled by hatred, casual murder, medieval-style torture, and a nearly pathological misogyny, where women are beaten on the street if they are caught showing an ankle, where they have their fingertips cut off if they wear nail polish, and where they face a death sentence exact word of Allah. This would, of course, include passage 4:34, which says, "Men are in charge of women, because Allah hath made the one of them to excel the other," and passage 67:5, which says, "Allah made the stars in the sky into missiles to throw at devils."

7. The Qur'an enshrines the institution of slavery, and Muhammad said that slaves—particularly female slaves—taken in battles of conquest are a "gift from Allah." (Review previous entry for more information about CAIR's beliefs about the accuracy of the Qur'an.)

8. There are more actual slaves serving Muslim masters in the world today than there were in the United States at the beginning of the Civil War.

9. The headscarves worn by Muslim women in Iran and in many other parts of the world are Christian, not Islamic, religious symbols. Thus, some of the Muslims in France and Germany now suing the European governments to keep their religious headgear are fighting for the right to wear Christian attire, once again proving the desperate need for irony education and awareness in the radical Islamic world.

10. Though Islam has been called the Religion of Tolerance, the historical Islamic system under which the "People of the Book" were "protected" and "tolerated" by Muslim rulers was actually the largest and most pervasive system of religious-based persecution in history and served as a partial inspiration for the Nazi treatment of the Jews in the 1930s.

if they are even suspected of talking to or meeting with a man who is not their husband.

And what is the reward in the afterlife for men who live piously according to radical Islamic principles? The company of beautiful and highly sexualized young women, specifically seventy-two extremely hot virgins with renewable virginities. This, of course, once again proves the desperate need for a mandatory course in Irony Awareness and Education in the radical world.

By the time we're done, we'll have a pretty good idea of who the bad guys are in this new/old war. And with our new Radical Eye, we'll also see just how deeply their thinking has permeated the larger body of the billion-plus Muslims in the world.

Some of the things I will show you will probably surprise you. There is much about Islamic history and current events that no one likes to talk about. Likewise, some of the things I will tell you will be uncomfortable or inconvenient in the context of the Western dream of multiculturalism in which no culture or religion is superior to any other, but the truth is the truth, and, as we will see, it can play an important part in the ongoing struggle against international terrorism.

Now let's pop in our Radical Eye, take a closer look, and see what we find peeking up over the skyline.

Chapter One

WAR PART I

Or, How to Found a Religion of Peace and Declare War on the Rest of the World

"Fight in the name of Allah and in the way of Allah. Fight against those who disbelieve in Allah. Make a Holy war . . ."[4]

—The Prophet Muhammad

IN SEARCH OF TRUE ISLAM

On 9/11 more than two thousand innocent men, women, and children were murdered by devoutly religious men who claimed they were doing God's work. But "Islam is a religion of peace," George Bush assured us, as did several other world leaders and various "experts" on Islam.

That tragic day was for many Americans and Westerners the first introduction to Islam. Maybe it was an aberration; maybe it was as the experts described—just a few sick people twisting a perfectly peaceful religion to their evil ends.

Then, when the United States invaded Afghanistan we learned that the Taliban, who had built their society on their understanding of Islamic principles, had been terrorizing the Afghani people for seven years, murdering dissenters, confiscating property, beating people publicly for minor religious infractions, and selling women into sexual slavery.

But Islam is a religion of peace.

Then we noticed that there was a spate of homicidal bombers killing innocents in Israel. Apparently, this had been going on since 1994, when Yasser Arafat signed the framework of agreements designed to bring peace between the Palestinians and Israel.

But Islam is a religion of peace.

In Bali, Indonesia, on October 12, 2002, over two hundred people were killed and hundreds more injured in an attack directed at the infidels in a nightclub. Most of the victims were vacationing mothers from Australia.

But Islam is a religion of peace.

In March of 2003, United States and coalition forces invaded Iraq and quickly deposed dictator Saddam Hussein. The coalition found overwhelming evidence of systematic murder and torture of innocents, as well as hundreds of thousands of bodies in mass graves—many of whom were women and small children. When the world learned of this, many Islamic governments as well as large sectors of the Muslim "street" responded with outrage—directed *against* the United States. From virtually all Islamic nations, terrorists flocked to Iraq to fight the coalition and reinstate the murderous Ba'athist regime. These fighters cite the call of Islam as their motivation. In fact, Osama bin Laden himself said that his primary reason for his war against America and 9/11 was religious—the presence of American Infidel soldiers on the "holy" Arabian peninsula.

But Islam is a religion of peace.

Also in March 2004, Muslim terrorists bombed a train station in Madrid, Spain, killing 191 people and injuring 1,800. The terrorists were motivated by a desire for their own Muslim nation.

But Islam is a religion of peace.

In September 2004, Muslim Chechnyan separatists attacked a school in Beslan, Russia and took hundreds of students and adults hostage. They denied their captives food and water, subjecting them to extreme physical and psychological abuse for three days. When the terrorists caused an explosion and the surviving children ran for their lives, the attackers shot them in the back. Later we learned that the Chechnyan murderers had international support from Muslims in Saudi Arabia and elsewhere.

But Islam is a religion of peace.

Also in 2004, we learned about the crisis in the Darfur region of the Sudan, where Arab Muslims committed genocide, rape, and general abuse against the local black Muslim population. We also heard about the previous Sudanese genocide committed against Christians in that nation, where the victims number in the millions.

But Islam is a religion of peace.

In July 2005, Islamic terrorists killed fifty-two people when they bombed three London subway trains and a bus. Two weeks later, another group of Muslim radicals attempted, and failed, to repeat the attack. And then, almost exactly one year later, in July 2006, militant Islamists killed more than two hundred people in a mass transit attack in Mumbai, India.

But Islam is a religion of peace.

Unsophisticated people without a full understanding of the context, history, and nuance of each of these situations might conclude that Islam is not really peaceful—or at least not *primarily* so. In fact, it's tempting to conclude that Islam is downright pugnacious.

But which is it? The overwhelming number of acts of murder and brutality, or the handful of experts who tell us about Islam? The question remains: Is Islam really a religion of peace?

Here's an illuminating statistic: Muslims were involved in twenty-six of the fifty ethnic conflicts of the 1990s, according to Harvard's Samuel P. Huntington, author of *The Clash of Civilization and the Remaking of World Order*. He goes on to say, "Muslims make up about one-fifth of the world's population, but in the 1990s they have been far more involved in inter-group violence than the people of any other civilization. The evidence is overwhelming."[5]

By now, we can almost hear the voice of political correctness asking: *But Islam is a religion of peace. It has been perverted, or something . . . um, right?*

Most Americans and westerners would like to believe that Islam is intrinsically peaceful, but plenty of evidence has been piling up to suggest otherwise. Terrorists and radical Muslim spiritual leaders are singularly unhelpful in convincing the world of their tranquil, nonsectarian agenda. And they virtually always evoke their religion of peace when they commit or justify murder. In fact, "Allah Akbar!" (God is Great!) are the last words of almost all homicide bombers. Clearly, these radicals all think *they* are practicing "true Islam."

Who's right? The experts we see on TV, or the terrorists themselves? Are radicals practicing "true Islam" or fake, brutal, and murderous not-really-real Islam?

The search for true Islam takes us to the Muslim prophet Muhammad, who founded Islam and the first Islamic state. We'll also look at the Qur'an, the holy book the Prophet revealed to the world, which is the basis of Islam. Muslims believe that the Prophet Muhammad was Allah's chosen messenger and today still consider him "the perfect role model in all situations." Thus, if terrorists have really hijacked a noble, peaceful religion, then we can't go wrong by going back to these two sources, Muhammad and the Qur'an, which are the basis of everything that followed.

MUHAMMAD: ISLAM'S GROUND ZERO

Born in what is now Saudi Arabia in 570, Muhammad was a merchant in the pagan town of Mecca, whose chief industry was catering to the many pilgrims who came to worship their different gods, see various pagan artifacts, and visit shrines—including the "black stone" that now sits in the cube-shaped building called the Ka'ba that is at the center of the Mosque in Mecca, the holiest mosque in all of Islam.

Apparently, Muhammad would often seek the solitude of a cave in the nearby mountains and on one of these trips in 610 he was visited by the angel Gabriel who told him that he was the Prophet of Allah, the one true God, and that it would be his responsibility to spread Allah's final revelation to man. Gabriel would visit Muhammad from time to time for the rest of his life, revealing more of Allah's will, which he conveniently provided in Arabic.

Since Muhammad could neither read nor write, he would recite the verses given to him by Gabriel to friends who wrote them down on whatever was handy—anything from leaves, to rocks, to goat and camel bones. These verses, or *Suras*, form the Qur'an (a word which means, literally, *recitation*). According to Islamic doctrine, the Qur'an follows and supercedes Allah's previous revelations of the Old and New Testaments of the Bible, which Muslims also recognize but see as precursors to the "true faith," Islam.

Now, you could make the argument that even if he did speak to an angel, Muhammad might not have remembered Allah's words precisely and that the people writing them down might have changed things slightly, as happens in the children's game "telephone." According to Paul Fregosi in his book *Jihad in the West*, one of the transcribers, Abdallah ibn Saad, would invent his own verses to add to the ones that the Prophet dictated to him. When he was found out, he fled and barely escaped Muhammad's wrath.[6]

A few years after Muhammad's death there was an effort made to compile a definitive record of the Qur'an, and all other versions were destroyed. This new Qur'an was not organized by theme, or even chronologically, but its 114 Suras were organized—more or less—from the longest to the shortest.

The Suras vary wildly in form and structure and, according to Qur'anic scholar Gerd R. Puin, "every fifth sentence or so simply doesn't make sense . . . the fact is that a fifth of the Qur'anic text is *just incomprehensible*"[7] (italics in original), even in Arabic. The Islamic holy book is also replete with contradictions, the most famous being the conflicting messages to "kill the Infidel where you find him," and other, more tolerant statements to respect "People of the Book," or to "bear with them and wish them Peace."

Islamic scholars invented a concept called *abrogation* to explain these apparent and sometimes egregious contradictions. Abrogation says that being all-powerful, Allah is more than able to revise his revelation as he sees fit, and that later suras will supersede earlier ones. The problem is that since the suras are not organized chronologically, there's no reliable way to know which ones came first. Careful readers will remember that Allah and the Qur'an are eternal and unchanging, and they might ask why Allah would want or need to revise his own will over time if He is eternal and stands outside time, but that kind of talk will not get you invited to many dinner parties in Saudi Arabia.

Reason would lead you to conclude that perhaps, just perhaps, the Qur'an is not the precise word of God. Even if Muhammad did speak to an angel, maybe there was a bit of human error in the dictation and/or the transcription and compilation of the book.

In fact, according to Qur'anic scholar Toby Lester, "a major theological debate in fact arose within Islam in the later eighth century, pitting those who believed in the Koran as the 'uncreated' and eternal Word of God against those who believed in it as created in time, like anything that isn't God himself." But after a brief period where the Qur'an was believed to be metaphorical rather than literal, by the end of the tenth century the doctrine of "inimitability" was firmly established, making it clear that the Qur'an was the actual Word of Allah and, in fact, part of Allah himself. Thus, to deny the accuracy of any part of the Qur'an is to deny God himself.[8]

Though Muslims believe that Muhammad was accurately relaying the word and will of Allah, some historians have speculated that he wasn't actually visited by the angel Gabriel and was simply trying to bring Judeo-Christian–style monotheism to the Arab people. Unquestionably, Muhammad was an Arab patriot and wanted his people to have the stature and political might he thought they deserved. As such, he wanted to forge a new Arab empire on par with the Persian and Byzantine empires. Thus, some of the verses in the Qur'an—like the prohibition against the common Bedouin practice of killing female babies at birth—are seen by some as an effort to eliminate some of the more barbaric practices of the time. And the murdering of female infants was one of the customs that cost Arabs significant respect from the other civilizations of the day.

The Qur'an also codified many seventh-century Arab customs and norms. Doing this in a religious text insured not only that the spiritual elements of Islam could be spread, but that many cultural aspects of Arab society could be propagated as well.

Many of the people who maintain that Islam is a religion of peace point to the various sections of the Qur'an that talk about peace or mercy, though a number of these were cribbed more or less directly from the Old and New Testaments of the Bible. The bottom line is that the Qur'an is about 135,000 words (about twice as long as this book) and is thus reasonably complex and can support a number of different interpretations. You could certainly cobble together a theology from the gentler parts of the book, but you would have to do quite a bit of work to ignore the clearly barbaric portions.

The point is there is some wiggle room in the Qur'an, so the best place to start in the search for "true Islam" is the life and works of Muhammad himself. All devout Muslims believe him to be nearly a "perfect man" whose life they can only hope to emulate. Certainly, the Prophet himself must have practiced true Islam or something pretty darn close to it.

IT'S NOT JUST A SET OF
RELIGIOUS AND SPIRITUAL PRINCIPLES,
IT'S THE LAW

In the early days of this new religion, Muhammad started amassing followers among his friends and family in Mecca. His monotheistic religion was immediately at odds with the old guard in Mecca, whose life and economy were built around the business generated by pilgrims visiting the pagan shrines, and monotheism would dramatically hurt that business.

In 622, twelve to thirteen years after Muhammad's first meeting with Gabriel, he moved himself, his family, and about sixty families of his followers to the city of Medina where he was welcomed. This would become an important event in Islamic history and the year of the migration is the beginning of the Islamic calendar.

In Medina, Muhammad functioned as both a political and religious leader. As scholar Bernard Lewis puts it in his book *The Middle East: A Brief History of the Last 2,000 Years*, as head of the Muslim *Umma*, or community, Muhammad "promulgated laws, dispensed justice, collected taxes, conducted diplomacy, made war, and made peace. The *Umma*, which began as a community, had become a state. It would soon become an empire."[9] This status set Muhammad firmly apart from previous religious leaders like Jesus or Moses. It created a precedent that has continued to the present day in many Islamic nations like Iran, where leaders hold both political and religious power.

The Qur'an, as it continued to be revealed to Muhammad, expressed Allah's will in a number of religious, social, political, legal, and economic areas. People in the West tend to see Islam as just one of the three monotheistic religions and not really so different from Judaism or Christianity, but Islam is fundamentally different in that it is as much a political system as it is a religious one. Saudi Arabia, for instance, has no constitution other than the Qur'an and Islamic holy law (called *Shariah*), which is derived from a few books of collected stories from Muhammad's life. There can be no separation of church and state because they are one and the same.

It was Jesus Christ himself who gave us the notion of a separation of church and state when he said, "Render unto Caesar the things that are Caesar's and to God the things that are God's." For Muhammad and for anyone who follows his example, there is no such distinction. In fact, there cannot be.

When people talk about moderate or reformed Islam, they discuss making it compatible with Western notions of religion as an individual matter between the worshiper and his or her God, and a key to individual and personal human comfort and salvation. But for many Muslims, devotion must include strict adherence to Islamic holy law, which spells out—among other things—specific punishments for certain crimes like the amputation of hands for thieves and the death penalty for people who leave Islam. It also details the proper treatment of slaves.

So getting back to my wife's friend's suggestion that the rest of the world convert to Islam to make peace with Muslims, it's clear that conversion would entail more than just praying five times a day while facing Mecca.

There's a special term for a version of Islam that is strictly spiritual and not concerned with politics or law, it's called *Not-Islam*. Certainly it's not Islam as it was practiced by the Prophet.

Again, we can almost hear the PC voices saying: *That's absurd! You don't expect us to believe that anyone outside of a small group of radicals are really fundamentalists, do you?*

For an answer, I'll point you to the best-known self-styled "moderate" Muslim group in the United States, the Council on American-Islamic Relations or CAIR. On their Web site they say very clearly that "Islam is both a religion and a *complete way of life*"[10] (italics mine). We're still early in our journey, but even our developing Radical Eye has no trouble seeing through that radical doublespeak.

True, there are some Muslims who prefer to ignore the political and legal side of Islam and call for the elimination of the nonspiritual aspects of the faith. In many traditional Muslim countries, people who express this view publicly are often characterized by a general lividity of the soft tissues followed by a stiffening of the muscles—*also known as rigor mortis*. In Islam, leaving the faith, known as apostasy, or even disavowing a portion of Islamic teachings can be punishable by death. Thus, apostates often suffer from a condition I call S.L.O.H. or Sudden Loss of Head.

Thus, Muslims who are not fundamentalists fall into the category of "Not Muslims." If they happen to live in many parts of the Middle East, they also fall into the category of not alive.

MASSACRING FOR PEACE

Early in his career as a religious leader and a statesman, the Prophet made the first use of what would become an important political and economic tool in the ongoing effort to spread Islam: the massacre. Early in his days in Medina, he was confronted with the problem of the Jewish Beni Qoreiga tribe who unreasonably withheld their support of his absolute rule in all matters. In response, the Prophet had between six hundred and eight hundred men of the tribe beheaded, an ambitious task that "started in the morning and went on all day and into the night by torchlight,"[11] according to an account in the book *Jihad in the West*. However, Muhammad didn't stay the whole time. He left the execution early to force himself on the pretty young wife of one of the victims.

The rest of the women and children were sold into slavery—which for attractive women and young boys was often sexual in nature. All of the property from the tribe was taken by the Muslim faithful and divided equally, except for a 20 percent cut that went to the Prophet himself. Fans of the *The Sopranos* will recognize this sort of arrangement, in which members of the organization "kick up" a set percentage to the boss.

You could argue that, though harsh, this sort of thing went on all the time in that part of the world in those days and that's true. Some critics might say that telling this story is unfair and doesn't provide relevant historical and cultural context. This is what I call the *anything sounds bad when you put it* that *way defense*. But I would argue there are some things that sound bad no matter how you say them and I think widowing and then forcing himself on a woman in the same day falls pretty squarely into that category.

And remember, to this day the Prophet is revered as the "perfect role model in all situations" whose life ordinary Muslims can only hope to emulate. Moreover, the Qur'an mentions this massacre directly. "God praised the killings and Muhammad became a foe to be feared,"[12] says Fregosi. And don't forget that since the Qur'an is the uncreated word of Allah and accurately represents Allah's will, Allah himself must have approved of the massacre.

Muhammad's life as a religious leader and a statesman is remarkably well documented because of a massive effort a century or two after his death to collect everything he said and did. These narratives and quotes are called the *Hadith*, or traditions, and form the other Islamic holy texts that are the basis for Islamic holy law. As a result, it is impossible to separate Muhammad's example as enshrined in the Hadith from the practice of Islam by most devout Muslims.

The problem here is that Muhammad, from an objective perspective, was very much a product of his time. And seventh-century Arabia (like seventh-century Europe, or Africa, or South America, etc.) was a tough neighborhood run by tyrants. What made Muhammad unique among Arab leaders of the day was his commitment to monotheism. But like his peers, he was a political ruler who was as harsh as any of his day.

The sad fact is that radicals who wish to justify murder can find many examples from the Prophet's life. In a recent interview, London-based radical Dr. Hani Al-Siba'i justified slaughter as an Islamic tactic because Muhammad used it as well. Dr. Al-Siba'i said, "The Prophet drove nails into and gouged out the eyes of people from the 'Urayna Tribe. They were merely a group of thieves who stole from sheepherders, and the Prophet drove nails into them and threw them into the Al-Hrara area, and left them there to die. He blinded them and cut off their opposite legs and arms. This is what the Prophet did on a trifling matter."[13]

SLAVERY: ISLAM'S HOLY INSTITUTION

The Qur'an also shows a cheerful acceptance of slavery. There are a number of verses pertaining to slaves. "Prophet, We have made lawful to you the wives to whom you have granted dowries and the slave girls whom God has given you as booty" (sura 33:50). Thus, slaves are not only allowed, but they should be considered a gift from Allah.

WHAT WOULD MUHAMMAD DO? #1

A few years ago, bracelets and T-shirts with the legend WWJD? (What Would Jesus Do?) became popular among Christians, mostly young people. The idea was for the faithful to measure their own behavior against what they think Jesus himself would do in a given situation. Even those most fearful of the dreaded Christian right would argue that it's not a bad way to think. Whatever your opinion of Christianity in practice, during his life Christ himself gave the world a peaceful example and the instruction to "love thy neighbor as thyself."

For Muslims, the Hadith serves the same purpose, revealing standards of behavior based on what the Prophet himself said and did over the course of his lifetime. Imagine this scenario: you are the ruler of a big seventh-century Arabian town. You hear that a local Jewish merchant has a large sum of gold buried somewhere. Naturally, you have your lieutenants bring him before you and demand he give up the gold. When the man refuses, you have him tortured, gradually increasing the level of the physical abuse until he dies, never revealing the hiding place of the gold. After having him beheaded, you order that his attractive young wife be brought to you.

Confronted with this recent widow do you:

a. Beg her forgiveness for your overenthusiastic gold collection practices.

b. Try to cheer her up by pretending to pull a coin from her ear.

c. Ask her to help clean up the terrible mess her husband left in the torture chamber.

d. Take her to your bed and force her to become your concubine, later expressing surprise when she refuses to become one of your wives.[14]

If you chose option "d" you have chosen the path Muhammad took when confronted with the same situation.

Again, we can hear the PC voices asking: *Okay, what about the Old Testament of the Bible? There was plenty of barbarity and even slavery there, right?*

As a matter of fact, there's a letter running around the Internet that pokes fun at Christian fundamentalist thinking that says, "Leviticus 25:44 states that I may indeed possess slaves, both male and female, provided they are purchased from neighboring nations. A friend of mine claims this applies to Mexicans, but not Canadians. Can you clarify? Why can't I own Canadians?"

It's funny but not relevant here because nobody today even in the much-maligned Christian right is trying to take us back to the days of Leviticus. However, there are a number of Islamic countries in the world where seventh-century Islamic law is in force, with more than half a billion people living under its rule in some form. Slavery is openly practiced with the full backing and support of the Muslim elite in the Sudan, Niger, parts of Nigeria, and a number of provinces in sub-Saharan Africa. There are also a large number of Muslims working day and night to bring Shariah to relatively secular states like Pakistan and Turkey—and even Canada.

Interestingly, in the West, the antislavery and abolitionist movements were mostly led by Christian religious groups. In the Islamic world, the most religious states like Saudi Arabia were the most reluctant to give up the institution because it so clearly meets with Muhammad's and the Qur'an's approval. In fact, it was only under pressure from the West that slavery was finally made illegal in Saudi Arabia in the 1960s.

Imagine that. When the Beatles were first storming the charts, there were still legal slaves on the Arabian Peninsula. Today, Saudi Arabia is a country of twenty-four million people that imports an almost exclusively infidel labor force of eight million, and some Islamic traditions refuse to die completely there. According to Human Rights Watch, "Migrant workers in the purportedly modern society that the kingdom has become continue to suffer extreme forms of labor exploitation that sometimes rise to slavery-like conditions."[15]

Human trafficking has been in the news quite a bit lately. Certainly, there are non-Muslim slavers and traffickers in the world today. However, only Muslims can claim to be operating in accordance with their religion and God's will. According to news reports, in 2004 in Iraq, radical Shiite cleric Muqtada al-Sadr told his followers that anyone capturing a female British soldier could keep her as a slave. In 2002, prominent Saudi Arabian government official cleric Shaikh Saad al-Buraik said, "Muslim Brothers in Palestine, do not have any mercy neither compassion on the Jews, their blood, their money, their flesh. Their women are yours to take, legitimately. God made them yours. Why don't you enslave their women?"[16]

I don't want to force my Western values on anyone else, but I feel very comfortable maintaining that slavery is just plain wrong, even with respect to Canadians.

ISLAM: IT'S NOT JUST FOR MUSLIMS!

Getting back to the Prophet's massacre of an entire tribe in the name of Allah, you could also argue that all that killing and enslaving was an unpleasant but necessary move to remove political opposition. However, murder was a tool that Muhammad also used for personal gain. In fact, that massacre made him a rich man overnight and established another reason to spread Islam through violence: the profit motive.

The institution of the raid goes way back in Arabian Bedouin history. In fact, in pre-Islamic times raids on neighboring tribes and caravans were a significant factor in Bedouin economic life. In that regard, Muhammad was no different than his forefathers, but to give credit where credit is due, he managed to combine his desire to spread his religious and political system with this Arab tradition, making plundering an art form and creating a historically unprecedented method of capturing treasure and slaves: the jihad, the spread of Islam by force or any other means.

Through the Qur'an, Muhammad firmly established the idea of the supremacy of Islam and the responsibility of Muslims to wage jihad. Scholar Bat Ye'or identified a number of key Qur'anic principles that form the building blocks of jihad ideology: "The pre-eminence of Islam over other religions (9:33); Islam is the true religion of Allah (3:17) and it should reign over all mankind (34:27); the *Umma* [Islamic community] forms the party of Allah and is perfect (3:106), having been chosen above all peoples on earth it alone is qualified to rule, and thus elected by Allah to guide the world (35:37). The pursuit of *Jihad*, until this goal [the *Umma* ruling the world] will be achieved, is an obligation (8:40)."[17]

Taken together, these passages of the Qur'an form the basis of jihad ideology (or theology, if you prefer), which is nothing less than a declaration of war on the rest of the world. And with these clear imperatives came the promise, in the Qur'an, of a guarantee of victory from Allah himself. As the Qur'an says, "And never will Allah grant to the unbelievers a way (to triumph) over the believers." And this is not idle boasting on Muhammad's part. For a thousand years, the jihad was a serious threat to the Western world; it has emerged as one of the most destructive forces in history, overrunning the Middle East, Africa, Asia, and fully half of Europe before it was finally stopped in the seventeenth century, only to reappear in the twentieth.

Here is a favorite sura from the Qur'an for people who like to defend Islam as a religion of peace: "Fight in the way of Allah against those who fight against you, but begin not hostilities. Lo! Allah loveth not aggressors" (2:190). That sounds pleasant and peaceful and suggests that Islam tells believers they may fight only in self-defense. However, once again, we run into the troubling reality of Muhammad's example.

The fact is that from the beginning Muhammad interpreted self-defense fairly, um, broadly and decided that it included the right to attack unarmed settlements that were absolutely no threat to him, his territory, or to Islam. Within ten years after his migration from Mecca to Medina, Muhammad and his followers had conquered half of the

MYTH ABOUT ISLAM #1:
The True Meaning of "Jihad"
Is a Personal or Spiritual Struggle.

You may have heard this refrain from Western-media-friendly Muslim clerics and experts. According to these sources, the term *jihad* has been perverted or "hijacked" to become synonymous with an armed holy war to spread Islam by force. You may also have heard of a young Harvard student named Zayed Yasin who caused some controversy when he planned to deliver a commencement speech called "My American Jihad"—less than a year after the 9/11 terrorist attack.

Yasin was apparently dumbfounded by the negative reaction to his use of the term *jihad*, which makes us wonder if Harvard's standards are perhaps getting a tad lax. Remember, Yasin was not only graduating from Harvard, but he had accomplished enough there that he was invited to give a commencement speech. And he really thought this topic would be a good idea.

Regardless, Yasin said he wanted to take back the *real* meaning of the word and present "Jihad as a moral and a personal struggle to do the right thing."[18] The problem is that a *moral struggle* has nothing to do with the *real* meaning of *jihad*, which—as it turns out—really *is* an armed struggle to spread Islam by force. According to Bernard Lewis, the Islamic concept of jihad has from the beginning been about holy war—emphasis on *war*—that was "a religious obligation that would continue until all the world had either adopted the Muslim faith or submitted to Muslim rule."[19]

To be fair, one of the relatively new and relatively minor

Arabian Peninsula, including the Prophet's home city of Mecca. It's worth pointing out that virtually all of Muhammad's battles were ones he started. During his ten years of conquest, the Prophet divided the world into two distinct units, *Dar al-Islam* (House of Islam), where meanings of the word *jihad* may have something to do with a spiritual struggle, but unfortunately Osama bin Laden and his friends hadn't gotten the memo on the peaceful nature of jihad and went ahead with their plans for 9/11. According to European author Wolfgang Bruno, the notion that jihad refers to an "inner, spiritual struggle" comes from a "single, weak Hadith of doubtful authenticity." Whereas "there are nearly 200 references to Jihad in the most standard collection of *Hadith*, Sahih al-Bukhari, and all assume that Jihad means warfare."[20]

And today there are the many wild-eyed radical Muslim clerics living in both the Middle East and the West who preach violent not-so-much-spiritual jihad, like the British imam who recently implored Muslim youth in England to join the jihad, saying that dead mujahideen (holy warriors) are "calling you and shouting to you from far distant places: al jihad, al jihad. They say to you my dear Muslim brothers, 'Where is your weapon, where is your weapon?' Come on to the jihad."[21] An astute reader will see that he is almost certainly not using *jihad* to refer to a spiritual struggle.

No one has a problem with pious people having nice quiet, spiritual struggles. It's when they commit mass murder in the name of their God and their religion that we get upset. So I say we make a deal with the Muslim community: we'll accept that the term *jihad* has nothing to do with violence—when large numbers of Muslims themselves stop defining the word exclusively by violence and use it to justify the beheading of our mechanics, telecommunications workers, aid workers, and journalists as well as the disemboweling of our women on their highways as they cry, "Allah Akbar!"

Muslims were required to play nicely with one another, and *Dar al-Harb* (House of War), where Muslims were not only free to make war but required to do so to spread Islam.

Muhammad died in 632 and was immediately succeeded as

FUN FACTS ABOUT MUHAMMAD

- Though the Qur'an, as relayed by Muhammad himself, allows Muslim men to take no more than four wives, Muhammad had eleven. According to the Qur'an, this was a right to be reserved only for him.
- Muhammad's youngest wife was six when he married her, though to be fair the marriage was not consummated until three years later.
- The Prophet once saw his daughter-in-law bathing (she was the wife of his adopted son) and wanted to marry her. However, public and family opinion was against the union. Miraculously, Muhammad revealed a new verse of the Qur'an that allowed a man to marry his daughter-in-law provided she divorced his son first.
- After a squabble with a few of his wives, Muhammad revealed a new verse of the Qur'an that said that if Muhammad divorced any of his wives, Allah would give him even better ones.
- In still another verse of the Qur'an, Muhammad revealed that his wives would be punished doubly for lewdness "and that is easy for Allah."
- Muhammad was a big believer in slavery and owned many slaves himself.
- The founder of the "Religion of Peace" led more military campaigns than Napoleon Bonaparte.[22]

caliph—religious and political ruler of the growing empire—by the father of his favorite wife, Aisha. Caliphs were absolute rulers of the Islamic Empire for life—though not for long in many cases, but more on that in a moment. The first four successors to Muhammad are, according to Bernard Lewis, "the rightly guided ones," and the period of their combined reigns is regarded by Sunni Muslims as a "golden age, second in sanctity, only to the lifetime of the Prophet himself."[23]

It is worth pointing out that it is impossible to overstate the reverence that Muslims hold for this period in their history.

It is also worth pointing out that by any reasonable standard this was a remarkably violent time and three of the four first caliphs were murdered.

There you have it. At best, the Qur'an seems ambiguous on the issue of peace. And Muhammad's example is certainly not a peaceful one. Getting back to the question "Is Islam a religion of peace?" well, it's doesn't look good for peace so far. And certainly, if you define "true Islam" as the kind of Islam practiced by the Prophet, then it's hard to make a case for peace. However, the religion has had a long history since the death of the Prophet. Let's see what Muslims did with Muhammad's legacy before we rush to judgment.

Chapter Two

WOMEN'S RIGHTS

Or, What Size Stick to Use to Beat Your Wife

Permitting women to leave the home, so that they rub up against men in the marketplaces and talk with people other than their chaperones—with some even exposing parts of their bodies prohibited from exposure—are forbidden acts, a disgrace, and lead to destruction.[24]

—Sheikh Muhammad Al-Nimr,
leading Saudi cleric

WOMEN: PROTECTING ISLAM'S DELICATE FLOWERS

Recently a Saudi Arabian television channel ran a program on wife beating as part of a show hosted by an Islamic expert named Jasem Muhammad Al-Mutawah. This was a family program and it was instructional: the host explained in detail when it is appropriate for a husband to mete out physical punishment to his wife and how severe that punishment should be depending on the infraction. A fair amount of airtime was given to the width of the stick a man should use when "correcting" his wife. As an example, Al-Mutawah held out a ten-foot pool cue that he said some families keep at the ready in the home.[25]

Corporal punishment is prevalent and accepted even in mainstream Islamic culture. Some have argued that the beating of women is a cultural tradition that predates Islam, and this is true. However, it is specifically encouraged by the Qur'an. This is what I call the "Death Star Defense" because it's like arguing that the Evil Empire in *Star Wars* is not really responsible for using the Death Star to destroy the entire planet of Alderaan because it did not invent murder.

There are a number of recent examples of Islam-based mistreatment of women in the Muslim world. There was the recent case of the woman from Nigeria (which is now under Islamic law) who was sentenced to be stoned to death for having a child out of wedlock. She had been raped by an acquaintance after being abandoned by her husband and was, thus, guilty of "adultery." Imprisoned for years, she narrowly escaped death only because of international pressure. Other, less lucky, women face stoning on similar charges.

Why punish a woman for a "sin" that's not her fault? Because in "conservative" Islamic countries like Saudi Arabia and Iran (or Afghanistan under the Taliban) women are not considered full people who are equal to men. And by unequal, I do not mean they earn seventy-two cents on the man's wage dollar, or that they keep hitting a glass ceiling in the corporate world. I mean they are not considered fully human.

As women, they are judged by their family and society according to two important criteria. The first is how many sons they produce for their husbands. The second is how they reflect the honor of their male relatives—a husband if they are married, fathers and brothers if they are not. In fact, a man's honor, and thus his status in the community, is largely determined by the behavior (read: chastity) of the women in his family.

If a young woman remains a virgin until she is married, she does not put a stain on her father and brother's honor. When she marries, her fidelity ensures that her husband's honor remains intact.

KEEPING THE FAMILY HOME AND HONOR SPOTLESS

If a woman is raped, she brings the same dishonor to her family as if she went out and had an affair. Thus, she is guilty of a capital crime. Interestingly, while being the victim of rape is punishable by death, committing rape in almost all Islamic countries is not. To be fair, this discrepancy in punishment does not come directly from the Qur'an, but it is part of an Islamic tradition that puts far greater value on the lives of men than those of women. And that dynamic comes from numerous passages in both the Qur'an and the Hadith.

Just after 9/11 there was a widely reported case of a young woman named Mukhtar Mai in Pakistan. She was eighteen and living in a small village in Pakistan's southern tribal lands when she ran afoul of the law. In her village, as in much of the Arab and Islamic worlds, the primary law is religious law as interpreted by the local clerics. In her case, these religious men ordered her brought before them and sentenced her to be gang-raped.

Remarkably, this young woman was guilty of no crime. She had not stolen anything, or hurt anyone, or shared music on the Internet. She hadn't even been accused of one of those lame non–prima facie cases based on circumstantial evidence that should never have gone to trial, and even if it did and you somehow got a conviction, it would get overturned in the state supreme court before you could say ex post facto.

No, this woman was punished because of an "alleged" crime committed by her brother. Apparently, the woman and her brother were members of the lower-class Gujar tribe. Her brother was accused of walking unchaperoned with a girl from the higher-class Mastoi clan. This was considered a great stain on the Mastoi tribe's honor and could only be avenged by the gang rape of the young Gujar man's sister.

Perhaps this would be a good place to mention that at the time of his crime the wayward young man was eleven years old.

The case got even stranger when Mukhtar Mai revealed that her brother's crime had been invented to cover up her brother's sexual assault at the hands of Mastoi men. Whatever the initial motivation for the sentence, the main reason the gang-rape punishment was meted out was so that the Mastoi tribe could restore its honor. Now, you might legitimately ask how the gang rape of a young woman could *improve* the honor of a people, but I'm afraid that's a subject beyond the scope of this book.

The secondary reason for the rape sentence was to destroy the honor of the young man, his family, and his tribe.

Of course, the fact that the young woman herself was guilty of no crime at all was immaterial since she was, by virtue of her gender, not considered a full person with rights equal to those of men under the law.

It's worth mentioning that this sentence was not rendered and carried out by a "tiny minority of extremists." While the attack was happening, there were hundreds of Mastoi standing outside the tent laughing and cheering.

Ultimately, you can view this whole incident in a number of ways. One would be in the context of the historical and cultural history of the people involved. Another would be from a psychological point of view, and clinical psychologists have a term for the mental state of the people who would authorize, commit, and encourage this kind of attack: batshit crazy.

Under international pressure, the Pakistani government finally charged and convicted the Mastoi village elder and four other men who had raped the woman, sentencing them to death. However, the story was in the news again in 2005 when a court overturned the convictions of the Mastoi men. A higher court later reversed the reversal and the conviction stands.

Though this young woman's case has been the most widely reported, Mukhtar Mai is far from being the only such victim. Her case represents both a historical and an ongoing trend in Pakistan. In a CBS news report on the story, Pakistani women's rights activist Naeem Mirza said, "Women are often punished for the crimes committed by male members of their families." Furthermore, "Mostly, those who commit gang-rapes or kill women in the name of honor are influential tribesmen . . . therefore they escape punishment."[26]

According to a *New York Newsday* report on the repression of women in Pakistan, "This system's treatment of women like property is nowhere more routine than in the southern Punjab province. . . . Here, a man controls the lives of his daughters or sisters, and often marries them off to other men to resolve debts, land disputes, or family feuds." According to a Pakistani human rights lawyer, "We have a saying that a woman is like a pair of shoes—you can change her any time."[27]

THE ETERNAL WORD OF ALLAH ON WOMEN'S RIGHTS

Where does the eternal and unchanging Qur'an stand on women's issues? As usual, the Islamic Holy Book sends mixed messages—sometimes in the same verse. Sura 2:228 says, "And women shall have rights similar to the rights against them, according to what is equitable," which sounds fair enough until you read the rest: "but men have a degree (of advantage) over them." Guess which part of that quote is given more credence in the Muslim world?

In case there was any doubt about which gender was dominant, there's sura 4:34, which says, "Men are in charge of women, because Allah hath made the one of them to excel the other." The same sura gives permission for a husband to beat or "scourge" rebellious women.

In the Hadith, Muhammad is even tougher on women and says, "After me I have not left any affliction more harmful to men than women."

The Qur'an does have a few passages that speak respectfully of women, but no one could read the book and conclude that it is a treatise on gender equality. Staunch belief in the notion that the Qur'an is the eternal and unchanging word of Allah makes change difficult. And even if it were possible to ignore the sillier and more outdated verses and cobble together a more fair system, there seems to be no significant movement—even among the "moderate majority" of Muslims—to do this.

FUN FACTS ABOUT WOMEN IN THE QUR'AN

- A woman shall receive half the inheritance of a man.
- It takes two female witnesses to equal one male witness. However, women are not allowed to give testimony if a male witness is available.
- Though Muslim men may marry non-Muslim women, Muslim women may only marry believers.
- A man may strike his wife if he has already "admonished" her and "banished" her from his bed in an effort to make her obedient.
- Though men may have up to four wives and an unlimited number of slaves and concubines, women are limited to no more than one husband.
- A man may not "forcibly inherit" a woman, unless she is guilty of "flagrant lewdness."
- Menstruation is an "illness" and men should not touch menstruating women until the women "have purified themselves."
- Lewd women should be confined to their homes until they die. The Qur'an does not specify what constitutes lewdness here, but Islamic courts have defined it as anything from holding hands or kissing before marriage to improper dress and premarital sex.
- If a man wishes to divorce a wife to whom he has given a sum of money, he should not try to take part or all of that money back.
- If a man has recently gone to the bathroom or come into close contact with a woman, he should wash before prayer.

Looking at Muhammad's own life, he did apparently treat his eleven wives and numerous concubines reasonably well, but, then again, he had *eleven wives and numerous concubines* so it's hard to give him points for sensitivity to women's issues.

He also made it clear through the Hadith that it was perfectly acceptable for men to rape their female slaves. In a Hadith from Sahih al-Bukhari, volume 7, book 62, number 137, he instructs his men that while it is okay to force themselves on the slaves they have recently taken in battle, they should *not* practice birth control while doing it.

KILLING WOMEN FOR THEIR OWN GOOD

One of the holdovers from Muslim history and Bedouin culture is the ironically named practice of "honor killing" whereby a young woman who has brought shame on her family is murdered by the men of the family to restore their honor. Again, since a man's honor is inextricably linked to the chastity of the women in his family, the capital crimes in these cases are always sexual and include but are not limited to: having sexual relations with a man before marriage, having an extramarital affair, dating a non-Muslim man, or meeting a man alone and unchaperoned—or being suspected of committing any of the preceding.

In these situations the woman is promptly murdered by her father, brother, or husband. This happens every day across the Islamic world. Estimates put the total number of women murdered by close relatives at over two thousand per year but most experts agree that the actual number is much higher. In Pakistan alone, conservative estimates put the average number of honor killings at three per day.[28] There is no doubt that in many parts of the world, murder by a family member is a leading cause of death for young Muslim women.

These murders are almost always handled privately and the authorities tend to look the other way. However, in many of these countries murder is (technically at least) against the law and sometimes the man is arrested. This happens in places like Jordan, which has in recent years engineered an international public relations campaign and made quite a show of its American-born and blonde-haired Queen Noor (who reigned until the death of her husband, King Hussein, in 1999), its cooperation in the War on Terror, and its efforts to modernize its society.

When an arrest is made, the man almost always escapes with either no punishment or a short prison term of a few months. When released, the man is greeted by his family and community as a hero.

Recently, there's been a disturbing development in Pakistan and other parts of the Muslim world where attacks in which men disfigure their wives' faces with acid have been "growing alarmingly over the past three years . . . most notably in southern Punjab,"[29] according to a report by the Human Rights Commission of Pakistan. Why are these women being attacked? Because of their husband's *suspicion* that they may have spoken to or met with another man.

MYTH ABOUT ISLAM #2
The Headscarf, or *Hijab*, Worn by Iranian and Some Other Muslim Women Is an Islamic Religious Symbol of Long Standing

As we like to say in my family: this is the opposite of true. The headscarf that is causing such a fuss in France is not a religious symbol, or at least it's not a *Muslim* religious symbol. The fact is that it is *Christian headgear* and is never mentioned in the Qur'an or the Hadith.

Iranian author Amir Taheri dates the current headscarf all the way back to the time of KC and the Sunshine Band. According to Taheri, "This headgear was invented in the 1970s by Mussa Sadr, an Iranian mullah who had won the leadership of the Lebanese Shiite community."

The invention was born of necessity because in the seventies, while the West was struggling with leisure suits and roller disco, the Lebanese were struggling at the hands of Yasser Arafat and his Palestinian gunmen, who controlled southern Lebanon and were sexually harassing and raping the women there. Sadr invented the *hijab* so that "Shiite women would be clearly marked out, and thus spared" by Arafat and his goons. As Taheri learned, the headscarves were inspired by the headgear of the Lebanese Catholic

---

SPREADING THE GOOD NEWS OF WOMEN'S RIGHTS

Unfortunately for the West, these sorts of women's rights issues are no longer limited to the Islamic world. With large numbers of Muslims emigrating from their native lands every day, they are bringing in many of their quirky and quaint little customs to the West. Many European countries have large and growing Muslim populations, leading to a number of serious assimilation problems. Muslim attitudes toward women are often at the crux of these situations.

The recent headscarf-ban controversy in France is a reaction to

nuns, whose own attire was based on clothes worn by Christian women in classical Western paintings.[30]

So there you have it. Some of the Muslims in France and Germany are now suing the European governments to keep their *Christian* religious headgear. If the ruling elite in Iran is aware of the humor and irony there, they have made no public statements to that effect. In fact, they have given no indication that they possess either a sense of humor *or* a sense of irony.

To be fair, the Qur'an and the Hadith do have passages that instruct both women and men to dress modestly, and women's headgear is part of a number of cultural traditions from Muslim nations. In fact, in some cases, some of what we consider Islamic clothing actually predates Islam. But the fact is that the specific headgear now worn by Iranian women is a new invention.

However, don't expect the mullahs in Iran to relax the rules on the *hijab* now that the story is out. Recent advances in *Advanced Islamic Religious Science* have alerted the Iranian ruling elite to a new danger posed by women's uncovered hair. As the *New York Post* reported in a 2004 article on Muslim female athletes (I swear I am not making this up): "*Hijab* theoreticians agree on one claim: a woman's hair emanates dangerous rays that could drive men wild with sexual lust and thus undermine social peace."[31]

this problem. The French have the largest Muslim population in Europe because of their colonial and historical ties with Morocco. Like much of Europe, the French are having a terrible time assimilating Muslim immigrants. The headscarf ban is an awkward and feeble attempt to try to do just that.

One of the least-talked about problems resulting from the growing Muslim population in the West is rape. In Denmark, the majority of the rapes of non-Muslim women are perpetrated by young Muslim men who make up only 2 percent of the country's population.[32] And according to one report, in Norway, "65 percent of rapes of Norwegian women were performed by 'non-Western' immigrants—a category that, in Norway, consists mostly of Muslims"[33] Clearly, there's a huge problem right now and it will likely only get worse since in forty years one estimate says that one Dane in three will be Muslim.

In Australia there was a well-known case of a group of Lebanese Muslim gang rapists who terrorized Sydney in 2002. The gang would seek out non-Muslim victims and subject them to hours of sexual torture. The women—as young as fourteen—were "sluts" and "Aussie pigs," according to the rapists. Seven men were convicted of rape.

"I looked in his eyes. I had never seen such indifference," said one eighteen-year-old victim, remembering one of the fourteen men who raped her a total of twenty-five times over a six-hour period,[34] according to the *Sun Herald* of Australia.

Now are crimes like these the result of individual pathologies or because of cultural norms that are in direct conflict with Western values, particularly regarding the rights of women? The answer to both questions is yes. Clearly the individual men have, um, issues, but there is no denying that the misogynist tendencies of Muslim cultures—supported by a perfectly reasonable interpretation of Muslim holy texts—are also directly responsible for the treatment of women both in their home countries and in their adopted lands. Remember, as we established above, in a number of Islamic societies a female rape victim will be subject to the death penalty but her attacker will not. And the Prophet himself sanctioned the rape of female slaves.

The PC voices might say: *Okay, but the Australian case is an aberration, it's unfair to paint a whole group of people with that brush.*

Possibly, but remember that Muslims in Norway and Denmark are small percentages of the population, yet Muslim men commit the majority of the rapes in those nations. That's not an aberration, that's an epidemic.

Not surprisingly, Muslims have also brought honor killing to other shores as well. There have been well-publicized honor killings in Europe, with a number of notable cases in England. One of the most disturbing was the murder of a young woman in Sweden.

Her name was Fadime Sahindal, she was twenty-six, and her family had moved from a small Kurdish community in Turkey more than twenty years earlier. Fadime had spent most of her life in her adopted land and spoke fluent Swedish. Yet, despite their decades in Sweden, Fadime's family remained strict and did not want her to mix with Swedes. Neither of her parents ever learned Swedish.

The parents also kept close ties to Turkey and their Islamic traditions. Both of her older sisters entered into arranged marriages with first cousins who lived in the old country (in Arabic and Islamic patriarchal cultures a marriage between first cousins on the father's side is considered an ideal match).

But Fadime resisted an arranged marriage and began secretly dating a Swedish boy. One day her father saw the couple holding hands on the street and exploded in anger. From that moment, Fadime's life changed completely. According to Leiff Ericksson, who is one of Sweden's best-known lawyers and was Fadime's attorney, "Fadime said she knew from that instant that she could never live with her family again, that she could never be secure again."

Immediately, Fadime moved away and only returned home to collect her things, which she did under police escort. Her father and brother now hated her intensely and regularly threatened her over the phone. When Fadime went to the authorities, her father and brother were put on trial. At one point, during a break and with television cameras rolling, her brother tried to attack her.

Later, he was given a suspended jail sentence and the father was ordered to pay a fine.

By now Fadime had become a celebrity who had evoked the sympathy of the Swedish people when she publicly asked them to help her escape the death sentence her father had imposed. Fadime went into hiding and moved in with her boyfriend to live under an assumed name. Tragically, her boyfriend was killed a few weeks later in a car crash. Just two days after his death, her brother attacked her on the street and put her in the hospital. On trial again, he testified in court that his sister was "a whore."

Authorities then brokered a deal where Fadime's father pledged not to harm her if she stayed away from home and stopped talking to the news media. The only tie she kept to her family was with her sister Songul, a frail young woman of twenty-four who had long battled psychiatric problems.

The sisters often spoke on the phone and Fadime would occasionally risk a visit to Songul's apartment. Her father found out she was there, confronted her, and shot her in the head, killing her. Though the shooting was witnessed by at least three people—Fadime's mother, her teenage sister, and Songul—only Songul tried to help, administering CPR.

Of the witnesses to Fadime's murder, only Songul would testify.

According to a *New York Times* report, at the hospital moments after the doctor came to tell the family that Fadime was dead, "one of her older sisters phones a male member of the family . . . and says, 'The whore is dead now.'"[35]

GROWING UP FEMALE PART 1, THE EARLY YEARS

Okay, stoning, honor killing, gang rape . . . these are terrible crimes, sure, but how relevant are they to the daily lives of most Muslim women, even those who live in so-called radical countries?

As it turns out, very relevant. For the thousands of Muslim female victims, these incidents represent just a small portion of the problems they face. Of course, defenders of Islam have maintained that, like wife abuse, traditions like honor killing are vestiges of pre-Islamic tribal customs. And to a point, this is true; the Qur'an was, in many ways, Mohammed's effort to eliminate some of the most barbaric Arab customs, even as it codified others. The problem is that whatever its origin, honor killing is now sanctioned by many Islamic societies. And once again, the fact that Muslims didn't invent this sort of murder doesn't absolve them from responsibility for practicing it. (See previous note on the inadmissibility of the *Star Wars* "Death Star defense.")

The religious and cultural norms that underscore honor killing and the stoning of women for adultery as well as the misogyny that underlies so much of Islamic culture are controlling forces in the daily lives of the vast majority of Muslim women.

From birth, toxic attitudes toward women guide a woman's entire life and in many ways she suffers more as she ages. In the pre-Islamic past, it was common for Arab tribes to kill female babies at birth by burying them in the sand—partly because each new female might eventually dishonor the men in the family and partly because so little value was placed on girls that raising them was often deemed too much trouble.[36]

In the Qur'an, Mohammed tried to discourage this practice and seems to have largely succeeded, though it probably continues to this day in some tribal territories. Today, a man who has only daughters in Saudi Arabia will likely be taunted as an *abu banat* or "father of daughters."[37] However, female babies are regarded primarily as a failure on the part of the mother who bore them. In fact, a woman's failure to bear sons is considered a fair reason for her husband to divorce her. Of course, science has told us for years that it is the man who determines the gender of the baby, but don't get me started.

Speaking of divorce, a Muslim man can divorce a wife simply by saying "I divorce you" three times. To be fair he must say it out loud and in front of adult male witnesses. For women, divorce is possible but in real life is virtually never granted by the male clerics who make the decisions in these matters.

A WOMAN'S WORTH IN SAUDI ARABIA

The Old Testament of the Bible places the value of a virtuous woman "far above rubies." In her book *A Woman's Worth*, Marianne Williamson explored a woman's value and place in society in both spiritual and naturalistic terms, calling women goddesses with cosmic functions.

Since the dawn of time, writers, poets, and philosophers have sought to define both the real and intangible value of women. For most of us, the question is an imponderable—interesting to explore but ultimately unfathomable.

Not any more.

According to the Saudi Arabian religious court system, a woman has a very clearly definable value. She is worth, *precisely*, the same as *the leg of one man*. Saudi Islamic jurists turned their attention to this question in January of 2005 when a Saudi Arabian court was asked to consider damages payable to a Syrian man who lost both his legs and his wife in a traffic accident in Saudi Arabia.

Using the latest in Qur'anic gender- and limb-valuation techniques, the court ruled that the guilty Saudi had to pay $13,500 to the Syrian man for the loss of his wife, the same amount he had to pay for each lost leg.[38]

FEMALE GENITAL MUTILATION

Many Muslim women face an ordeal immediately after birth or as young girls: female circumcision or, more accurately, female genital mutilation, abbreviated as FGM by Amnesty International and other human rights organizations.

There are a number of different kinds of FGM. Almost all of the procedures involve the removal of the clitoris, some the removal of the labia, and in the most extreme form the removal of most or all of the external vaginal tissue and the sewing together of the vagina with catgut or thread, leaving only a small opening for urination and menstruation.

According to Amnesty International, FGM is practiced mostly in the twenty-eight North African countries. Currently, about 135 million women have suffered through the procedure and thousands of girls are targeted every day for mutilation.[39]

FGM is not exclusively a Muslim practice. It also comes from pre-Islamic traditions and is never mentioned in the Qur'an. However, the fact is that most of the girls currently at risk are Muslim. And FGM is a part of many Islamic cultures.

Why? Well, mostly FGM seems to be about control. Some of the strangest justifications for the procedure in Africa include a preternatural fear of the clitoris, which has the power to give grown men nightmares because of the belief that it can cause sickness or death for those unlucky enough to come into contact with it. However, the majority of the FGM procedures performed in the Islamic world are done to reduce female pleasure during sex in order to help maintain chastity, which, of course, reduces the risk that the women will bring dishonor to the family.

In the most extreme cases of FGM, where the vagina is sewn shut, premarital sex becomes a physical impossibility and the vagina has to be cut open on the wedding night and sewn shut again after intercourse.

In our culture, the sexual mutilation of women is the domain of psychopaths and serial killers. In the Islamic world, it is part of many Muslim cultures and is sanctioned and performed by large numbers of people. Astonishingly, most of the procedures are performed by women.

Most leading clerics in radical countries like Saudi Arabia refuse to rule directly on the practice since it is not mentioned in the Qur'an. Instead, they publicly defer to doctors like the, um, expert Dr. Muhammad Rif'at Al-Bawwab, a surgical specialist at Al-Azhar University in Saudi Arabia who defended FGM in a public statement translated by memri.org: "The clitoris protrudes more than other parts of a woman's genitalia, and this protrusion causes it to rub against clothing and other things, which diverts the attention of the adolescent girl toward unnatural pleasure that is likely to make her addicted to it in an abnormal and damaging way. . . . After marriage, it is difficult to prevent this from happening to a woman who has become accustomed to it. The only way to deal with this situation is to conduct sexual relations in an abnormal way, in which her clitoris is rubbed forcefully, as she has become accustomed thus leading to her moral degradation."

The practice was also defended by Muslim writer Dr. Ahmed Abd Al-Rahman, who said in another statement translated by memri.org, "Not circumcising girls opens the gate to the spread of depravity and prostitution, as happened in the West as a result of ignoring this normal, human demand. Do we want to be like the West?"[40]

For the victims, there is, of course, the obvious pain and resultant sexual dysfunction and the inability to achieve orgasm. There are also many attendant psychological effects and physical complications, including scarring, excessive bleeding, and persistent infections. It's important to note that large numbers of the procedures are performed by midwives with no medical training who do not clean their instruments, which are often no more than pieces of broken glass. Because of these unsanitary practices, FGM has become a significant method of transmission of the AIDS virus in Africa because of the nonsterile instruments used to circumcise numerous girls.

GROWING UP FEMALE PART 2: DRIVING WHILE UNDER THE INFLUENCE OF ESTROGEN

Even if women are lucky enough to avoid infanticide and FGM, from birth, young girls in virtually all Muslim cultures are treated very differently from young boys, who, for starters, are usually breast-fed for about twice as long as girls. According to Raphael Patai in his book *The Arab Mind*, boys receive much more nurturing than a female infant, who from the time she is weaned "is well on the way to internalizing the role she will play in life as a woman: a subordinate, a person of little importance, destined to remain most of her life in a servile position in relation to the menfolk who will dominate her life: her father, brothers, husband, sons."[41]

In more "conservative" Muslim countries and certainly in Saudi Arabia, many girls will receive no schooling and will never even learn to read. As a result, the twenty-two countries that make up the Arab League have a female illiteracy rate of more than 50 percent.[42] That's why it was such a big deal in postwar Afghanistan when girls were finally allowed to go to school again.

Many girls in Saudi Arabia are still waiting. The illiteracy rate for women in that country is 50 percent, though you can call that figure progress because just thirty years ago it was 100 percent.

Part of the reason for keeping girls illiterate and uneducated is that schooling is of no use to women in meeting their responsibilities within the culture: cooking and cleaning for their fathers, brothers, or husbands and taking care of the children.

Since work outside the home is out of the question for almost all women in Saudi Arabia, there's no need to educate women so they can pursue careers. But the biggest reason to keep women uneducated is that it makes it easier to keep them in the dark about how women live in the rest of the world, particularly in the West.

There is no such thing as a free press or media in the overwhelming majority of the Islamic and Arab countries. Saudi Arabia, in particular, maintains tight controls on information to keep out the West's secular, evil ways. Probably the most heavily censored information is that which deals with the life and role of women in Western society.

Men, who work and sometimes travel, lead a much more cosmopolitan life and inevitably learn about the outside world. This is not of great concern to Saudi authorities because it represents no threat to the status quo. But keeping women in the dark is a top priority because the entire social system is built upon keeping women in their place.

Now, you might argue that Arab men would benefit from more satisfying relationships with women who are their intellectual and social equals and that society would benefit from releasing the talent and energy of half its population, but, apparently, the Saudis don't see it that way, nor do the Iranians, or the Jordanians, or the Yemenis . . .

In fact, the Saudis maintain extensive propaganda campaigns to convince Saudi Arabian women that American women are all immoral harlots who want nothing more than to corrupt and steal their virtuous Saudi men.

A very telling incident occurred during the first Gulf War in 1991, when Saddam Hussein invaded Kuwait. He mobilized the largest army in the Islamic world and overran the small nation in no time. After taking Kuwait City, he was just hours from the Saudi capital of Riyadh and control of that nation's oil reserves—the largest in the world. Since the Saudis have no military to speak of, the royal family did the only thing they could think of: they pleaded with their business partner, the United States, to come save them.

The United States immediately sent troops to defend Saudi Arabia and push Saddam back into Iraq. Included in the American force were, of course, female soldiers, and even the best efforts of the Saudi censors could not keep this a secret. Talk began immediately: American women were walking around "unveiled!" "in shorts!" and "driving cars!" Driving is, of course, illegal for Saudi women, who are deemed "too emotional" to handle an automobile—though it is common for twelve- and thirteen-year-old boys to drive.

News of the American women swept the country and despite the decades of propaganda a rebellious spirit erupted, particularly in the cities. Then in Riyadh the unthinkable happened, forty-seven women decided to throw off their shackles and actually got behind the wheels of their family cars. They enjoyed a few precious minutes of exhilarating freedom driving the streets of the nation's capital.

According to a *Washington Post* report, the punishment those women faced was swift and severe: "They lost their jobs and passports for two years, and they were denounced in flyers written by religious groups as 'fallen women calling for vice.' Those who returned to work have been denied promotions."[43]

RADICAL FASHION SENSE

As they grow older, things go sharply downhill for Saudi women. Once a girl has her first period, Saudi Arabian law (not custom, mind you, but law) dictates that she must wear a veil completely covering every inch of her skin whenever she is in public. In years past, the black veil covered even the eyes, giving women severely limited visibility. Now, women are allowed to keep their eyes uncovered.

When the Taliban took control of Afghanistan, they brought forced veiling with them. All women had to be veiled from head to toe or face the roving religious police who would beat them on the spot with long sticks if they showed any of their skin.

Why veil your women? Well, veiling is a custom that goes back to the ancient and revered Bedouin traditions, and the Qur'an does instruct women to be modest, but the real answer seems pretty obvious. Physical attractiveness and sexuality would be one of the few sources of power for uneducated women with little or no social or legal standing. Keeping women veiled insures that even in this way, they remain completely powerless.

How strict is the enforcement of this rule? Pretty strict. There was the widely reported case of the Saudi girls who died in a fire in March 2002. According to a Saudi press report quoted by Human Rights Watch, "There were 835 students and fifty-five women teachers in Intermediate School No. 31 when the blaze started at about 8:00 in the morning." The report noted that *mutawwa'in* (Saudi religious police) were at the school's main gate and "intentionally obstructed the efforts to evacuate the girls. This resulted in the increased number of casualties." The religious police reportedly tried to block the entry of Civil Defense officers into the building.

"We told them that the situation was dangerous and it was not the time to discuss religious issues, but they refused and started shouting at us. Whenever the girls got out through the main gate, these people forced them to return via another. Instead of extending a helping hand for the rescue work, they were using their hands to beat us," *Arab*

News quoted Civil Defense officers as saying, "The officers also said they saw three people beating girls who had evacuated the school without proper dress. A Saudi journalist told Human Rights Watch that the *mutawwa'in* at the scene also turned away parents and other residents who came to assist."[44]

Fourteen young women died in that fire.

PROTECTING WOMEN THE TALIBAN WAY

The Taliban were members of the Wahhabist school of Islam, something they shared with Saudi Arabia and their friend and patron Osama bin Laden. For the Taliban, protecting women was a primary concern. A US State Department report in 1998 showed how the Taliban accomplished historic levels of protection by:

- Forbidding women to work outside the home, and thus protecting them from the workplace's many dangers. Of course, this was tricky for Afghanistan's many single mothers, of which there were thirty thousand in Kabul alone.
- Forcing women to cover themselves from head to toe with a burqa that cost a month's pay. This was again difficult for single women given their limited earning potential as per the first rule.
- Forbidding women to use hospitals and medical facilities reserved for men, which meant they were forbidden to use pretty much all hospitals and medical facilities. This was to protect women from the dangers of being close to sick people.
- Cutting off women's fingertips if they were caught wearing nail polish. This obviously protected women from nail polish's many dangers. After all, both nail polish and nail

A RADICAL'S GUIDE TO PROTECTING WOMEN

In many Islamic cultures, clerics and apologists maintain that the rules governing women's lives are for their protection. As a result of this protection, women in Saudi Arabia cannot leave their homes without the permission of their father or husband and, even then, they must be accompanied by a close male relative. Being alone with a male who is not a close relative is called *khilwa* and is a crime. To be fair, it is also a crime for the men. However, guess which gender is on the receiving end of the majority of the enforcement?

polish remover contain the warning "Harmful or Fatal If Swallowed."

- Painting over the windows of houses that contained women. This was a clear and amazingly enlightened effort to protect women from the well-known dangers of overexposure to ultraviolet light.
- Beating women on the spot if they were caught outside, unchaperoned by men. This helped deter them from putting themselves in danger in the future. This also provided additional protection from harmful UV rays.
- Stoning women for adultery. This had the obvious value of protecting women from dishonoring themselves in the future.[45]

Though the Taliban no longer govern Afghanistan, they are still fighting US forces as well as the Afghani government, so there is always the danger that if the United States left, they might return to power. Of course, their spiritual brothers and financial patrons in Saudi Arabia are still active in the desert kingdom protecting Saudi women from the dangers posed by Western vices like makeup and shorts.

If you said men, you haven't been paying attention.

The reason for the unequal application of the law is that there is an immediate assumption that the woman is alone with a man for immoral purposes, meaning sex for pleasure or prostitution.

Not surprisingly, the Saudi ruling religious elite claims that the veil and Islamic law regarding the role of women in society are there out of respect for women and solely function to protect them. Before September 11, this was a favorite refrain of the Taliban, who were severely criticized by human rights groups (including one chaired by Jay Leno's wife, Mavis) for their treatment of women.

"Protecting women" is one of those terms that should send up a big red flag for our Radical Eye. After America invaded Afghanistan and the true horrors of the Taliban's religious rule were revealed, the world saw a systematic abuse of women by Taliban leaders that was staggering and included the buying and selling of women into slavery—not the virtual slavery of oppression, but actual slavery, usually sexual in nature.

RADICAL FAMILY VALUES

In Saudi Arabia and much of the Islamic world, women have no say in whom they marry (unless such say is granted by their fathers). Marriages are arranged for them by their fathers, and as we saw earlier the favored matches are between first cousins. In fact, across the Islamic world, marriages between relatives stands at about 45 percent. In some regions of Saudi Arabia it's between 55 and 75 percent,[46] according to a *New York Times* report.

This same report says that these numbers lead to remarkably high instances of genetic abnormalities, from sickle cell anemia and diabetes to severely debilitating diseases like spinal muscular atrophy. In Saudi Arabia, where women have an average of six children, the chances of having one or more with some kind of genetic problem is higher than any other country in the world.

What are the psychological effects of many generations of inter-breeding? Is there some sort of correlation between extensive, multi-generational incest and the seemingly irrational fervor that drives the most radical nations? Well, no studies have been done, but I would be willing to go out on a limb and say that the practice doesn't help.

Women also face the problem of "child marriages" and a large percentage of girls throughout the Muslim world are married before they reach the age of eighteen. According to Arabist Raphael Patai, for many Arab countries including Saudi Arabia, "the average age at marriage is only now slowly climbing toward the time of puberty."[47] How serious is this problem? According to a recent UN report, "Pregnancy-related death is the single leading cause of mortality worldwide for girls aged fifteen to nineteen."[48] Then, of course, there is polygamy. In Saudi Arabia, polygamy is legal and a young girl will often find herself sharing her husband with another wife, or two, or three. Of course, this practice is again designed to reduce the power of women, who in a polygamous marriage cannot even maintain the status of being the sole provider of sons.

As wives, women are expected to cook and keep the house, bear as many sons as possible, and raise the children. At meals, the women will serve the men of the family first and then eat the leftovers later. It is common for women in countries from Saudi Arabia to Jordan to leave the home only a few times after they are married. In some cases they never leave. At all times a woman can only leave the house if so permitted by the man in charge of her, father or husband. Traveling abroad is allowed only if the woman has the written permission of her father or husband and then she will probably have to be accompanied by a male relative. There are some exceptions: if a Saudi family goes out to a restaurant together, women and children can come but they are ushered into a separate section, segregated from the men. Oh, and a Saudi woman cannot receive treatment at a hospital unless she has written permission from her father or husband.

Since Saudi Arabia is a wealthy country, women can go shopping in surprisingly modern malls and stores, and this is one of the few ways for them to see the outside of the house. Of course, they will be chaperoned at all times if there will be men present, even in a market. To be fair, in some wealthy, progressive Saudi families women are educated, allowed to work, and given freedom to travel abroad. They are able to maintain relatively equal marriages where they are the only wife and are treated with respect. This happens every day to a small number of women even in so-called conservative Islamic countries. However, in these cases a woman's personal freedom (if you can call it that) and happiness is always dependent on the graces of her husband or father—and can be rescinded at any time.

Even with a loving father and an enlightened husband, women in Saudi Arabia and in much of the Islamic world live under the constant threat of violence or severe legal repercussions for publicly or privately deviating from their assigned place in society. And there is always the specter of murder at the hands of the men in their lives if they are even suspected of bringing dishonor to their family. Radical clerics and public relations experts are working round the clock to develop an explanation for honor killing that describes it as part of the "protection" they offer women. Progress has been slow, but work continues.

RADICALS WOULD RATHER FIGHT THAN SWITCH

How bad is life for women in radical Islamic countries? Well, Iraq makes a useful comparison. The human rights abuses under Saddam Hussein have now been widely reported, including rape rooms for the abuse and torture of women. However, on the whole, women still fared better under Saddam's Ba'athist Party rule than they do in Saudi Arabia today. The Iraqi constitution gave women full equality with men and specific legal rights in areas of marriage, divorce, custody, and inheritance. Women were educated and had freedom of movement and the freedom to work.

Why is this? Because, for all of its abuses, Saddam's Iraq was a *secular* country. And while women suffered repression, they suffered more or less equally with the men and for the same reasons, usually political. As long as a woman and her family stayed away from anti-Saddam politics, she could live a life that most women in Saudi Arabia cannot even dream about because they don't know it exists. The biggest danger facing Iraqi women today is the threat of the rise of Islamic holy law, which could eliminate many if not all of the freedoms they had in the past.

The fact is that the more religious and authentically Islamic a Muslim country, the greater the repression and abuse of its women; the more secular the nation, the better the women in that society will fare. As a result, probably the best Muslim nation for women to live in today is Turkey because it is the most secular. Of course, Turkey has its share of problems with religious extremists but it has a secular government with a secular legal system that guarantees women a certain amount of basic freedoms.

You can make a useful comparison between women in radical Islamic countries (as well as a number of the so-called moderate nations) and people who are eligible to receive political asylum in the United States. An asylum candidate must meet the definition of a refugee, which is "a person outside of his or her country of nationality who is unable or unwilling to return because of persecution or a well-founded fear of persecution on account of race, religion, nationality, membership in a particular social group, or political opinions."[49]

Now if we define women as a "social group," it's pretty clear from the preceding chapter that many millions of Muslim women would meet that standard. In fact, the entire female population of Saudi Arabia and quite a few other Islamic countries would qualify.

So, while we debate whether or not women in the West are treated fairly in all areas and earn enough money and respect for the work they do, women in the Muslim world live a life of repression and cruelty that defies our belief and understanding. Meanwhile, throughout the Islamic world it is the behavior of Western women and our liberal attitudes toward gender roles that radical Muslims view with the most bile and hate with the greatest religious fervor.

While the Middle Eastern countries are ground zero for the worst misogynistic pathologies, we've seen there are disturbing trends in Europe where Islamic communities are enforcing their own notion of women's rights in secular countries.

What about America, where we are told that the vast majority of Muslims are moderate? Well, in February of 2005, there was a piece in the *Daily News* of Baton Rouge, Louisiana, about the friendly Muslims in the area. The story was about a talk given by Imam Jehad Mahmoud, the president of the Islamic Center of Baton Rouge, who talked about how moderate and peaceful Muslims really are. His explanation for why the congregation was segregated during prayer with men in the front and women in the back was not because women are considered inferior to men, but rather "out of respect and protection."[50]

Sound familiar?

They make women stay together in the back of the mosque out of "respect"? And what are they being protected from? What sort of dangers await women who might venture to the front of the congregation?

The answer to that question came a month later when there was an announcement that Amina Wadud, a female Islamic scholar who wrote the book *Qur'an and Woman: Rereading the Sacred Text from a Woman's Perspective*, would lead Friday prayers at a Muslim service in New York City. Now, there is no injunction against women leading mixed-gender prayers in the Qur'an, but it had never happened before in a Muslim service. One would think it wouldn't be a problem, what with all the "respect" and "protection" going on in moderate and tolerant Muslim mosques.

It turns out that it *was* a bit of a problem. The service was originally supposed to be held at a Manhattan gallery, but, according to a press report, the venue "pulled out in the face of mounting threats, including one promising to 'blow you up.'" Interestingly, at least three of New York's "moderate, tolerant, and peaceful" mosques turned down the event, as did a number of Muslim groups at various colleges. In fact, no major Muslim group in New York would even comment on the situation.

Finally, a venue was found at an Anglican church and Amina Wadud may have become the first woman in history to lead the ritual Friday prayer. She spoke for a few moments about the fact that Allah stands above human concepts of gender. While no major Muslim groups wanted to talk about the event, on the streets of New York "a dozen screaming protesters waved angry signs from behind sawhorses." One of those signs read, "Mixed-Gender Prayers Today, Hellfire Tomorrow." And one member of the ironically named Muslim Thinkers said, "If this was an Islamic state, this woman would be hanged."[51] As it turns out, women do need protection in a mosque. In this case, Amina Wadud's protection came in the form of two helmeted police officers with automatic rifles held across their chests. Make no mistake, if this is what happens in America over a prayer that violates no part of the Qur'an, imagine what the threat of full equal rights for women would do in predominantly Muslim countries. Did Osama bin Laden and the 9/11 hijackers crash those planes because we let our women wear shorts, go to school, drive a car, and go to work? Though these were not his stated reasons, I think they were a large part of his motivation. Equal rights for women is one of the greatest threats to their seventh-century values and, if affected in the Middle East, would cause revolutionary reordering of every institution of their male-dominated societies from government, to religion, to the family.

For many Muslim men a world in which they might have to cook their own food or in which a woman occasionally controlled the TV remote, or would be free to refuse to marry her first cousin, is a world too horrible to contemplate. Make no mistake. They will continue to fight to the death to keep that world from coming about.

Chapter Three

CRIME AND PUNISHMENT

Or, How to Cut Off Your Hand to Spite Your MTV

As for the thief, both male and female, cut off their
hands. It is the reward of their own deeds, an exemplary punishment from Allah. Allah is Mighty, Wise.

—Qur'an 5:38

HOLY LAW FOR DUMMIES:
AN INTRODUCTION TO RADICAL JURISPRUDENCE

In 2002, a Nigerian woman who was raped by a male acquaintance
and subsequently became pregnant was found guilty of "adultery"
and sentenced by an Islamic court applying Muslim *holy law* to be
buried up to the neck and stoned to death.

In 2003, a Qur'anic court in Iran ordered a man convicted of
armed robbery to have four fingers on his right hand amputated as
punishment. (The regular amputation of hands and fingers for the
crime of armed robbery shows once again the desperate need for irony
education and awareness in Islamic countries.)

In 2004, a Saudi Arabian airlines flight attendant was found smuggling eight bottles of liquor into the country and sentenced by the religious court system to forty-five days in prison and 150 lashes.

Later that year, a fourteen-year-old Iranian boy broke fast during Ramadan. He was apprehended by authorities and sentenced to eighty-five lashes to be administered in public. The boy died during the punishment.

Welcome to Shariah, or Islamic holy law.

It's brutal, it's medieval, and it's completely incompatible with any reasonable standard of human rights. And for hundreds of millions of Muslims, it's the law.

If radical Islam is an ideology, Shariah is a central part of its belief system. It is also at the heart of the ideological battle between Islam and the West. Since the overwhelming majority of Muslims believe the Qur'an is the word of Allah, and accurately represents Allah's will, it's perfectly logical to codify the rules set down in the Qur'an into law. And since the Hadith are, if not the precise words of Allah, close enough for theocratic government work, we might as well throw those in, too.

The fact is that many Muslims believe the West's various legal systems have no validity because they clearly contradict the word and will of Allah. Given the widespread belief in the inimitability of the Qur'an and Muhammad as "the perfect role model in all situations," this is, again, perfectly logical.

The belief in Shariah is one of the defining characteristics of radical Islam. Robert Spencer, author of *Islam Unveiled* and a number of other books on Islam, has made the point again and again that many Muslims believe Islamic holy law is "superior to all other ways to order societies, and must be pressed forward by force."[52] If this is the case, Shariah is irrevocably intertwined with the concept of jihad because the spread of political Islam and the imposition of Islamic rule is the only way to insure that Allah's law is observed on Earth.

But don't let Western analysts put words in anyone's mouth. As the Ayatollah Khomeini put it, "Islam makes it incumbent on all adult males, provided they are not disabled or incapacitated, to prepare themselves for the conquest of countries so that the writ of Islam is obeyed in every country in the world. . . . Those who study Islamic Holy War will understand why Islam wants to conquer the whole world."

In case we fail to see the importance of political Islam in this mix, Khomeini adds, "What is the good of us [i.e., the mullahs] asking for the hand of a thief to be severed or an adulteress to be stoned to death when all we can do is recommend such punishments, having no power to implement them?"[53]

Crazy? Not at all. It's actually perfectly reasonable if one accepts that the Qur'an accurately represents the uncreated word and will of Allah. If that is true, then radicals like Khomeini are doing the people of the world a favor by strictly enforcing Allah's will.

It's tempting to write off Khomeini, or bin Laden, or the entire radical movement as crazy, but they're not. The fact is they are simply taking their deeply held, if irrational, convictions to their logical conclusion. I call this the difference between barking mad and raving mad. Someone who is raving mad isn't good for anything other than, well, raving—beating his head against the wall and eating the occasional fly. Whereas, someone who is barking mad starts from a crazy or irrational principle and aggressively defends it. Some scholars prefer the term *howling mad* to describe this condition.

I would put Osama bin Laden and Khomeini in the barking mad category. Thus, you could argue that their belief in the Qur'an as the exact word of God is irrational or at least unlikely, but it's not crazy. And, thus, neither is stoning or amputation, which are clearly called for in Islamic tradition and holy texts.

THE ETERNAL AND UNCHANGING LEGAL CODE OF ALLAH

Surely, true Islam—the one I've heard so much about—doesn't allow for these barbaric punishments.

Guess again. The problem is that the point of Islamic holy law is to

FUN FACTS ABOUT SLAVERY IN THE QUR'AN

- A man may keep slaves as concubines.
- A man may have sex with his slave anytime he wishes.
- A man may marry his slave.
- Slave owners may not force their slaves into prostitution.
- As punishment for some crimes, a man may be forced to free a slave.
- Under certain circumstances, a slave may buy his or her freedom.

re-create as accurately as possible true Islam, or Islam as practiced by Muhammad and his early followers. And the simple fact is that the more authentic the Islam, the more brutal it is in terms of crime and punishment.

But I've heard Islam is all about mercy.

Well, the Qur'an does say a few things about mercy. However, it sets a lot of standards for personal behavior that fall pretty low on the "mercy index." And the Qur'an is the primary source of Islamic law. Islam's holiest book was designed to be a blueprint for a social and legal system as well as a religious system. Thanks to the widespread fundamentalist interpretation of the Qur'an, there is no questioning the contents without being subject to another important tenet of Islamic law: the death penalty for apostasy.

In the end, it's impossible to reconcile Qur'anic-based Shariah with Western laws like those against slavery, which, as we have seen, has the cheerful approval of Islam's holiest book.

THE PROPHET ON LAW AND ORDER

The Qur'an is not the only source for Islamic holy law. Since Muhammad was and is considered the most perfect practitioner of Islam, the Muslim faithful also have the example he has set for them, which is called the *Sunnah*. We've already discussed the Hadith, which are part of the Sunnah in that the collected tales of the Prophet include many of his direct quotes. These Hadith were compiled in a series of massive efforts that took place about a hundred years after Muhammad's death. These anecdotes form a set of books that are considered second only to the Qur'an in their expression of Islamic principles.

Together, the Qur'an and Hadith are the basis for Islamic holy law. In Saudi Arabia, for instance, there is almost no criminal code—at least none outside of these two sources, which are considered enough law for the people.

Most of the discussion about "reforming" Islam centers on changing or de-emphasizing certain Hadith, at least the ones that form the basis for the most barbaric parts of Shariah. However, this is impractical for a number of reasons. First, there is no central authority in Islam analogous to the Vatican that could make such a ruling and give it weight. Second, like it or not, the Hadith seems to be a fairly accurate representation of the life of the Prophet, and few Muslims are willing to admit there is anything wrong with his example. Or, if they are, they are unwilling to say it out loud—at least in one of the number of Muslim nations where insulting Muhammad is a crime and can lead to that medical condition we discussed earlier called S.L.O.H. (Sudden Loss Of Head). And finally, the Hadith often simply reiterate or expand upon passages from the Qur'an, which—as we know—is believed to be the exact word and will of Allah.

So, it seems like the Muslim world is stuck with holy law as it stands now. And just as political power is necessary for the mullahs to enforce Shariah, the same holy law gives Muslim leaders their legitimacy with the faithful. As Bernard Lewis says, "The caliph's supreme purpose was to safeguard the heritage of the Prophet and to enforce the Holy Law."[54]

Without Shariah, there is no need for political Islam. This is why Islamic rulers like the Ayatollah Khomeini and clerics throughout the Muslim world regard the notion of "human rights" as an abomination, which is a reasonable position for them to take given their beliefs.

For one, human rights put the law of man above the law of Allah. Second, they eliminate the basis for the religious leaders' great social and political power. And third, the fact that the fundamental precepts of human rights are so much more humane than their holy law makes even the most pious and devout cleric ask uncomfortable questions about the legitimacy of his seventh-century religious legal code. And once you start questioning that, you are shaking the foundation of all Islamic belief.

PUTTING A HUMAN FACE ON ALLAH'S LAW: SHARIAH IN THE REAL WORLD

Okay, but you are picking the worst example to prove a point. Outside of stoning and amputation, how bad is holy law? After all, it has holy *right in the name.*

Well, we already talked a little about the sanctity of slavery in the Qur'an. There are literally hundreds of Hadith that lay out remarkably complex and detailed Islamic rules about slavery. As we mentioned earlier, in one Hadith, Muhammad makes it clear that it is perfectly acceptable for his men to rape their newly captured slave girls. However, he continues, they should not engage in coitus interruptus to prevent pregnancy because "it is better for you not to do so, for if any soul (till the Day of Resurrection) is predestined to exist, it will exist."

Are we clear on this? Rape is perfectly fine, but using birth control during rape is not. For me, this is another one of those things that sounds bad no matter how you say it. Passages like this would be comical if they didn't have very real and tragic implications. Not just throughout history; even today, there's the Sudan, where rape has been a weapon of the jihad since Shariah was established in 1987.

Slavery is perhaps the worst institution to come out of Islamic holy law. In the United States, there is still much discussion of the tragedy of the African slave trade that operated from the sixteenth to the nineteenth centuries—and rightly so. In that time, about 10.5 million Africans were taken from their homelands to the West. However, according to a report in the *American Thinker*, the "composite of the trans-Saharan, Red Sea, and Indian Ocean traffic generated by the Islamic slave trade from 650 through 1905 C.E., is 17,000,000 [Africans]."[55] And, of course, this number does not include the millions of Europeans and other non-Africans who were swallowed by Islam's holy institution.

And the problem of slavery is not just historical. There's the current situation in the East African country of Mauritania, which finally outlawed slavery in 1980 but which still has a large percentage of its black population serving Arab masters as slaves. And finally, there's Niger, an overwhelmingly Muslim country, where slavery was very recently outlawed but is still widely practiced.

A recent report on Niger by the BBC News found the following:

- Almost 8 percent of the population (of nearly a million people) remain slaves, despite the fact that slavery was outlawed all the way back *in 2004*.
- The children of slaves are taken away "from their parents before they are two years old, to break the bonds between parent and child and to eliminate any sense of identity."
- Slave owners encourage slaves to have children and determine when they have sex.
- Masters use frequent beatings for small infractions.
- Female slaves are frequently raped by their owners.
- Male slaves are castrated as punishment for a number of crimes.[56]

And the reason that the abolition of slavery in the Muslim world has been difficult is that the institution is enshrined in both the Qur'an and the Hadith. This is why there are more slaves serving Muslim masters *today* than there were slaves in the United States on the eve of the Civil War. Yes, you read that correctly. And of course, there's the kind of informal slavery we have already discussed that exists in Saudi Arabia.

Speaking of the Saudis, their commitment to Shariah gives them another important distinction: they are the beheading capital of the world. Saudi religious courts apply this punishment for a number of offenses, including homosexuality, drug smuggling, murder, armed robbery, and—I swear I'm not making this up—"sorcery," according to Human Rights Watch. It's worth pointing out that since homosexuality is a capital crime in Saudi Arabia, there is very little impassioned debate on the issue of gay marriage. According to the Saudi Institute, fifty people were beheaded for various crimes in Saudi Arabia in 2003.

Of course, Shariah-based capital punishment is common throughout the Muslim world, which holds the distinction of being a world leader in the execution of children. Like adults, children are subject to capital punishment in quite a few Muslim countries. Most of the executions are for murder, some are for armed robbery, and some are for nonviolent crimes, like the case of Azizullah Shenwari, a fourteen-year-old Pakistani sentenced to die in 2004 for drug offenses and then freed in 2005 because of international pressure. And there's the case of Leyla Mafi, a nineteen-year-old mentally handicapped young woman who was forced into prostitution as a child and had given birth to an illegitimate baby by the age of nine. This woman, who has a mental age of eight, was sentenced to death by stoning in 2003 by Iran's religious courts for "acts contrary to chastity."[57]

Recently, under pressure from the European Union, Iran has agreed to halt the practice of executing children. In a compromise that has been heralded as a major victory for human rights, the mullahs in Iran have agreed to stop executing children and to wait until they turn eighteen to kill them.

Perhaps the most chilling part of these extreme forms of punishment is the public nature of the executions and amputations. In Saudi Arabia, the beheadings are carried out in the public square and are always well attended. In Iran, stonings are carried out by the entire community.

What are the psychological implications of this sort of bloodlust for Muslim societies? What does it show us about the community and

FUN FACTS ABOUT ADULTERY AND ISLAMIC HOLY LAW

- Albania, Bosnia, the Russian Federation, and Turkey still have the death penalty on the books for adultery—though they haven't enforced it for some time.
- Stoning is never mentioned as a punishment for adultery in the Qur'an. However, more than twenty years after his death, one of Muhammad's wives suddenly remembered seeing a sura to that effect lying around the house years before. The missing verse was not found, but the penalty was added to Islamic holy law. (Astute readers will remember that the Qur'an is considered the exact word and will of Allah and not subject to change. As such, you may be asking yourself how a sura could have been lost if this is true. I would remind you that there's nothing radicals hate more than a wiseguy.)
- A conviction for adultery requires a freely given confession, four adult male witnesses, or eight adult female witnesses (because a female witness is worth exactly one-half of a male witness). Because this is often difficult to achieve, one of the few reliable methods of establishing guilt is pregnancy, which explains why stoning victims are almost always women.
- Shariah courts do not recognize DNA evidence that could establish the guilt of a man in the cases of a rape or adultery that causes a pregnancy.
- An obscure tenet of Islamic law allows that an embryo can "sleep" for up to seven years. This has saved the lives of many women who became pregnant after being widowed or divorced.
- Women who claim they were raped but are unable to prove it are subject to severe punishment (usually one hundred lashes) for making a false accusation.[58]

the individual psyches involved? Now you might argue that it is unfair to apply our moral standards to another culture. The concept of cultural relativism asks us to judge cultures according to their standards, not ours. (Of course, the radical world judges the West plenty, particularly for the shameful way we let our women go to school, drive cars, work, and wear shorts.)

To that argument, I respond that whatever these public spectacles say about the individuals who participate in them, it isn't good.

THE LONG ARM OF THE HOLY LAW

Under Shariah, there are capital crimes that require little or no physical activity. One of these "thought" crimes is leaving Islam by converting to another religion. As we have discussed, this is called apostasy, and it is illegal in at least fourteen Islamic nations and punishable by death in eight. In one recent and much-publicized case, an Afghani man named Abdul Rahman converted to Christianity and narrowly escaped the death penalty for his crime against Islam. Though he was finally released from his high-security prison in March of 2006, it was not because authorities recognized that there was nothing wrong with him changing his religion, but because there was a lack of evidence and suspicion that he was insane. Because his life was in danger from the Muslim community in his home country, Rahman fled to Italy, where he was granted asylum.[59]

Even in the West, Muslims who leave the faith endure constant threats and intimidation. Salman Rushdie still faces a death sentence rendered by Ayatollah Khomeini in 1989. In fact, Ayatollah Khomeini's successor, Ayatollah Khamenei, recently grumbled that Westerners "talk of respect for all religions but they support an apostate worthy of death like Rushdie."[60]

According to recent news reports, in England, thousands of Muslim converts to Christianity feel the reach of Shariah and "face not just being shunned by family and community, but attacked, kidnapped, and in some cases killed. There is even a secret underground network to support and protect those who leave Islam." One man and his family "have been regularly jostled, abused, attacked, shouted at to move out of the area, and given death threats in the street. His wife has been held hostage inside their home for two hours by a mob. His car, walls, and windows have been daubed in graffiti that reads: 'Christian bastard.'"[61]

Did I make it clear that this is not happening in the tribal no-man's-land between Afghanistan and Pakistan but in England, the land of Monty Python and the Fab Four? The fact is that even outside the bounds of Islam's political spheres, individual Muslims and Islamic communities will often try to enforce Shariah on their own. There is a powerful book by Ibn Warraq called *Leaving Islam* that tells the stories of a number of former Muslims, including some living in the West, who have suffered extreme harassment and now must live under the constant threat of death for their beliefs.

Insulting the Prophet or criticizing Islam is another good way to get yourself killed in the Muslim world, or in nations with a big enough Muslim community, as we learned from the recent murder of Dutch filmmaker Theo van Gogh, whose film *Submission* criticized Islam's treatment of women. Author Robert Spencer has a term for this sort of radical thinking. He calls it "Say We're Peaceful or We'll Kill You."

This behavior and this thinking are not limited to people who "misunderstand" the Religion of Peace. Muhammad himself was a big believer in murdering poets who criticized him; he killed his first poet early in his career when he was still consolidating his power in Mecca. Clearly, the murder of Theo Van Gogh and the Danish cartoon controversy show that many Muslims today well remember this important lesson in literary criticism.

EXTREMIST FAMILY LAW

Unfortunately, holy law also enshrines some of the most dangerous cultural traditions in the Muslim world—like the unequal treatment of women. The Qur'an says, in 2:228, "And women shall have rights similar to the rights against them, according to what is equitable; but men have a degree (of advantage) over them." Okay, this doesn't sound too bad; after all, it does say that women have "similar" rights to men. But in another sura, the Qur'an clearly puts men in charge of women saying, "Your women are a tilt for you (to cultivate) so go to your tilt as ye will" (2:223). And in case that is too vague: "Men are in charge of women, because Allah hath made the one of them to excel the other" (4:34).

The Hadith take a generally harsher view of women. According to Muhammad, "A woman in many ways is deprived of the possession of her own body. Even her milk belongs to her husband" (Sahih al-Bukhari P 27). And then there's Muhammad's "After me I have not left any affliction more harmful to men than women" (Sahih al-Bukhari, volume 7, book 62, number 33). But Shariah isn't all about executions and misogyny; it also regulates an amazing number of behaviors, from divorce and inheritance law to food preparation.

In addition to the capital crimes of murder, apostasy, adultery, and defaming Islam or Muhammad, there are other serious crimes that will usually get you one hundred lashes. These include fornication or sodomy, making a false accusation (usually an accusation of adultery or fornication), and the consumption of alcohol.

Together, these are the gravest crimes, called *Hud* in Islamic religious jurisprudence. The term for lesser crimes is *Tazir*, and these are more or less equivalent to misdemeanors and include everything from listening to rock music, dancing, or reading unapproved books. The Qur'an provides no set punishment for *Tazir*, so penalties vary pretty wildly by country and infraction and could be anything from a fine to flogging to amputation.

SPREADING THE JOY

Though extreme, Shariah is far from rare and is not limited to the most radical countries like Saudi Arabia and Iran. Harsh forms of Shariah are practiced in the Sudan, Nigeria, Niger, and a number of other nations. Holy law is squarely in the mainstream of Muslim life, with more than half of the world's 1.2 billion Muslims living under some form of Shariah.

To be fair, not all iterations of Qur'anic law include stonings and amputations, and the practice of it varies quite a bit from country to country. However, it's important to remember that holy law is not a quaint and outmoded system but is actually on the rise in the world with more people living under some form of it today than have at any other time in history.

And for many of those people, Shariah is plenty harsh and getting even harsher over time. Nigeria started reintroducing holy law in some provinces in 2000 and since that time has seen an increase in both its reach and severity. Amputations for adults and children have already begun, and women have been sentenced to stoning.

In 1987, the imposition of Shariah in the Sudan began one of the greatest human rights disasters in history. In the years that followed, millions of Catholic Sudanese were killed or sold into slavery under the nose of the UN and most of the world.

Indonesia is another country seeing a resurgence of Muslim holy law. The globe's most populous Muslim nation at nearly 240 million people is shifting to a religious system more in line with Islam. According to a news report, "The campaign against kissing is part of a proposal of sweeping reforms to laws adopted by the country's Dutch colonial rulers in the late nineteenth century."[62]

In an effort to free themselves from secular Dutch laws, Indonesia is borrowing a page from the legal book of its neighbors Malaysia and Brunei who "already enforce laws defining 'khalwat' or 'close proximity,' a crime akin to adultery for unchaperoned meetings between Muslim men and women."

Now that they're throwing off the yoke of Dutch Infidel law, Indonesians can look forward to:

- Police raids on the homes of nonmarried couples suspected of living together.

- The outlawing of pornography and displays of "certain sensual body parts."
- Aggressive censorship of films, television, and music.

If the recent history of nations like Nigeria and the Sudan are any indication, *Shariah* will only become more extreme in Indonesia over time, with a real danger of a move to stonings and amputations.

After the Iraqi elections of early 2005, there has been great discussion of the increasing role of Islamic holy law in that country. According to the *New York Times*, almost immediately after the Shiite majority won in the elections, leading Shiite clerics began pushing for Islam to be "recognized as the guiding principle of the new constitution."

Some are advocating for *Shariah*-based laws "overseeing personal matters like marriage, divorce, and family inheritance" (be afraid). And some clerics are "insisting that *Shariah* be the foundation for all legislation"[63] (be very afraid).

This is a very important issue because one of the key reasons for the invasion of Iraq was to bring democracy to a Muslim nation in the center of the Middle East. *Shariah*, even a watered-down family-court-only version, is incompatible with a number of important democratic principles, including gender equality. Remember, in Islamic Law, women receive half the inheritance of men, among other disadvantages.

With increasing Muslim populations in Europe, there has been an increase in incidents in which single as well as groups of Muslims begin enforcing their holy law in the form of honor killings and the harassment of Muslim converts to Christianity. As we will see in our discussion of Islamic tolerance, there have been efforts by Muslims to impose their standards on the larger non-Muslim community around them in areas as mundane as advertising. There have also been serious efforts to bring more formalized Islamic law to the growing Muslim communities in Europe.

In fact, Muslim groups tried to bring a limited form of Islamic religious law to Muslim enclaves in Canada, giving the Muslims living there the special brand of tolerance that only Islamic holy law can provide.

BLAME CANADA: HOLY LAW COMES TO NORTH AMERICA

The story starts in 1991, when Canada passed the Ontario Arbitration Act, which gave citizens the right to seek religious arbitration for civil disputes and matters of family law like divorce and inheritance, provided that both parties agreed to seek religious arbitration and the decision could later be appealed in the Canadian courts. This system seems like a nice multicultural approach. It gives weight and respect to different religions and has been used successfully by Christians, Jews, and Canadian native tribes. It was only logical to extend the same rights to Muslims. As Shabir Ally, president of the Islamic Information Institute, said in a Fox News report, "If Muslims have a civil dispute among themselves, they would want to settle the matter within the community rather than take it outside."[64]

Yet some of the quirks of Islamic culture suggest that this voluntary system might not be entirely voluntary for Muslim women. Critics raised the issue of whether a Canadian Muslim woman would realistically have a choice on whether or not to enter the religious arbitration process. "They will be oppressed in a sense because they'll be coerced into feeling they need to follow this process of binding arbitration, implementing *Shariah*. Otherwise, they're deemed as blasphemous and labeled by the community, and then where will she go?" said Imam Zebian, who sits on the board of the Canadian Council of Muslim Women.[65] This is a legitimate concern in Muslim culture, where women are routinely killed when they are even suspected of "honor crimes," and where apostasy is punishable by death.

But come on, those are extreme situations mostly limited to Muslim majority nations, and this is friggin' Canada.

The Canadian Council of Muslim Theologians would have been one possible source of authority for Shariah in Canada and would have decided which of the many forms and interpretations of Islamic holy law would be used. In 2005, on its Web site, the council gave the public an idea of the mind-set that might guide Canadian Shariah when it answered a question about whether women should be "allowed" to drive: "To the extent of necessity, it is permissible for a woman to drive . . . driving will not be permissible for leisure and going around unnecessarily."[66]

The president of the Canadian Society of Muslims, Syed Mumtaz Ali, recently defended Canadian Shariah. He was quoted in *Commentary* magazine, saying, "Freedom of religion as guaranteed under Canada's constitution means not only freedom to practice and propagate religion but also to be able to be governed by one's religious laws in all aspects of one's life—spiritual as well as temporal."

That's sort of multicultural and doesn't sound too bad, and Mumtaz is a well-respected member of the Muslim mainstream in Canada who has been practicing law in Ontario for more than forty years. But then he said he openly supported the traditional Muslim belief that converts from Islam must "choose between Islam and the sword." In other words, he supports death for apostates. And, according to Mumtaz, not only is this reasonable, but it's *imperative* because "if Canada is to be true to its own Charter of Rights and Freedoms [the Canadian equivalent of the United States' Bill of Rights], it must allow the country's Muslim community to punish those members who renounce or traduce their faith."[67]

Thus, according to Mumtaz, the only way Canada (which doesn't have a death penalty for murder—or for any other offense for that matter) can live up to its ideals of religious tolerance is for the country to allow Muslims to kill people who leave Islam and/or criticize the religion.

Any questions?

Fortunately, apostates in Canada are safe from state-sanctioned murder, at least for now. In September 2005, Ontario Premier Dalton McGuinty ended the controversy when, in a Fox News report, he said unequivocally, "There will be no Shariah law in Ontario. There will be no religious arbitration in Ontario. There will be one law for all Ontarians."[68]

Unfortunately, Christian, Jewish, and native Canadian communities will have to give up their limited and successful use of religious arbitration. As a practical matter, it is impossible to deny arbitration to

WHAT WOULD MUHAMMAD DO?

Imagine this scenario: You are walking down the street, and you come upon a group of wild-eyed, angry townspeople who have buried a young woman up to her waist in the ground and are in the process of collecting stones to execute her for "whoredom."

Now, you might argue that this rarely, if ever, comes up in contemporary Western life. However, it does happen with some regularity in the Muslim world. As a test of your understanding of Islamic holy law as revealed by the Prophet and the principles of Muslim peace and tolerance as shown in his example, choose which of these courses of action you would take if you were following the example of the Prophet:

a. Run for the nearest phone and call the police.

b. Walk on by, opting to not get involved, knowing that later you may face criticism from Obi Wan Kenobi that this was just your "uncle talking."

c. Execute a daring rescue of the woman and succeed against all odds while the angry townspeople as well as a team of ninja assassins try to stop you.

d. Take the opportunity to teach the would-be execution mob a lesson. Instruct them that if they choose rocks that are too small, they will be there all day, and if they choose rocks that are too large, the stoning will be over too quickly and will not inflict either enough pain or fear on the condemned to be worthwhile. Pick up a medium-sized rock as an example, showing them the right tool for the job.

Well, according to the Hadith, when faced with just this situation in real life, Muhammad opted for option *d*. Incidentally, when Jesus Christ faced a similar situation, he saved the woman's life by shaming the mob, saying, "He that is without sin among you, let him cast the first stone at her."

only one religious group, even if their beliefs are clearly at odds with the rights guaranteed to Canadian citizens. Still, in the sometimes painfully politically correct Canada, the rejection of Shariah is a tremendous victory.

Ladies and gentlemen, I give you Shariah, where stonings, amputations, and floggings are not just a good idea; they're the law.

Chapter Four

WAR PART II

Or, Europe on Five Massacres a Day

> Make War on them until idolatry shall cease and
> God's religion shall reign supreme.
>
> —Qur'an 8:39

JIHAD: WHEN PEACEFUL INNER STRUGGLES TURN BAD

From the early, glorious days of Muhammad until September 11 in 1683, the story of the expansion of the Muslim world is the story of the success of the jihad as a way to spread Islam's religious and political rule as well as a way to make jihadists rich in plunder. Today, everyone has heard the Muslim world's universal condemnation of the Israeli "occupation" of the Palestinian territories and their many complaints about the relatively brief European colonization of the Middle East. Astonishingly, the important piece of information left out by all sides in these discussions is the fact that Islam, through the various Muslim empires, constitutes the biggest and most successful imperial power in world history.

Yes, you read that correctly. The Muslim Empire of the Middle East and the later North African and Ottoman empires controlled a larger percentage of the known world (as well as of the world's population) than the empires built by the Persians, the Romans, the Byzantines, and the British.

The empire founded by Muhammad did not spread through peace; it spread through the sword, more specifically through the jihad. For centuries, the conquering Muslim armies seemed unstoppable, extending their theocratic rule throughout the Middle East, taking North Africa in the west, large parts of western and eastern Europe in the north, and moving as far as India and Pakistan in the east.

The jihad was also a major fact of life for a thousand years of European history, with much of Europe either under Muslim rule, under a jihad attack, or under threat of war. For some reason, this falls under the category of subjects people don't want to talk about. The Muslim world has decided that they are the perpetual victims of Western aggression and both historians and journalists seem to have no interest in setting the record straight, or at least in applying some sort of historical perspective.

Here's an interesting comparison: Muslim invaders occupied and ruled Christian Spain for more than seven centuries, which meant that Islamic rule over a Christian, European country lasted longer than the entire five-hundred-year history of the Roman Empire, from its founding in 27 BCE until the fall of Rome in 476 CE.

Holocaust denial (which is very popular in the Muslim world) is a school of, um, thought that maintains that the atrocities committed by the Nazis against the Jews either didn't happen or were vastly overstated. Besides the moral qualms we might have with Holocaust deniers, there is also a more subtle danger that the lessons of the Holocaust will be lost if we can't agree that it really happened.

In that spirit, let's coin the term *jihad denial* to describe the mindset that denies or ignores the reality of the Islamic jihad waged for centuries against the rest of the world, or the *House of War* as Muhammad called it. The untold millions of victims of the jihad—from the countless Europeans massacred or kidnapped into slavery over centuries to the innocent victims of 9/11—deserve to have their lives and deaths remembered in the spirit of truth so that the lessons of the tragedy of the jihad are not lost.

In the more than thirteen-century history of Islamic aggression against the rest of the world, there have been far too many battles and massacres to do justice to them all, but we'll hit the high points and talk about the ones most relevant to Western history and the current trouble the West is having with Islamic radicals.

FIGHTING FOR VIRGINITY

After Muhammad's death, Muslims continued his war of conquest, exploding outward throughout the Arabian Peninsula, the Near East, and the Middle East. In those days, the Muslim jihadists were fearsome soldiers fighting to spread Islam and collect booty in the form of treasure and slaves from the vanquished.

They also had a secret weapon: virgins.

Muslims were assured by Muhammad himself that dying for the cause of Islam would make them martyrs and guarantee them immediate entry into Paradise, where each Muslim man would enjoy the sexual attention of seventy-two virginal wives.

There has been a high-level theological dispute within Islam about whether the virgins, or the "houris," are there for sexual pleasure or not, or even whether sex is possible at all in Paradise. However, one thing is very clear, all of Muhammad's early followers believed it to be true. Thus, before battle, the early commanders of jihadist forces would shout, "The *houris* are waiting for you!"[69] Today, the families of Palestinian, Iraqi, and other homicide bombers regularly have a celebration called the "Wedding of the Martyr," to commemorate their sons' arrival at Islamic Paradise and his marriage to seventy-two virgins.

Muslim warriors rode into battle to spread their religion knowing that if they won they would receive booty, slaves, and/or women, and if they died they would go to Paradise. It was a no-lose scenario that led the conquering Islamic armies from successful campaign to successful campaign. Thus, for the jihadists, virgins were just the beginning.

TOP TEN THINGS TO LOOK FORWARD TO IN ISLAMIC PARADISE

According to Islamic tradition, faithful men can expect the following in the afterlife:

1. Seventy-two virgins, called *houris*, who have *renewable* virginities.
2. Orgasms that last a thousand years. (Later Islamic theologians would reduce this number to a still respectable twenty-four years.)
3. Three hundred servants.
4. A ruby horse with two wings.
5. Plenty of soft carpets and *green* cushions.
6. According to the Muslim holy texts, "In Paradise, there is a tree under the shadow of which a rider can travel for a hundred years." In other words, there is a *really* big tree.
7. Gold and silver utensils *and* combs.
8. Eternal youth and clothes that don't wear out.
9. People who enter Paradise are remade sixty cubits high, which is somewhere between eight and eleven feet, since a cubit is the distance from the elbow to the tip of the middle finger. According to Islamic tradition, this is the height that God made Adam, though humans have apparently shrunk significantly since Adam's time.
10. According to Islamic holy texts, "The inmates of Paradise would eat and drink but would neither spit, nor pass water, nor void excrement." Digestion is accomplished by belching and sweating.[70]

OUT WITH THE OLD, IN WITH THE MEDIEVAL

After the Prophet's death, the Muslim sphere was bounded by the world's two great empires, the Persian and the Byzantine. At its height in the early 500s, the Persian Empire, centered in what is now Iran, stretched from a large part of Egypt in the west to what is now Pakistan in the east, and from the Persian Gulf in the south to the Caucus Mountains in the north.

The Byzantine Empire was the Christian heir to the Roman Empire. Its capital was Constantinople (Istanbul today) and it was largely made up of the territory that now comprises Turkey and Greece, as well as some portions of southern Europe, including parts of Italy and Spain as well as the Balkan coasts.

Fortunately for the Muslims, the two empires had weakened themselves by decades of fighting against each other as well as internal squabbles. By 639, Muslim conquerors invaded Egypt, then a Christian country and part of the Byzantine Empire. In 641, less than ten years after the death of Muhammad, Persia and its empire that had stood for two hundred years fell to the Arabs.

By 644, the Muslims had captured the formerly Greek Syria, Israel (including Jerusalem), and most of Iraq. From there, the growing empire spread out from Egypt to North Africa. The holy warriors left a path of bloodshed and destruction in their wake and took countless people captive to be kept or sold as slaves. With each new victory, as Paul Fregosi tells us in his book *Jihad in the West*, "The conquered populations were given three choices: Islam, the sword, or tribute."[71]

The Muslim Empire experienced some internal strife. After the murder of the fourth caliph, Islam suffered a significant split when Muhammad's son-in-law Ali was involved in a battle for succession with a man named Muawiya, the son of one of the Prophet's first blood enemies, Abi Sufyan, who had tried to crush Islam in its earliest days.

Muhammad's son-in-law lost the contest and Islam was permanently divided into two main rival groups, the Sunnis—who had supported the son of Muhammad's greatest enemy—and the Shiites, who had supported Muhammad's son-in-law. The bitterness between the two groups continues today. In the 1980s, Shiite-majority Iran and Sunni-dominated Iraq fought a war that cost nearly two million lives. And the current Iraqi "insurgency" is driven largely by Sunnis who had ruled over the Shiite majority under Saddam Hussein and then lost power after the United States and the coalition invaded.

Muawiya is an important historical figure who founded the Umayyad dynasty, which ruled the growing empire for a hundred years and would later rule the second Islamic empire, in Spain. Muawiya was a conqueror who greatly expanded the territory of the "Religion of Peace."

LAUNCHING A FULL-SCALE INNER, SPIRITUAL STRUGGLE ON EUROPE

In 649, eight years before Muawiya took power, Muslim invaders had already visited Christian Europe, when they raided the island of Crete, but their only motive then was plunder. According to Paul Fregosi, the island was attacked by seventeen hundred ships. "The raiders took and sacked the town of Constantia and massacred most of the population."[72] This would be the first of many massacres of Europeans by Muslim invaders.

No effort was made to take political control of Crete or convert anyone to Islam. The invaders, or more accurately pirates, butchered the population and simply took what wealth they could, including as many slaves as their ships could carry. As slaves, attractive young women and boys were highly sought after and could look forward to sexual servitude that Fregosi characterizes as "the inevitable fate worse than death." This despite the Islamic prohibitions against homosexuality.

Barbaric? Certainly, but these early Muslims firmly believed they were doing the work of Allah. Next on the agenda was another raid on Crete in 651, then on Cyprus in 652, which would face raids until the late 900s. The island of Rhodes was next on the hit list and the remains of the famous Colossus of Rhodes (formerly one of the Seven Wonders of the World) was carted away and sold for scrap. From there, the jihadists moved on to Sicily in 668, which was sacked and had many of its people carried off into slavery.

Though presented to the faithful as part of the jihad, these raids were nothing more than acts of piracy against the outer reaches of the Byzantine Empire. When Muawiya was firmly established as caliph, he thought it was time to set his sights on the big prize: the Byzantine Empire's capital, Constantinople. The sacking of Constantinople had been a dream of the Prophet himself, who had once demanded the Byzantine emperor's submission to Islam. When the emperor refused, Muhammad started planning to conquer the city and, according to Fregosi, "decreed shortly before his death that all who took part in the attack on the Christian capital would be forgiven their sins, and those who died in the campaign would go straight to Paradise."

In or around 668, an invading force of about fifty thousand jihadists sailed from Syria for the capital of the Eastern Roman Empire. The first Muslim siege against Constantinople is one of the true epic tales of ancient warfare. Though it has been largely forgotten, it rivals the battle for Troy in its importance and scope. However, unlike the battle for Troy, in this tale, the defenders win, at least this time. The Muslim invaders laid siege to the city for seven years and were finally turned back. The Byzantines saved themselves, in part, with a novel piece of military technology called "Greek fire."

Greek fire was a chemical mixture that burned with extreme heat and would continue burning even when it hit water. Though the formula has been lost, it was probably made up of a combination of liquid petroleum, resin, and sulfur. The Byzantines shot their secret weapon out of tubes and on arrows to hit targets at a distance and also tossed containers filled with the burning chemical stew on their enemies.

According to Fregosi in *Jihad in the West*, Greek fire "obliterated many of the attackers and their ships as well." After seven years, twenty thousand of the Arab invaders had died and the surviving thirty thousand had had enough. In their retreat, the Muslims split into two groups: one group took to the seas in their remaining ships and the other headed for home on foot.

Much of the fleet was destroyed in a storm and many of the soldiers on land were killed by pursuing Byzantines. Finally, the Muslim caliph had to offer treasure and slaves to the Christian emperor so his surviving soldiers could return home. The Arabs would be back years later, but something important had happened: the jihad had just suffered a major defeat and the first full-scale attack on Europe had failed.

No doubt this must have been hard for the Muslim Empire's leaders to accept because the Qur'an had promised Muslims that "never will Allah grant to the unbelievers a way (to triumph) over the believers" (4:141). The jihadists consoled themselves over the next few years by raiding European coastal towns, plundering their treasure and carrying off as many Christians into slavery as they could. Islamic forces were also consolidating their gains in Africa and by the early 700s had overrun North Africa, taking Libya, Tunisia, Algeria, and Morocco, which gave the Muslim jihadists a new launching point from which to attack continental Europe.

In 711, Muslims sent a few trial raids from North Africa and struck Spain. Their ships returned "loaded with booty and pretty girls."[73] A full-scale invasion fleet was amassed and soon landed on Gibraltar. By 718, the Muslim forces had control of virtually all of Spain except for the relatively small mountain region in the north.

The story of the Arab colonization of Spain and the subsequent "Reconquest" by Christian forces is another epic tale that spans nearly eight centuries of active occupation and fighting. It is still relevant today because the loss of Spain is a very sore point for Osama bin Laden, al Qaeda, and other radical Islamic groups, who believe that once a region has come under Muslim control, it must always remain, by right, Islamic territory.

Thus, there is still an active terrorist movement in Spain's Basque region, and it was originally thought that Basque separatists (who want to create an Islamic state ruled by Shariah in the Pyrenees Mountains region on the border between France and Spain) were behind the Madrid train station bombings.

Fairly quickly, the Muslim powers in Spain grew almost as powerful as the central Islamic rule in Damascus. There, in 756, the Umayyad caliphate was ending after a century. A man named Abu al-Abbas overthrew the last Umayyad caliph, the line started by the once mortal enemy of Muhammad. The new caliph (who was known affectionately as "The Shedder of Blood" and "the Butcher") tried to have every single surviving Umayyad tracked down and murdered. In one particularly nasty piece of business, he invited about ninety Umayyad survivors to a banquet. Then "Abbas summoned his soldiers and executioners, who surrounded the ninety guests and flogged every one of them to death. Carpets were then rolled over the dead or dying victims and Abbas invited his followers to gorge themselves on the uneaten food which was thus served while the guests reclined on the bodies of the last of the Umayyads."[74] Did I mention that the caliph was not only the political ruler of Islamic territories, but the *holy* messenger of Allah on Earth?

The single surviving Umayyad, Abd al-Rahman, fled the Middle East and made his way to Spain where his forces defeated those of the Muslim ruler at the time. He then created a nearly autonomous Islamic mini-empire that answered to its own rulers.

The reconquest of Spain by the Spaniards, or the Reconquista, began in the 1000s in northern Spain and worked its way south over centuries. By the 1200s, Muslim rule was reduced to the Granada region. By the late 1400s, the Reconquista was successful and King Ferdinand and Queen Isabella were able to rule over a Christian and more or less united nation.

The most famous hero of the Reconquest was a figure known as El Cid, a military leader who was immortalized in *The Poem of the Cid*. He was probably the greatest warrior of his age, a sometime mercenary, and the man who freed the town of Valencia in 1094 from Muslim rule. For more on El Cid, see any number of books written about him as well as the classic film starring Charlton Heston—some of which is even true.

Meanwhile back in the rest of Europe, the Arabs made another assault on Constantinople in 717, nearly forty years after their first attack. This time, the power of the holy warriors was truly staggering: one hundred twenty thousand Arab and Persian Muslims set out for Constantinople on foot, horseback, and camelback. They crossed the Dardanelles straits—which separates the eastern and western portions of what is now Turkey—and surrounded the city. They planned to connect with another force of one hundred thousand Muslims who left from Syria and Egypt on eighteen hundred ships. But the plan started to go wrong quickly.

The Byzantines lured the invading fleet into their harbor, trapped them there, and then set on the Muslims with their "fireships" loaded with the dreaded Greek fire. The Byzantines quickly destroyed many of the invading ships, taking a great toll on the Muslim sailors.

One witness describes a Greek fire attack like this: "It came flying through the air like a winged long-tailed dragon, about the thickness of a hogshead, with the report of thunder and the velocity of lightning." The jihadists who had traveled on foot and the survivors of the debacle at sea decided to wait out and try to starve the Byzantines. However, the Muslims began to starve instead and then, when winter came, to freeze to death. Fregosi says that they "died of the cold in the tens of thousands, as well as their horses and camels."

In the spring, four hundred ships full of reinforcements from Egypt came to join the jihad against Constantinople, but they also faced the fireships. Meanwhile, Byzantine ground forces, with the support of the Bulgarians, "cut the weakened Arab troops to pieces."[75]

Finally, the invaders had to admit the inevitable and retreat. Out of the well over two hundred thousand jihadists who set out to conquer the city, only thirty thousand headed for home. Many of the surviving ships were destroyed in a storm and only five vessels finally returned to Syria.

However, the Muslims were far from finished with their assault on the West and, with the conquest of Spain, it did seem like the jihad was an unstoppable force. In fact, it would make continuous gains for the next nine centuries.

THE FRENCH SAVE EUROPE—NO, SERIOUSLY

Early in the eighth century, the Muslim Empire set its sights on France as its next addition to the family of believers. At the time, a man named Charles Martel (Charlemagne's grandfather) ruled much of northern France as well as nearby parts of Germany and Belgium.

In 721, jihadists started into France from the Pyrenees Mountains in the north of Muslim-ruled Spain. That year, invading Muslims took the town of Narbonne, murdered the men, and enslaved the women and children. According to Fregosi, the invaders' "preferred targets in France were usually the monasteries and churches, which they cheerfully plundered of all their holy objects, enslaving or killing the monks."[76]

These early excursions were simply raids and not a proper invasion effort, which would finally come in 732 when an invasion force of between twenty thousand and thirty thousand men, most on horseback, moved north. They met Charles Martel's force of about the same number of foot soldiers in a valley at Poitiers.

The Arab cavalry hit an impenetrable line of ground forces who stood side by side with their tough shields touching. The jihad had hit both a real and metaphorical wall in Europe. The Muslim warriors found that not only could they not make progress, but they also were pushed back by the overwhelming force of the French infantry.

As it turns out, the Muslim cavalry forces were ideal for raiding largely undefended villages and monasteries. However, they were less effective against the armored and shielded Franks, who were fighting for their homes and their families.

Accounts of the number of dead vary wildly, but one thing is clear: Martel won a decisive battle and the invaders executed a very speedy strategic withdrawal. According to military historian Victor Davis Hanson, they left behind "empty tents and booty—and their dead on the battlefield." He added, "Poitiers signaled a high watermark of Islamic advance in Europe: Muslim armies never again reached so far north. With the near simultaneous repulse of the Arabs from the harbors of Constantinople in 717, the Islamic wave of the prior century was at last checked at the periphery of Europe."[77] Martel would fight a few more battles, but the tide in France had already turned against the jihadists.

JIHAD, ITALIAN STYLE

Finding the French too tough an adversary, the jihad turned its attention to southern Italy, Sicily, and some of the big islands in the Mediterranean during the ninth and tenth centuries. Arab raiders had been attacking Sicily and plundering the island since the mid-600s but the full-scale invasion didn't start until 827. Sicily was no easy conquest. Fregosi describes it as "a slow occupation, marked by much fighting and many massacres. It took the Saracens seventy-five years to conquer the island."[78] In Sicily, the Muslims would stay for more than 250 years, until they were finally defeated by the same Normans who, in 1066, invaded England.

Not even Rome was spared from the jihad. In 848, jihadists looted St. Peter's Basilica, and the pope had to buy off the invaders with the promised tribute of twenty-five thousand silver coins a year.

Through much of the tenth century, Muslims attacked and harassed a swath of Europe from St. Tropez through southern France, including Marseille, Genoa, and up into Switzerland, Germany, and part of Italy. As usual, their progress was marked by massacres, looting, and the taking of slaves—though they were finally pushed out by the end of the 900s.

During this time, the Islamic Empire fractured. The Abbasids in the Middle East ruled from the new center of power in Baghdad. Theoretically, they had dominion over the entire Muslim world, but in reality, there were two other autonomous caliphates: the Umayyads in Spain and the Fatimids in North Africa.

And though the *Umma* had split, the faithful kept important Muslim traditions alive, including the jihad.

CHRISTIANITY STRIKES BACK

Meanwhile, back in Arabia, in 1031, the Umayyad caliphate collapsed and was replaced by dozens of small Islamic fiefdoms run by local rulers. This confusion served the ongoing effort to reconquer both Spain and Portugal. While the Muslims in Spain were fighting that battle, the Muslims of the Middle East were faced with a counter-jihad in their own backyard: the Crusades. Without a doubt the most misunderstood conflict in world history, the Crusades have the reputation of being the first example of European imperialist aggression against the Middle East.

That is what we call in my family, the opposite of true. It's like calling the Allied invasion of Berlin in World War II another example of American imperialism against the peace-loving German people. The fact is that the Crusades were a direct response to the jihad in Europe, particularly its success in Spain, and were purely *defensive* wars. Besides addressing the general and quite reasonable concern about the Islamic invasions across Europe, the Crusades had an important immediate cause: the Muslim closing of the route to the Holy Land used by Europeans making religious pilgrimages there. Here's a thought experiment: imagine that the United States invades and takes over Saudi Arabia and then cuts off access to Mecca, where each Muslim is supposed to make a pilgrimage in his or her lifetime. Can you hear the high-pitched shrieks accusing America of religious intolerance, the loud calls for a religious war? And that would just be in the United States. If the Muslim "street" got hysterical when America and its partners liberated more than fifty million Muslims from the Taliban and Saddam Hussein's tyranny, imagine how the same "street" would react if the United States denied Muslims the right to visit their holiest site.

And there you have the first Crusade.

Another major reason for the Crusades was that the Byzantine emperor, who faced a constant—and as we know very credible—threat from Muslim invaders, asked Pope Urban II for help.

From the beginning, the Crusades were very different from the jihad as practiced by Muslims, which was a perpetual state of warfare

THE CRUSADES VS. THE JIHAD: BATTLE OF THE HOLY WARS

The Crusades

Year begun: 1096.

Declared by: Pope Urban II at the request of embattled Byzantine emperor Alexius Comnenus.

Reason for Hostility: Response to massive gains in southern Europe by Muslim invaders waging jihad, as well as the Muslim Empire's cutting off of the Christian route to the Holy Land.

Disputed Area: A few square miles of Jerusalem.

Duration: On and off for 214 years.

Number of Campaigns: 8.

Number Enslaved: Very, very few if any.

Number Killed: In the thousands.

Status: Long over.

The Jihad

Year begun: Circa 645.

Declared by: Muhammad, at the request of Allah.

Reason for Hostility: To subject the rest of the world to either conversion to Islam or Muslim rule.

Disputed Area: The Earth. There has been actual fighting in most of the Middle East, the Near East, Africa, pretty much all of eastern and western Europe, as well as Asia, Indonesia, the United States, and . . . well, most of the globe really.

Duration: Continuous for over 1,350 years.

Number of Campaigns: In the thousands.

Number Enslaved: Millions.

Number Killed: Far, far too many to count because the jihadists lacked the record-keeping skills and attention to detail that characterized the Nazi Party's "atrocity management." However, this number is well into the millions.

Status: Ongoing.

with a goal of bringing the world under Islamic rule. The Crusades, on the other hand, had very limited objectives. According to Bernard Lewis, the objectives were, quite simply, "the conquest of the promised land, the defense of Christendom against non-Christian attack."[79]

The first Crusade was successful in 1099 and Jerusalem was claimed by the Christians. By 1144, Christian rule of Jerusalem was threatened and there were a number of subsequent Crusades to defend it. In 1187, the famed Islamic warrior Saladin recovered Jerusalem for Muslims. Though there would be a few more Christian campaigns over the next eighty years, they would be ultimately unsuccessful.

Considering the actual history, it's remarkable how much of a hot button the word *Crusade* has become. It's such a sore point that the media pilloried George Bush for using the term after 9/11. There is a strange sense that the Western world should be embarrassed by its behavior during that time. But the fact is that, as writer Thomas Madden, author of *A Concise History of the Crusades,* put it, "The crusades were in every way a *defensive war.* They were the West's belated response to the Muslim conquest of fully two-thirds of the Christian world."[80]

The constant bleating by Islamic militants and radical clerics reveals some interesting things about them. They claim every US military operation in a Muslim country (including the efforts of US soldiers to feed the starving people of Somalia) is an aggressive, imperialistic "Crusade" against Islam. This is, of course, fraught with irony when you consider that the Crusades were defensive in nature. This pattern shows that radicals are like bullies who absolutely cannot stand a taste of their own medicine.

This inability to cope with setbacks or counterattacks is a surprisingly consistent theme in Islamic history. As we discussed, the Qur'an says very clearly that Allah promises he will not allow infidels to triumph over Muslims. So these setbacks create both a psychological problem for the bully who can't believe the class weakling is kicking his butt, and a theological problem that calls into question the unchanging and perfect nature of the Qur'an. If the Qur'an could be wrong about the inevitability of Muslim victory, it could be wrong about other deeply held beliefs like the notion that Allah made the stars in the sky into missiles to throw at devils (Qur'an 67:5) and that Allah created the jinn, or demons, out of smokeless fire (Qur'an 55:15). And then there are the numerous suggestions that the world is flat and the Sun circles the Earth.

Once you start questioning clear truths like that . . . well, you have complete anarchy! Cats and dogs living together. . . .

SPREADING PEACE EVEN FARTHER

After the loss of Jerusalem, the twelfth century was marked by the continued and slow push by the Spaniards to free their country from Muslim rule. By the thirteenth century, Muslims would suffer another setback, this time in the heart of the remains of the Caliphate: Baghdad. In 1258, the city was taken by Mongols commanded by the grandson of Genghis Khan. According to Bernard Lewis, "The city was stormed, looted, and burnt."[81] In five hundred years the Abbasid caliphs had waged jihad and brought countless massacres and destruction on the House of War. Yet, now they were at the mercy of the Mongolian hordes that rounded up the caliph and as many of his family as they could find and butchered them. The Mongols would dissipate, but the Caliphate would never return. In the Middle East, the Abbasids' remaining power would be assumed by a number of regional Muslim rulers.

A new center of power for the Islamic Empire would form in Turkey where the aggressive pagan Turks started converting to Islam in the 1200s. The Ottoman Empire was founded by Othman I near the end of the thirteenth century. This new empire, on the doorstep of western Europe, would reinvigorate the jihad because in this new Islamic nation "continuous Holy War was the fundamental principle of the state," says Turkish historian Halil Inalcik.[82]

One of Othman's primary contributions to the jihad was the formation of the Janissary Corps, a military force made up of Christian men who had been taken from their parents when they were young, forcibly converted to Islam, and heavily indoctrinated and trained. According to Edward Creasy, author of the 1878 *History of the Ottoman Turks* (still a standard reference on the Ottoman Empire), "This military brotherhood grew up to be the strongest and fiercest instrument of imperial ambition, which remorseless fanaticism . . . ever devised upon earth."[83]

With the emerging Ottoman Empire, dark times were ahead for Europe. "Within a century, Holy War was to penetrate and overwhelm most of southeastern Europe and transform it for centuries into the Land of Islam,"[84] says Paul Fregosi. Dark times, indeed. The near-constant onslaught by the jihadists was punctuated by a series of massacres and heartbreaking losses all over Europe.

The early conquests of the Ottoman Empire were in what is now eastern Turkey, the large mountainous region called Asia Minor. Othman I personally took the town of Bursa, which would become the first Ottoman capital until it was moved in the mid-1300s to the city of Adrianople, just northwest of Constantinople. This was not an accident, because the Ottomans still had their eye on Constantinople.

The European jihad began when Othman's forces made their first steps into Europe and started taking territory in the Thrace region, which is the northeastern part of Greece, but the real gains for the Ottomans came when Othman's son Murad brought the jihad to Europe. As Fregosi puts it, "Murad not only led the first Turkish mass invasion force into the Balkans, he also tripled the size of the Ottoman Empire. He made Islam, and the Jihad, a seemingly permanent political force on the European continent."[85]

In 1371, a group of twenty thousand Christian Serbians and Hungarians set out to meet the Ottomans at their new capital of Andrianople. They were literally caught napping by Ottoman soldiers and most were massacred in their tents. There was a real sense of danger to all of Christendom, since Rome now lay between the Turks to the east and the North African Muslims to the west.

By the late fourteenth century, the Mongolian horde that had conquered Russia in the early to mid-thirteenth century had converted to Islam (now there's a picture: Mongols getting "civilized" by jihadists) and the Russian people were ready to fight back. A Russian force defeated an army of two hundred thousand Muslim Mongols and, according to Fregosi, "at the battle of Kulikove Pole in 1380 [they] sent them reeling back into their own territory."[86] After that, the Mongols, now called Tartars, developed closer ties to the Ottomans and fought Russians and Poles for another two hundred years.

The Ottomans turned their attention to Greece, and by 1387, the cradle of Western civilization was almost completely under Ottoman control, as it would be for another five hundred years. If you've seen the movie *My Big Fat Greek Wedding*, the film gets a fair amount of laughs by having the grandmother make a number of references to "bloodthirsty Turks." It's a funny bit in a funny movie, but we'll talk more later about what life was like for Greek and other non-Muslim Europeans living under Muslim masters when we talk about Islamic tolerance in chapter 5.

Next comes the fall of Kosovo in 1389, a tragic defeat for Europe. Combined with the previous defeat of the Serbian-Hungarian force in 1371, these two events "brought a large part of the Balkan peninsula under Ottoman rule, and reduced most of the rest to vassalage,"[87] according to Bernard Lewis.

Paul Fregosi says of the battle, "The date: June 15, 1389. A battle and a date that are universally mourned throughout the Balkans and even today . . . and that explains much of what is now happening in the Balkans."[88] A large pan-Balkan force of twenty thousand to thirty thousand Christian soldiers led by King Lazar of Serbia met a smaller force of invading Turks led by the Ottoman sultan Murad near the Kosovo Mountains. Though Murad was mortally wounded, the Ottomans won the day and Murad's oldest son, Bajazet, took power.

After Kosovo, next on the Ottoman hit list was Hungary, which knew it would soon face a force of forty thousand jihadist invaders. Since Hungary was a Catholic country, the Hungarians appealed to the pope for help, which came in the form of ten thousand French knights, who set out in 1396 and fought bravely in an effort to push the Ottomans out of Europe but were defeated in Bulgaria. True to form, Sultan Bajazet ordered thousands of surviving Christian troops beheaded on the spot.

This would be only the beginning of the Hungarian struggle

OTTOMAN FAMILY VALUES[89]

A new tradition was begun for Ottoman rulers at the battlefields of Kosovo. The Muslims had just won a major victory for the jihad, defeating a larger force and dramatically increasing the Ottoman domain. Apply your Radical Eye to the following question:

How did the new sultan and supreme ruler of the recently expanded Ottoman Empire celebrate this great victory?

a. By praying to Allah to thank him for this success and this opportunity to further spread His word and law on Earth.

b. By taking his victorious forces out for ice cream.

c. By setting aside some *alone time* to reflect on the great loss of life around him and to rethink the whole jihad business.

d. By ordering his brother strangled on the spot.

If you answered "d" you are correct. Though this may seem counterintuitive to most of us with a limited Western viewpoint, it makes perfect sense given the verse in the Qur'an that reads, "Unrest is worse than death." In this context, the murder of potential challengers to the throne not only makes good political sense, it is also—wait for it—a *religious* duty. As Paul Fregosi put it, "Peace and quiet are preferable to strife and trouble, and killing a potential troublemaker is therefore an act of great piety."[90]

Any questions?

Following is a select history of these Ottoman Religious Family Values as applied by the various sultans throughout the history of the empire.

SULTAN	REIGN	LEAST FAMILY-FRIENDLY MOMENT
Bajazet aka "The Thunderbolt"	1389–1402	Had his younger brother, Yakub, strangled within minutes of his father's death from wounds sustained in the Battle of Kosovo in 1389. The murder took place in the presence of their father's corpse. Strangulation would become the method of choice for disposing of unwanted relatives of the new sultan because it respected the taboo against spilling noble blood.
Mahomet I	1402–1421	Mahomet conspired with his brother Musa to overthrow and murder their brother Rumelia. After that, Mahomet joined forces with the Byzantine emperor to overthrow and kill Musa. Then, showing a rare compassion for an Ottoman sultan, Mahomet I had his sole surviving brother blinded instead of killed.
Murad II	1421–1451	Ordered his thirteen-year-old brother Mustafa executed. To be fair, Mustafa had actually rebelled against his brother and led an army to besiege part of Murad's territory.
Mahomet II aka "The Conqueror" and "The Drinker of Blood"	1451–1481	Took immediate and decisive action upon taking office and executed his chief rival, his infant brother. Cleverly, he had the boy drowned while the boy's mother was busy congratulating Mahomet on ascending to the throne. Mahomet then ordered the grieving woman married off to a slave.
Selim I aka "The Grim" and "The Brave"	1512–1520	After taking the throne by successfully rebelling against his father, Selim executed his two brothers. He also ordered his five nephews killed and watched them die as the youngest of them begged his uncle for his life.

Suleiman I aka "The Magnificent" and "The Lawgiver"	1520– 1566	Believing that his son Mustafa was plotting against him, Suleiman had the young man strangled while Suleiman was nearby in the same tent. Suleiman later learned that he had been too hard on the boy, who was not actually trying to overthrow him. In another succession dispute, Suleiman later had his second son, Bajazet (who had actually rebelled against his father), killed as well as the young man's four infant sons.
Murad III	1574– 1595	In his first act as sultan, he ordered the execution of his five brothers.
Mahomet III	1595– 1603	On taking office, Mahomet immediately ordered his nineteen brothers strangled. For good measure, he eliminated his father's seven pregnant concubines by having them thrown into the sea. Before he died, he feared one of his sons was plotting to overthrow him and had the young man killed as well.
Ahmed I	1603– 1617	Ahmed distinguished himself because he refused to put his mentally handicapped brother Mustafa to death. Technically, he doesn't belong in this column, but I thought he deserved mention for being one of the very few Ottoman rulers who declined to murder a close family member.
Murad IV	1623– 1640	During his reign, Murad had three of his brothers killed. He also ordered some of his own concubines drowned and would use women for target practice, firing at them with arrows and bullets. A vicious drunk, he would sometimes cut strangers down on the street with his sword. With his dying breath, he ordered his brother Ibrahim killed. Ibrahim hid until his brother died and then he became sultan.

against the jihad. Like the battle for Spain, it is full of great heroes like the Hungarian warrior Janos Hunyadi, who joined the fight against the jihad in 1444 and, according to Fregosi, "probably has done more than any other individual in history to stem the Muslim invasion that, in the fifteenth century, threatened to overwhelm Europe." Together, "the Hungarian and Albanian heroes brought to a grinding halt the Muslim assault on Europe for a quarter century."[91] However, after decades of Islamic onslaught, and weakened by internal divisions, Hungary was finally defeated by Ottoman forces in 1526. According to Creasy, the victorious holy warriors "drove before them a miserable herd of 100,000 Christians, men, women, and little children, destined for sale in the Turkish slave-markets."[92]

Even as Hunyadi and others were resisting the jihad in the mid-fifteenth century, the Ottomans were planning once again to try to take the last remnant of the Byzantine Empire. "Besieging Constantinople had become . . . almost a permanent fixture of Ottoman political and military activity,"[93] says Fregosi. When new sultan Mahomet II took power in 1451, he decided to finish the job once and for all.

As it turned out, he chose a good time for his assault. France and England were still smarting after their Hundred Years' War and didn't answer the city's desperate calls for help. Only three European bodies did respond. One was the Republic of Genoa, which sent seven hundred men; the others were the Vatican, which sent two hundred men, and the Christian patriarch of Venice, who also sent two hundred men. This to help defend a city of one hundred thousand people whose own defensive forces numbered about five thousand.

Mahomet II, who was a devout pederast and whose nickname around the empire was "The Drinker of Blood," sent a force of between one hundred thousand and one hundred and fifty thousand to take the city. The stage was set and, once again, the odds were overwhelming.

As before, the Muslim attackers decided to amass their forces around the city to starve the people out. Though this tactic had failed spectacularly in the past, this time the Muslims had something new: Western-made cannons they used against the city's walls for several weeks beginning in April of 1453. Yet the defenders stood firm and held off a force of fifty thousand Ottoman soldiers who attacked on the city's gates in May.

To picture the kind of struggle the residents of Constantinople faced, imagine the Battle of Helm's Deep in the second *Lord of the Rings* book and film, where a small group of defenders faced an army of tens of thousands of Orcs. Like Tolkien's heroes, the defenders of the city knew that if they failed their own lives would be lost, as would the lives of their wives and children—for the Ottomans, like the Orcs, would give no quarter to the vanquished.

Come on, you are not really comparing the Ottoman jihadists to Orcs?
You bet I am.

The defenders hoped that help would come from Europe. Unfortunately, however, for them, no help came from the men of the West, as it did when the wizard Gandalf rode in with the men of Rohan.

Knowing the end was near, on October 28, a final mass was celebrated in the great nine-hundred-year-old cathedral Hagia Sophia, then one of the greatest churches in Christendom. As Fregosi describes the scene, "In the crowded church, in the dim light, the candle flames fluttering in the drafts; men, women, and children, entire families, crowded together, praying and sobbing and hugging one another and singing hymns to beseech mercy."

The next day, the Turks made their final attack, sending an endless stream of soldiers, and after a day of brutal fighting they were victorious. Hagia Sophia, Christianity's most spectacular church after St. Peter's in Rome, was now the final refuge for several thousand people—men, women, and children from all walks of life who locked the doors and prayed.

According to Fregosi, when the Ottomans stormed in, "they raped, of course, the nuns being the first victims, and slaughtered. At least four thousand were killed before Mahomet (the sultan) stopped the massacre." Then the great leader of the Orcs—I mean jihadists—ordered a cleric to dedicate the cathedral to Allah. For nearly five centuries it remained a mosque where Muslims prayed five times a day on the site where thousands were raped and murdered by warriors for their faith. In the end, fifty thousand of the city's survivors were rounded up and sold into slavery.

It was over for the last vestige of the once great Byzantine Empire, and the dream of the Prophet himself had been fulfilled. With all of the rape, murder, and enslavement out of the way, the religion of peace now reigned supreme in Constantinople. The city was renamed Istanbul and immediately made the capital of the Ottoman Empire.

VIENNA PART 1: THE JIHAD GETS A SURPRISE

The fall of Constantinople was widely regarded as a disaster throughout the Christian world. In fact, it is impossible to overstate the sense of grief felt in Europe, both because of the horrors inflicted on the inhabitants of the city and the sense of loss at what Constantinople represented about a shared European past. Of course, Europeans had good reason to fear that they might also share the fate of the people of Constantinople.

Despite the fact that most studies of the Renaissance ignore the jihad completely, the truth is that jihad and the fall of Constantinople cast a dark shadow over the entire Renaissance. We remember very well the great period of art dominated by the works of Michelangelo, Raphael, and Leonardo da Vinci, as well as the explosion of new work in literature, architecture, and philosophy—including the rise of humanism. However, history ignores the fact that, as Paul Fregosi puts it, "The Turkish threat was for centuries the main concern of all the European nations, and every European man and woman lived in terror of the Turks."

Energized by his great victory at Constantinople, Mahomet II next planned to take Rome and bragged that his forces would "stable their horses by the high altar of St. Peter's."[94] He consolidated his hold on the Balkans, taking firm control of Serbia and Bosnia.

In Sultan Mahomet's push to Rome, the next major stop was in

Belgrade, which is now the capital and largest city in Serbia. The same cannons that had brought down the walls of Constantinople were turned on the walls of Belgrade. However, the defense of this city had taken on the air of a Crusade and the battle was joined by Hungarian hero Janos Hunyadi and a Franciscan friar named Juan de Capistrano, who would later become a saint.

The Ottoman forces were again led by Mahomet II himself. Friar Capistrano led a counterattack against tens of thousands of Turks with one thousand crusaders. As Fregosi describes it, "The Turks fled, panic stricken, calling on Allah for help."[95] Besides losing the battle, Mahomet's forces suffered twenty-five thousand casualties.

After that defeat, Mahomet decided to get serious about taking Rome. He first attacked the Greek island of Rhodes, was unsuccessful, and then attempted to take the heel of Italy only to be repelled by another mini-Crusade in 1481. However, Mahomet's grandson Suleiman would succeed where his grandfather had failed and take Belgrade in 1521 and Rhodes in 1522—though he would never see Rome.

Suleiman also finished the job in Hungary, whose population got to experience Islamic tolerance firsthand. According to Fregosi, "Probably three million Hungarians were enslaved and deported all over the Ottoman Empire."[96]

In the context of these victories, the jihad seemed to once again be an unstoppable force and Christian Europe had very good reason to fear the Ottomans. The sultan's new target was Vienna. It was the capital of the Holy Roman Empire, which had been ruled by the Hapsburgs for four hundred years starting in the mid-900s, and which included Germany, most of Italy, and parts of France, Poland, and Hungary. In 1529, the Ottomans attacked, and though the Viennese were outnumbered ten to one, the city held and the jihad was kept at bay.

The Ottomans spent the next two decades focused on harassing the Mediterranean with raids to capture slaves and other booty. There was also a parallel effort at piracy by the Algerians of North Africa who, according to Creasy, "infested the western parts of the English Channel and the Irish Sea for many years; and the Algerian rovers more than once landed in Ireland, and sacked towns and villages, and carried off captives into slavery. They even ventured as far as Iceland and Scandinavia."

In 1566, an Ottoman army of two hundred thousand men set out to try to take Vienna again but was turned back en route when it stopped to take a Hungarian town and was repelled. However, as with Constantinople, the jihad was not finished with Vienna.

There was still more than a hundred years of jihad before the next battle for Vienna. In 1571, the Ottomans attacked the Greek island of Cyprus, which was a Venetian colony. After laying siege to the city of Famagusta, they captured the town and started with the usual torturing, massacring, and enslaving. It was business as usual for the jihadists, but forces were gathering against them.

VIENNA PART 2, DÉJÀ VU ALL OVER AGAIN

Pope Pius V put together an alliance called the Holy League, which included Venice, Spain, and the Vatican. Europe was reeling from the loss of Cyprus, and after decades of extensive Muslim slave raids on the Mediterranean coast, the pope decided that it was time to take action. In the fall of 1571, a combined naval force was put together to stop the menace of the Ottoman fleet. It included two hundred and forty warships and seventy-six smaller ships carrying fifty thousand rowers and thirty thousand soldiers. According to military historian Victor Davis Hanson, this was a "pan-Christian force in size not seen since the crusades."[97]

This force met the larger Ottoman fleet in the Mediterranean, just off of Lepanto, Greece. The Ottomans had two hundred and thirty fullsized warships, eighty more gunships, and one hundred thousand men. The Holy League was outnumbered but it had the advantage of a few pieces of technological and tactical innovation that helped win the day, including more and better cannons, and four new ships, called galleasses, that were significantly larger and better armed than any in the sultan's fleet. According to Hanson, because of the efforts of these gal-leasses, "a third of the Ottoman armada was scattered, disabled, or sunk" before the proper battle between both fleets was begun. "As many as 10,000 Turkish seamen were thrown into the sea when their galleys were obliterated in thirty minutes of firing from just four Euro-pean ships."[98] The Holy League prevailed. According to Fregosi, "The Turks had lost 210 ships of which 130 had been captured and eight sunk. Twenty-five thousand Muslims and some 7,500 Christians had been killed."[99]

To put that into perspective, Lepanto's forty thousand dead (count-ing galley slaves) and thousands wounded or missing would make Lepanto, according to Hanson, "one of the bloodiest single-day slaughters on land or sea in the history of warfare."[100] But it was not only historic because of its carnage, but because, as Hanson says, "Lepanto would be one of the last great battles in history in which a few Western powers united solely on the basis of shared culture and religion against Islam."[101]

Entering the seventeenth century, the jihad in Europe was high-lighted by continued fighting in the Balkans, including a revolt in Transylvania, a major defeat in Hungary, and a decades-long siege of Crete, which the Ottomans finally took in 1669. The jihadists were also successful in taking Poland in 1672, only to lose it again to the Poles and the Russians led by King John Sobieski of Poland in 1681.

Though the jihad seemed to have lost momentum, the Ottomans still represented a considerable threat that was much feared in Europe. Finally, Sultan Mahomet IV decided to go on the offensive in Europe and set his sights on Vienna.

The stakes were enormous. With control of Vienna, all of western Europe would be at the mercy of the Ottoman Empire. Stories of the brutality the jihad inflicted on the vanquished were legend, and Euro-peans well knew of the crushing oppression suffered by the Christians living under Islamic rule in Spain, Greece, and eastern Europe.

In many ways, the second siege of Vienna seemed like déjà vu all over again, with eerie comparisons to the final successful siege of Constantinople. The Ottoman grand vizier had a force of 250,000 troops prepared to "defend Islam" by attacking a city far from home that was no threat to the Ottomans. The quarter million jihadists encamped outside the city were determined to starve the inhabitants out while pounding the walls with cannon. Once again, the battle invites comparison to the defense of the Battle of Helm's Deep from the *Lord of the Rings* trilogy. Vienna had a small number of defenders—eleven thousand in this case—facing overwhelming odds and a large, brutal army of Orcs—I mean foot soldiers of the "Religion of Peace."

Come on, that's a cheap shot.

Well, sure, but the Ottomans do make it easy. And while you might argue that, like modern terrorists, the Ottoman rulers had hijacked or perverted Islam to suit their own evil purposes, you can hardly call the vast sixteenth-century Ottoman Empire and the quarter-million-man army a "tiny minority of extremists."

On the way to Vienna, the Islamic soldiers plundered the countryside and captured more than thirty thousand slaves. They also massacred the entire population of four thousand people in a nearby town to give the Viennese a taste of what would happen if their city fell. Like Constantinople in 1453, Vienna sent desperate pleas for help to the major powers of western Europe. Like Constantinople, they were mostly ignored, except for one significant exception: King John Sobieski of Poland, who had been the great hero of the successful Polish resistance to the jihad several years before.

Sobieski rode out with three thousand cavalry to face the massive Muslim force. On the way, he picked up thousands of soldiers in Poland and Germany until he had amassed a force of nearly sixty thousand men. They arrived on September 12, just in time, since, after two months of constant bombardment, the walls of the city were crumbling.[102]

Gandalf had arrived with the men of the West.

The Ottoman invaders still outnumbered the defenders nearly four to one but Vienna now had three key advantages. First, the Ottomans were caught between the soldiers in the city and Sobieski's forces, which had come racing down from the mountains. Second, the defenders knew they were fighting for their lives, their families, and, quite likely, the fate of what remained of Christian Europe. As Sobieski himself put it, "It is not a city alone that we have to save, but the whole of Christianity, of which the city of Vienna is the bulwark. The war is the holy one."[103] Just to be clear, it's worth pointing out that by "holy war" Sobieski did *not* mean a brutal war of aggression that involved systemic massacre, rape, and enslavement with the ultimate goal of subjugating and humiliating anyone who didn't share his religious views.

The third advantage Vienna had was that Sobieski scared the pants off the jihadists, who remembered their previous defeats at his hands.

Facing this new threat, the Ottoman military leader Grand Vizier Mustapha bravely sized up the situation and ran for his life, as did most of his forces. They were in such a rush to retreat that they neglected to perpetrate the traditional massacre of the 30,000 people they had enslaved on the way to battle. Now, the only soldiers left were the dreaded Janissaries who were still in front of the city. These were the most dedicated, or fanatical, troops in the empire. They had committed their whole lives to Allah and the jihad. Now that they were facing what was probably a fair fight, they, to quote the film *Monty Python and the Holy Grail*, "bravely turned their tails and fled." As Fregosi says, "It was no longer just a defeat, but a rout."[104]

Unlike the first siege of Vienna in which, as Bernard Lewis says, "The Turkish retreat was orderly, their defeat inconclusive. . . . This time the Turkish defeat was total and final."[105] Or, as Creasy put it, "Never was a victory more complete."[106]

As one contemporary Turkish chronicler wrote, "This was a calamitous defeat, of such magnitude that there has never been its like since the first appearance of the Ottoman state."[107]

The day that Sobieski and his forces arrived, September 12, 1683, marked the beginning of the end of the Ottoman Empire. Thus, September 11 was its last day of "greatness." There has been very credible speculation that Osama bin Laden and al Qaeda's choice of date for the 9/11 attacks was for just this reason.

SELECTED MASSACRES AND
OTHER ATROCITIES OF THE EUROPEAN JIHAD:
OR, EUROPE ON FIVE MASSACRES A DAY[108]

The jihad in Europe was marked by countless abuses committed against civilians, vanquished armies, and numerous others who had the misfortune to be in the wrong place at the wrong time.

To qualify for this list, the actions taken had to be vicious and serve no useful military or political purpose. Of course, this is an incomplete tally and represents only a sampling of the atrocities committed in the name of Allah in Europe. However, it gives a clear idea of the fate that befell many hundreds of thousands of innocent Europeans who had the misfortune of having the various Islamic powers declare their brand of "peace" on them.

649—Cyprus: In probably the first large-scale massacre by the jihad in Europe, almost the entire town of Constantine in Cyprus was massacred, with survivors taken away to be sold as slaves. The attack on Cyprus included seventeen hundred ships and was, according to Fregosi, "the first major Arab naval enterprise." Muslim slavers would wreak havoc in Mediterranean Europe until 1830 when the French conquered Algiers.

668—Sicily: Suffered much the same fate as Cyprus, with countless people massacred and many taken as slaves. The women of Sicily were highly prized in the Muslim slave markets.

721—France: After the successful invasion of Spain, Muslim forces turned their attention to France. Crossing the Pyrenees Mountains that separated Spain and France, holy warriors took the town of Septimania, in the Catalan province, killing every single man in the town and enslaving all of the women and children.

739—France: Hitting Lerins Island off of Cannes, Muslim raiders massacred nearly all of the five hundred monks at the famous Benedictine monastery, leaving just four alive.

792—Spain: After hearing rumors that some of the recent Christian converts to Islam were planning a rebellion, the Muslim leader al-Hakam invited as many as five thousand of them to a reception. The hapless new Muslims were led to a pit where they were slaughtered. One of al-Hakam's favorite forms of execution was crucifixion. According to Fregosi, "The dying or rotting corpses of dissidents, hanging from their crosses, dotted the Spanish landscape." In one case, al-Hakam revealed the typical radical Muslim inability to see irony by having his guards crucify ten people who were staging a demonstration against the crucifixions.

859—Sicily: The seventy-five-year battle to take Sicily was, according to Fregosi, "marked by much fighting and many massacres." In 859, the Muslims murdered eight thousand people in the Sicilian town of Castrogiovanni.

981—Spain: During the fighting in Spain, Muslim forces took the town of Zamora from the Christians and executed four thousand captives.

984—Spain: After taking Barcelona, jihadists massacred "most of the leading citizens and soldiers . . . the survivors [were] enslaved, and the city plundered and burned."[109]

1084—Sicily: In the town of Reggio, the jihadists burned down all of the churches. They also forced all of the monks at the Rocca d'Asino monastery into slavery.

1131—Spain: When jihadists captured the town of Escalona, they murdered all of the men and, true to form, enslaved the women and children.

1145—Algeria: Jihad was not restricted to the fight against the infidel. Often, Muslim leaders would declare a jihad in a battle against other Muslim forces. In 1145, after particularly vicious fighting between factions in Algeria, one hundred thousand Muslims were slaughtered. Okay, Algeria is not in Europe, but I include this entry in the interest of balance. Not all victims of the jihad were Christians and Jews.

1389—Kosovo: After the successful battle of conquest at Kosovo, the sultan Bajazet was so upset by the Muslim losses that he ordered all of the Christian prisoners beheaded. The task of chopping off so many heads proved exhausting and, after some hours, the executioners cut off the victims' opposing hands and feet (a trick they picked up from the Prophet himself) and let them bleed to death.

1396—Bulgaria: In the battle of Nicopolis, six thousand French soldiers who had responded to a cry for help from Hungary died to stop the jihad. Though the Muslim forces were victorious, Sultan Bajazet was so appalled at the great number of Muslim casualties that he ordered all the French Christian prisoners executed, killing as many as three thousand men.

1453—Constantinople: No survey of massacres of the European jihad would be complete without mention of the rape, wholesale murder, and enslavement that the victorious holy warriors inflicted on tens of thousands of Constantines. So many people were enslaved at once that the price of slaves hit historic lows in Turkey.

1512–1520—Throughout the Ottoman Empire and Beyond: Sultan Selim the Grim was an equal opportunity massacrer. The Sunni Muslim leader ordered the forty thousand Shiites in his realm executed. Then, he took Cairo, installed himself as caliph, and had fifty thousand citizens killed. Near the end of his life, he ordered all Christians in the Ottoman Empire put to death. Though the command was not carried out, it highlights the vulnerability of infidels living under Muslim rule.

1526—Hungary: After the Battle of Mohacs, in which Hungary fell to the invading Muslim soldiers, the victors executed more than two thousand prisoners. One hundred thousand people were sold into slavery after the battle.

Early to mid–1500s—Italy: The famous Muslim naval leader called Barbarossa or "Red Beard" by the Italians was "the greatest provider of laborers for the work force in Algeria and the greatest provider of concubines for the harems," according to Fregosi. In the town of Minorca, he carried off six thousand people into slavery. In Calabria, he killed anyone who resisted and his forces "raped, cowed, and abducted" all the attractive women. In Apulia, he enslaved ten thousand more people.

Landing in southern Italy at Otranto and planning to move on and sack Rome, he defeated the Italian defenders there, took many prisoners, promised to spare their lives, and then massacred them. Giving up on his dream of taking Rome, he returned home with ten thousand new slaves.

1529—Vienna: After failing to take Vienna in the first unsuccessful siege, the jihad forces killed the thousands of prisoners they had collected as they pillaged their way toward the city.

1570—Cyprus: After laying siege to the town of Nicosia for six weeks, the Muslim invaders promised to spare the lives of the defenders. Immediately upon their surrender, the jihadists tortured and killed them. Two thousand young boys and girls where then shipped back to Istanbul to live out lives of sexual servitude.

1571—Cyprus: At this time, Cyprus was a Venetian colony. The town of Famagusta fell after a long siege. The jihadists started torturing the local governor, Bragadino. They cut off his ears and nose and then threw him in a cell for two weeks. Then they dragged him out and abused him in public, eventually stringing him up for all to see. Finally, the Muslim torturers skinned him alive. When he was dead, the jihadists filled the skin with straw and displayed it in the streets. Then the stuffed skin was proudly displayed on the Muslim leader's ship. News of the treatment of Bragadino would later galvanize the Christian forces at the Battle of Lepanto.

1638—Baghdad: Ottoman Sultan Murad IV, who was mad as a hatter, took Baghdad and had all of the city's thirty thousand soldiers massacred.

1656–1661—Ottoman Empire: During his five-year reign as grand vizier of the empire, Mohammed Kiuprili declared war on corruption and executed more than thirty-six thousand Muslims.

1683—Germany: On the way to their great defeat in Vienna, the forces of the jihad pillaged the countryside, raping and killing many along the way and taking thirty thousand prisoners who they intended to later sell at the slave markets of Istanbul. Just a few miles from Vienna, they massacred four thousand people in the village of Perchtoldsdorf. Normally, a retreating Muslim army would kill all of its prisoners, but these holy warriors left in such haste that they only had time to behead a concubine who refused to go with them and kill an ostrich for undisclosed reasons.

By the time of the final battle for Vienna, the war that was declared by Muhammad himself was turning in favor of the infidels. As Bernard Lewis puts it, "For the first thousand years or so of the long struggle between the two world systems, the Muslims on the whole had the upper hand." Even the eventual loss of Spain, Portugal, and Sicily were "more than compensated by the Turkish advance into southeastern Europe and the creation of a new Muslim power on Christian soil, which for a while threatened the very heart of Europe."[110] Though some historians argue about how much of the decline of the Ottoman Empire was a direct result of the setback at Vienna, few deny that this battle was a major turning point in the thousand-year Christian struggle against the jihad.

Had Vienna fallen there was a very real danger that all of western Europe would have come under Islamic rule. I'll describe in the next chapter what life was like in eastern Europe for Christians and Jews, and what life would have been like had the Ottoman influence spread. For now, we'll enjoy the victory that started the fall of the Ottoman Empire, once the most powerful political force in the world. Until then, it had been a thousand-year journey up, filled with many conquests in the name of Allah.

It would be a long way down.

Chapter Five

TOLERANCE AND DIVERSITY

Or, The Right to Practice Any Religion as Long as It's Islam

Degradation of the Infidels in this world before the afterlife—where it is their fate [to be degraded]—is considered an act of piety.

—Caliph al-Amir bi-AhkanM Illah,
supreme ruler of the Muslim world
from 1101–1130[111]

TOLERANCE, RADICAL STYLE

"Islam is a religion of tolerance." We've heard this refrain almost as much as we've heard, "Islam is a religion of peace." In fact, if you listen only to the self-proclaimed experts from organizations like CAIR and MESA (the Middle Eastern Studies Association), you would be left thinking that the only real controversy with respect to Islam today is which is greater, its peacefulness or its tolerance.

The problem is that there are inconvenient facts and widely reported stories about the state of "tolerance" in the Islamic world. There is the famous case of Salman Rushdie, a British citizen, whose book *Satanic Verses* earned him a death sentence from the Ayatollah Khomeini himself in February of 1989 and a bounty of $2.8 million that remains on Rushdie's head seventeen years later.

But Islam is a religion of tolerance.

Sudan is in the news because Arab Muslims are committing atrocities against the black African Muslims in the Darfur region. Then there were the two million or more Christian Sudanese killed or sold into slavery in the years following the 1987 imposition of Islamic holy law.

But Islam is a religion of tolerance.

Vicious anti-Semitic, anti-Christian, and anti-American doctrine is taught in Muslim schools and is widely distributed even in American mosques. One pamphlet distributed in the Islamic Center of *Washington, DC*, reads: "To be dissociated from the infidels is to hate them for their religion . . . to be on one's guard against them, never to imitate them, and to always oppose them in every way according to *Islamic Law*"[112] (italics mine).

But Islam is a religion of tolerance.

Mein Kampf is a best seller throughout the Muslim world and topped the charts in 2005 in the great model of a secularized Muslim nation: Turkey.[113]

But Islam is a religion of tolerance.

In both Iran and Saudi Arabia it is against the law to publicly practice any religion other than Islam. In Iran, this year, an officer in the Iranian army was thrown in jail. His crime: practicing Christianity. Of course, it could have been worse: as we saw in 2006, a convert to Christianity in Afghanistan narrowly escaped the death penalty.

But Islam is a religion of tolerance.

The Islamic holy men running Iran have always been harsh with traditional journalists who criticize the regime or have unpopular politics. Recently, according to BBC News, the Iranian government has started persecuting Internet journalists, arresting at least two-dozen Webloggers, or "bloggers," over a period of six months.[114]

But Islam is a religion of tolerance.

Converts from Islam are being harassed and persecuted by members of the Muslim community *in England.*

But Islam is a religion of tolerance.

In September 2005, a Danish newspaper published a small number of political cartoons depicting the Prophet Muhammad. In early 2006, the entire Muslim world exploded in rage at the cartoons. Embassies were burned, Christians were murdered, and dozens died in violent riots.

But Islam is a religion of tolerance.

Taken together, these incidents make it seem like calling Islam a religion of tolerance is like calling Genghis Khan a man of peace. Or is there more to the story? Is this apparently intolerant form of the religion true Islam, or is it another example of *fake, brutal, and murderous not-really-real Islam?*

THE QUR'AN ON PEACE

Once again, our first stop in getting to the bottom of this mystery will be the Qur'an. Defenders of Islam point out that the religion's holiest book instructs the Muslim faithful to respect "People of the Book"— or followers of Judaism and Christianity. In fact, we are told that infidels were granted special, "protected" status in various Islamic empires throughout history.

Sura 109 of the Qur'an does say, "Unto you your religion, and unto me my religion" (109:6). There's sura 2, which says, "There is no compulsion in religion." These lines are promising and do suggest that people must come to Islam of their own free will.

Then there's sura 7, which clearly says that those who "deny Allah's revelation" are "evil." And another verse says, "The curse of Allah is on disbelievers" (2:89). Still another says, "Take not the Jews and the Christians for friends. They are friends to one another. He among you who taketh them for friends is (one) of them" (5:51). Got that? Non-Muslims are evil, cursed, and shouldn't be taken as friends.

This kind of thinking figures prominently in pamphlets and books being openly distributed in mosques and Islamic schools all over the United States, as per a recent study done by the human rights group Freedom House (more on that study in chapter 8, "Education").

There are also many verses of the Qur'an that refer to the nasty tortures Christians and Jews will face in hell. My favorite comes from sura 56: "Lo! Those who disbelieve Our revelations, We shall expose them to the Fire. As often as their skins are consumed We shall exchange them for fresh skins that they may taste the torment. Lo! Allah is ever Mighty, Wise."

My radical to English translation: infidels in hell will regularly have their skin burned off, replaced with new skin, and burned off again, etc. etc. Plus, Allah is mighty and wise.

Sura 4 is also pretty clear when it says to kill the infidels "wherever you find them."

But what about the protection the Qur'an *guarantees "People of the Book" living in Muslim territory? I've heard that the Muslim rulers were very tolerant of Jews and Christians in the lands they controlled.*

The source of some of the talk on this subject comes from Qur'an 9:29, which says: "Fight those who believe not in Allah nor the Last Day, nor hold that forbidden which hath been forbidden by Allah and His Messenger, nor acknowledge the religion of Truth, (even if they are) of the People of the Book, until they pay the *jizya* with willing submission, and feel themselves subdued." This verse calls for Muslims to fight infidels until the unbelievers either "acknowledge the religion of Truth" or pay a non-Muslim poll tax, called the *jizya*, and are properly "subdued" or subservient to their new Muslim masters. Under those circumstances, a Christian or a Jew, called a *dhimmi*, will be *tolerated*.

Think of it this way: a small group of Muslims launch an invasion of the United States and quickly overrun the country. Once the ruling Islamic minority is firmly in charge it announces that there is good news and bad news. The bad news is that Americans will now face death until they "feel themselves subdued" and pay a special infidel tax. The good news is that the Americans will then be *tolerated* in their own country.

Sound absurd? It happened all over the world during the more than thirteen hundred years of the jihad. Substitute the word *Spain* for *the United States* in the above paragraph and you see the system the Spanish had to live under for seven centuries.

Unfortunately, our study of the Qur'an is inconclusive. You can make a case for a tolerant Islam that doesn't force itself on non-Muslims, allows them to practice their religion, and even, sort of, protects them. Or you can make a case for a brutal, violent Islam that despises infidels, makes war on them because of their religion, and calls on the Muslim faithful to make sure infidels feel plenty subdued.

So, left without a clear map in the Qur'an, our next stop in the search for true Islam will be with the Prophet himself. Again, few if any Muslims would deny that Muhammad represents the true spirit of Islam. Let's see how he scores on the tolerance meter.

THE PROPHET INVENTS ISLAMIC TOLERANCE AND FOUNDS HIS OWN SCHOOL OF LITERARY CRITICISM

According to the Hadith, Muhammad made it very clear that the punishment for leaving Islam (called apostasy) was death. So, Muslims may not force you to join, but once you're in you might as well be a member of the Soprano or the Corleone crime families, because the only way out involves sleeping with the fishes.

Then there's the question of the apparent intolerance of the Islamic community for people like Salman Rushdie who criticize Islam. As it turns out, Muhammad also faced criticism in his early days as he was solidifying his rule in Medina. As we discussed briefly in chapter 3, poets were among Muhammad's first critics and his reaction to these writers explains a lot of Muslim history since. One of the first scores that the Prophet settled when he took power was with a female poet named Asma bint Marwan. As Paul Fregosi tells it, "She had spoken and written most disparagingly of the Prophet, whom she regarded with deep suspicion and, in memorable verse, had called upon her fellow citizens to throw him out."[115]

The Prophet was furious and his sentence was swift. The writer was killed in her sleep, her assassin plunging the dagger in so deep that she was "nailed to her couch." A male poet named Abu Afak was also killed in his sleep for insulting Muhammad. Still another poet named Cab, who traveled to Mecca to try to unite the people to take action against the Prophet, had his throat cut when he returned to Muhammad-ruled Medina.

Apparently, Muhammad was particularly sensitive to anything that made fun of him personally. According to Bernard Lewis, "In one case, not only was the composer of a satire executed, but a singing girl who had sung and recited the poem was also put to death."[116]

In seventh-century Arab culture, poetry was a very advanced and sophisticated literary form as well as an important method of disseminating political and social thought. It was also a primary method of spreading either propaganda or satire. For obvious reasons, Muhammad's reaction to dissent had an extremely chilling effect on this form of expression.

After Muhammad's experiences with poets, apparently Allah himself developed a distaste for them and revealed to the Prophet the following addition to the Qur'an, "As for poets, the erring follow them" (26:224).

Next, we'll look to Muhammad's life for the origins of the relationship between Muslims and the *protected* "People of the Book," living under Islamic rule. The ranking modern scholar on the subject is Bat Ye'or, who describes the relationship as a "ransom-protection" system, which is based on Muhammad's treatment of the Jews of Arabia. This, of course, does not include the Jews of Medina because Muhammad killed all of them between 624 and 627. Though, to be fair, after they were all dead, Muhammad tolerated them just fine.

The first Jews conquered by Muhammad and allowed to live were the Jews of Khaybar, which was an oasis about 140 miles from

Medina. According to Ye'or, the people there surrendered to Muhammad and the terms of the agreement they reached with the Prophet "formed the basis of the *dhimmi* status. The Prophet allowed the Jews to farm their lands, but only as tenants; he demanded delivery of half their harvest and reserved the right to drive them out when he wished."[117] Thus, they were not only "allowed" to live, but they would be granted the Prophet's protection. Similar protection contracts were offered in the next few years to other Jewish and Christian tribes on the Arabian Peninsula.

Theoretically, the special tax paid by the *dhimmis*, the *jizya*, funded the cost of protecting them; however, it's worth noting that though there was a danger of Bedouin raids, the greatest danger to the non-Muslims was from Muhammad's own forces. In that context, this system seems like a mob protection money scheme familiar to viewers of historical chronicles like *Baretta* and *Starsky and Hutch* as well as contemporary accounts from such sources as *The Sopranos*. So, yes, while technically the infidels living in Muslim-controlled lands were tolerated, it's not tolerance as we understand it today. Infidels were by no means thought of or treated as equals to Muslims, and they had no inalienable right to life, which is something we take for granted. Their continued existence, which was allowed only as long as they remained a financial asset to the *Umma*, was part of a business transaction, not a moral principle.

Nevertheless, it's tempting to think that this system was probably pretty enlightened considering the time and place. However, it's important to mention that given the widely held Muslim belief that the Qur'an is the unchanging Word of Allah and, according to a recent column by a Muslim journalist, Muhammad is "the perfect role model in all situations," there is a great prejudice against updating these principles. In fact, according to many Islamic jurists, doing so is a sin, a serious affront to Allah, and a denial of His message. This is dangerous ground because, as you will recall, apostasy is punishable by death.

In the end, Muhammad's life does not give much ammunition to the argument that Islam is a religion of tolerance. Thus, we will move on to take a look at the question of tolerance in Islamic history. Because of the success of the jihad at spreading Muslim rule, we have many good examples of how actual Muslims treated actual Christians, Jews, and others under their "protection" in different times and places.

TOLERANCE ON THE GROUND

As we stated in chapter 1, Bat Ye'or has identified six fundamental principles that establish Muslim supremacy and the relationship between Islam and the rest of the world: "The pre-eminence of Islam over other religions (9:33); Islam is the true religion of Allah (3:17) and it should reign over all mankind (34:27); the *Umma* [Islamic community] forms the party of Allah and is perfect (3:106), having been chosen above all peoples on earth it alone is qualified to rule, and thus elected by Allah to guide the world (35:37). The pursuit of *Jihad*, until this goal [the *Umma* ruling the world] will be achieved, is an obligation (8:40)."[118]

But don't most major religions profess to be the only "true" faith and superior to all others?

True, but let's take a look at how this brand of religious chauvinism manifested itself in the treatment of non-Muslims.

One of the things that people who purvey the myth that the ransom-protection relationship was actually a model of respect and tolerance don't discuss is the uncomfortable subject of forced conversions, which happened throughout the history of the various Islamic empires. In fact, in the case of the Ottoman Empire, forced conversions were essential to its political and military functioning as well as its continued expansion.

But I thought people had to come to Islam openly, of their own free will?

So says the Qur'an, but we are not discussing theoretical Islam, we are discussing Islam in the real world. The fact is that there were sporadic forced conversions of *dhimmis* throughout history based on the whim of the current caliph, sultan, or local ruler. You could argue that these were exceptions, but in some cases the conversions devastated the non-Muslim populations of entire regions as they did during the twelfth-century persecution of the Christians in southern Spain and the Jews in northern Africa, as per Ye'or. And after the conversions, Muslims doubted the sincerity of the converted Jews and removed Jewish children from their families.

In northwestern Africa and Morocco, "Jews were forced to convert in 1165, 1275, 1465, and 1790–92." Then there were the forced conversions in "Libya in the period of 1558–89 and Tabriz [now one of the largest cities in Iran] in 1291 and 1338, and in Baghdad in 1333 and 1344. In Persia, sporadic waves of forced conversions from the sixteenth to the beginning of the twentieth century decimated the Christian and particularly the Jewish communities."[119]

There are numerous other specific examples, but the point is that conversions were ordered by Muslim leaders fairly regularly. By all accounts, these leaders seemed to be untroubled by the fact that they were not practicing "true Islam." There is ample anecdotal evidence that they did not lose any sleep over whether or not their behavior would later meet the approval of modern Western analysts.

The most egregious example of forced conversion was the *devshirme* system in the Ottoman Empire, where, for centuries, the victims of this program were children taken from Christian villages in Muslim-occupied Europe. They formed a military corps called the Janissaries, which would become the most elite military arm of the Ottoman Empire, analogous to the highly trained SS troops of Nazi Germany. This group was founded in the early fourteenth century under Othman I, who also founded the Ottoman Empire. He created the Janissary Corps and firmly established the recruitment methods in which Christian children were taken from their communities and, according to Paul Fregosi, "cut off from all their roots and families, and turned into the finest fighting force of the age."[120]

Devshirme, euphemistically called the Ottoman "levy of boys" by some historians, "consisted of the regular conscription, as tribute, of one-fifth of Christian children from the conquered eastern and central European countries."[121] Yes, you read that correctly: *one-fifth* of all Christian boys were taken from their families. That meant that almost all infidel families lost a child to their Muslim rulers.

No one was safe. All male children ages fourteen to twenty could be taken. As per Bat Ye'or, "The Christian children were conscripted from among the aristocracy of Greeks, Serbs, Bulgarians, Albanians, Armenians, and from the sons of Orthodox priests. At a fixed date every father had to appear in the town square with his sons. There, in the presence of the *kadi*, the recruiting agents, themselves Janissaries, selected the handsomest and most robust. No father could avoid the child tribute."[122]

These children were sent for training and heavy indoctrination into the Islamic faith. For three centuries they formed the most feared fighting force in the world, and for centuries they were "supreme on every battlefield where they fought."[123] The Janissaries were essential to the success of the Ottomans in vastly extending the reach of the empire.

They were also responsible for many of the worst massacres and other atrocities in Islamic history, and played a significant part in the fall of Constantinople and the horrors that followed. It's easy to imagine the Ottoman rulers reveling in the irony of using the sons of the infidels to further the reach of Islam and allow the subjugation of more and more non-Muslim lands and people.

The Janissaries also proved—not that there was really ever any doubt—that there is no connection between the brutal behavior of Islamic radicals and biology. Properly indoctrinated, European children were just as capable of Islam-inspired inhumanity as the Arab originators of the religion, just as today we see murderous radical movements in places as geographically and genetically diverse as the Arabian Peninsula, Indonesia, the Philippines, and eastern Europe. All of these people are ethnically, historically, and culturally very different. They share only one thing: radical Islamic ideology.

The architect of the Janissary program was a royal named Kara Khalil Tschendereli (or Black Khalil), who justified the system this way: "The conquered are the property of the conqueror, who is the lawful master of them, of their lands, and their goods, of their wives, and of their children. We have a right to do what we will with our own; and by the treatment which I propose is not only lawful, but benevolent. By enforcing the conversion of these captive children to the true faith, and enrolling them in the ranks of the army of the true believers, we consult both their temporal and eternal interests; for, is it not written in the Qur'an that all children are, at their birth, naturally disposed to Islam?"[124]

In addition to the children taken and conscripted into the Janissaries, there was a parallel Ottoman program. This one took children of both sexes from the ages of six to ten, converted them to Islam, and put them in the regular army, harems, brothels, or some form of civil service. When they grew up, slaves recruited this way "supplied the Ottoman state with its top hierarchy of officials." Given the fact that "Islamized Christian slaves of both sexes formed a considerable population,"[125] they became another way to spread the religion through the subjugated lands.

Imagine the letters to friends from infidels in Muslim-occupied countries: *After the jihadists massacred half the town and took over I was worried, but then I saw how tolerant they were and I breathed a sigh of relief. Of course, they ripped Junior from my wife's arms, but then they promised that when they came back next year they'd get our little Pumpkin into a good harem.*

It's worth pointing out that "child tribute" programs under the Ottomans were far from the only context for the abduction of non-Muslim children. Children and adults could be taken under a number of pretexts, including real or imagined insults to Muslims, Islam, or the Prophet, as well as for nonpayment of the *jizya*. As per Bat Ye'or, "There was scarcely a place or period when slavery did not claim its harvest of *dhimmis*: men, women, and children."[126]

There was always the individual freelance kidnapping of infidel children, which was practiced in virtually all Muslim lands throughout Islamic history. As Bat Ye'or tells us, "*Dhimmi* sources from all quarters repeatedly mention the abduction of children of both sexes by nomads, soldiers, or individuals. This practice continued up to the twentieth century" in some places. There were also more formalized programs in places like Yemen where "fatherless Jewish children of both sexes were taken from the mother or family, forcibly converted, and placed in state orphanages where some of them underwent military training."

Whether or not these abuses were institutionalized or independent, they were possible because of the low standing of the infidels living in Muslim lands, even when they made up a majority of the population, as they often did. Children were most vulnerable because of the Qur'an, which says Islam is "religion in the right state—the nature made by Allah in which He has made men; there is no altering of Allah's creation; that is the right religion, but most people do not know." This basically says that Islam is not only the "right religion," but it is also the natural state of man. Thus, all children are born Muslim, so converting them (via abduction or any other method) is simply returning them to their natural state, which is part of the case that Black Khalil made for *devshirme*.

Certainly, other religions have had examples of abuses like forced conversion and the death penalty for heresy, both of which figure into the history of the Christian Church. However, these were relatively rare instances in a long history and the Church has since firmly rejected both. The size and scope of these abuses in the history of Islam is mind-boggling. Because of the fundamentalist nature of Islam and the literal reading of the Qur'an, it's very hard to let go of any practices that defined the Prophet or life in his time.

TOLERANCE WILL REQUIRE A SMALL FEE

Infidels had to pay another significant price to be "tolerated" in their own lands, the *jizya*, or as we have called it, the infidel tax. Now, it's tempting to underestimate the significance of this tax in the lives of the non-Muslims living under Islamic rule because, well, everyone had to pay some sort of taxes, right? Well, infidels were the only ones to pay the *jizya*, and they also paid far, far more in all forms of taxes and fees than their Muslim masters.

Certainly, other conquerors have required tribute from vanquished nations, but the *jizya* was different in important ways. First, it was mandated by the conqueror's most holy religious text and therefore was nonnegotiable. Second, it was in most cases absolutely ruinous to the native population. Infidels who couldn't pay or refused were either killed or enslaved along with their families.

Refusal to pay taxes was rare, but the taxes were often so large that the *inability* to pay was fairly common. Throughout the history of the Muslim empires the *jizya*, combined with additional taxes on everything from orchards to fishing to tolls, often represented, according to Bat Ye'or, "ruinous requisitions" that "reduced the peasant to poverty."[127]

An eighth-century Armenian historian described the situation like this: "Every individual, even by giving all he had, his clothes, his foodstuffs and prime necessities, did not succeed in paying his ransom and redeeming his person from torture. Gibbets, presses and gallows had been set up everywhere; nothing but fearful and continual torture was seen everywhere."[128]

In the Middle Ages, taxes were so ruinous that peasants would often flee their own land to escape the financial burden and the physical danger of nonpayment. Thus, severe penalties were devised to keep the peasants from running.

During the Ottoman rule, non-Muslims had to be ready to produce a receipt proving they had paid the *jizya* or they faced immediate imprisonment. Despite the fact that, theoretically, "women, the poor, the sick, and the infirm were exempt from the poll tax," there are many sources that show "the *jizya* was demanded from children, widows, orphans, and even the dead."[129]

Of course, not all people in all places under Muslim rule suffered equally at all times. However, "all *dhimmi* chronicles throughout the centuries mention the excessive rates the Muslims charge in order to

---

MYTH ABOUT ISLAM #3:
The Ottoman Empire Gave Refuge to Jews Being Persecuted in Spain

The myth that the Ottomans took in Jews during the Spanish Inquisition is a persistent one. It also happens to be true. During the Inquisition, Jews were subjected to persecution, forced conversion, and, in many cases, they were not allowed to raise their own children. It was a dark time in Christendom and it's true that the Ottoman Empire took in Jews fleeing the persecution.

Within the Muslim Empire life was certainly no multicultural extravaganza, and Jews were far from equal to the Muslims, but for a time they were treated somewhat better than they had been in Spain.

---

strip the community of its property."[130] The bottom line is that the infidels were at the mercy of Muslim overlords and completely dependent on their, um, good graces.

As late as 1844, terrible abuses were still occurring. As Bat Ye'or describes, the local ruler in Damascus "ran short of money for his troops and resorted to extreme measures. Soldiers stopped Christians and Jews in the streets and entered their homes at night to force them to pay the *ferde* (income tax)." According to a contemporary account from the French consul, "This soldiery committed the most deplorable violence against them and their families, and removed merchandise from shops as they pleased by sheer force."[131]

In addition to the abduction of their children, enslavement, and financial hardships, non-Muslims had to endure institutionalized degradation as the further price of Muslim "tolerance" of their existence. Meting out humiliation was considered to be not only appropriate by Muslim leaders but—wait for it—a religious obligation, and as we saw in the opening of the chapter, an "act of piety," the logic being that since infidels could look forward to many great humiliations courtesy of Allah in the afterlife, it was the responsibility of the Muslim faithful to get them used to the idea in this life.

Throughout more than thirteen centuries of Islamic rule over various *dhimmi* peoples, it's clear that Muslim leaders and their people took this particular act of piety very seriously. Humiliation was often part of everyday interaction between Muslims and their Christian and Jewish subjects—even in the payment of taxes, which some apparently did not consider harsh enough by themselves. Sixteenth-century Moroccan jurist al-Maghili had this to say about the collection of the *jizya*: "On the day of payment they [the *dhimmis*] shall be standing there waiting in the lowest and dirtiest place . . . our object is to degrade them by pretending to take their possessions. They will realize that we are doing them a favor again in accepting from them the *jizya* and letting them (thus) go Free. . . . When paying, the *dhimmi* will receive a blow and will be thrust aside so that he will think that he has escaped the sword through this (insult)." Now comes the big finish, the invocation of religious purpose for these tactics: "This is the way that the friends of the Lord, of the first and last generations, will act toward their Infidel enemies, for might belongs to Allah, to His Apostle, and to the Believers."[132]

Accounts by Jews, Europeans, American visitors, and other sources confirm that these practices were still in place in the late nineteenth century in both Morocco and central Asia. To be fair, the Ottoman Empire did not use this tax collection method, and, instead, used local infidel community leaders to do the collections.

Lest you think that humiliation and subjugation began and ended with child abductions, enslavement, and the ruinous—to say nothing of humiliating—collection of taxes, the Muslim rulers had numerous other means to make sure that infidels knew they were both apart from and vastly inferior to the Muslim faithful. Bat Ye'or concludes that this systemic "ignominy and degradation . . . provided irrefutable proof of the triumph of Islam. Its superiority inherent in the relationship between its strength and the humiliation forcibly imposed on others."[133]

So, in a blaze of fuzzy radical logic, Muslim leaders concluded that the fact that they could treat people so deplorably proved the intrinsic superiority of their people, religion, and system—when to a reasonable Westerner it proves exactly the opposite.

From a psychological point of view it makes a kind of sense. Bat Ye'or points out that the early Muslim soldiers had the supremacy of Islam drilled into them, yet when they invaded the Persian and Byzantine empires, they saw numerous examples of the economic, social, and technological superiority of the people they had conquered. Thus, the humiliation of the non-Muslims gave the *Umma* a way to settle this apparent mental conflict in their own favor. And to this day, we see radical clerics preaching the supremacy of Islam and the inferiority of the West against all sense, evidence, and reason. Even as they call the West inferior, they maintain that Muslims are constantly victimized by that inferior yet somehow more powerful West. Of course there is a paradox here, but it's one that radicals don't talk about, except to say that whatever is going on is the fault of the Jews and/or the United States.

HOW TO PROPERLY SUBJUGATE AN INFIDEL: A FIELD GUIDE FOR MUSLIMS

With over thirteen hundred years of experience in degrading non-Muslim subjects, the Islamic empires used complex methods, laws, and rules to make the infidel "feel subdued" in accordance with Qur'an 9:29. Some of the rules infidels were subjected to still appear in a manual of Islamic holy law that has the endorsement of Al-Azhar University, in Cairo, Egypt, the most respected authority in Sunni Islam. These were some of the basic rules for *dhimmis* in force for most of the history of the Muslim rule.

According to these holy laws, non-Muslims had to be "distinguished from Muslims in dress, wearing a wide cloth belt." Though the various rules for what infidels were forced to wear varied from place to place and period to period, some form of these rules was a fact of life for virtually all infidels in almost all periods of history.[134] The distinctive clothing served the same purpose as the yellow star that said "Juden" in 1930s Nazi Germany.

In Yemen, Jews had to abide by this method of labeling until 1950.[135] This rule was never eliminated; it was simply rendered moot when the Yemeni Jews had all finally escaped to Israel.

Non-Muslims could not be greeted with the traditional Muslim greeting, "Peace be with you." This one still shows up in some form in Islamic literature, including materials found in American mosques. One publication recently distributed in the Islamic Center in Washington, DC, says, "It is forbidden for a Muslim to be first in greeting an unbeliever."[136]

Infidels had to keep to the side of the street, avoiding the more prestigious center of the street, which was reserved for Muslims. Also, unbelievers could not build homes or other buildings that were higher than Muslim buildings. Open displays of wine and pork were big no-nos and still are in Saudi Arabia and Iran, as well as in other Muslim nations.

It was completely out of the question to recite the Torah or to talk about other infidel faiths in public. This is still verboten in Saudi Arabia, Iran, and other Muslim countries.

Infidels could not make public displays of their funerals or feast days, and they still can't in Saudi Arabia and Iran.

No new infidel churches or temples could be built. Even repairs on existing structures had to be approved, usually at great cost, by local Muslim rulers. This, of course, is still the law in Saudi Arabia as well as in—you guessed it—Iran. However, even that easygoing model of European secularism, Turkey, has had problems here, causing a recent press report to dub the building of a new Christian church in that country "Mission Impossible."[137]

Any faux pas with respect to these rules meant that the violators could be killed or enslaved depending on the whim of the Muslim ruler. And this was not an idle threat, like the outdated blue law that says women are not allowed to parachute on Sunday in Indiana. This

TEN SIMPLE RULES TO FOLLOW TO QUALIFY FOR THE MUSLIM EMPIRE'S "TOLERANCE" PROGRAM

Here are a few simple rules that infidels had to observe to receive Muslim mercy and protection. As a bonus, strict adherence would allow infidels to avoid enslavement, imprisonment, torture, and/or death.

1. *Dhimmis* could not carry weapons, as weapons were considered unnecessary since the Muslim community was giving infidels its "protection."
2. Infidels could not ride horses, though they were sometimes allowed to ride donkeys.
3. In many parts of the Islamic world, *dhimmis* were not allowed to wear shoes.
4. Claiming Jesus was divine was cause for instant execution.
5. Saying that Muhammad was not the Prophet of God was another shortcut to the afterlife.
6. Suggesting that the Qu'ran was not the exact word of Allah carried the death penalty.
7. Insulting Muhammad or Islam in any way meant immediate, well, you know . . .
8. Christian and Jewish religious processions, *including funeral processions*, were banned. And ringing church bells was forbidden.
9. An infidel had to stand aside if a Muslim passed him or her on the street.
10. If a *dhimmi* was assaulted by a Muslim, he or she was not allowed to fight back. However, infidels were not completely helpless; they were allowed to politely request that the Muslim stop beating them.[138]

rule was enforced, well, religiously. According to Ye'or, the ruling sultan was walking the streets of Constantinople one day in 1758 when he came upon a Jew wearing the wrong "colors" and immediately had the man beheaded.[139]

IT'S ALL ABOUT CARING AND SHARING: TOLERANCE IN THE ISLAMIC WORLD TODAY

In the Ottoman Empire, Janissaries would frequently physically abuse unbelievers on the street for no reason. If the infidel was foolish enough to complain, the Muslim would immediately accuse him of insulting Islam or the Prophet and the unlucky *dhimmi* would be killed. Today, Christians are still harassed in this way in Muslim countries. Pakistan's legal code prescribes "life imprisonment for desecrating the Qu'ran and death for insulting Muhammad, the prophet of Islam." And the laws are not just harmless throwbacks. According to one report, "Fresh allegations of blasphemy seem to be a weekly occurrence in Pakistan (107 people were accused in 2005)."[140]

The myth that the Muslim empires allowed the People of the Book to enjoy a historically unprecedented level of tolerance is an enduring one. There are exhaustive historical accounts of the treatment of infidels by Muslim masters. As Bat Ye'or says, "Periods of relief were exceptional and temporary."[141] Just as I'm sure that every once in a while the Romans gave the Christians a break and the lions a change of diet, that hardly means that the Romans were "tolerant" of early Christians.

Nevertheless, various contemporary press reports continue to enshrine this period. A 2005 report in the *Montgomery Advertiser* is typical of the kind of puff piece done on Islam today in the press. In an article titled "Entertainment Media's Muslims Bear Little Resemblance to Reality," the intrepid reporter Darryn Simmons writes (apparently with a straight face): "Muslims do not believe in converting people to their religion by force. In fact, the Qu'ran accepts religious pluralism and sees strength in diversity."[142]

Now, were there examples of Muslim kindness toward *dhimmis*? Certainly, just as there were no doubt many examples of kind slaveholders in America and perfectly nice white people in South Africa when apartheid was law. The South African system is actually a good analogy for *dhimmi*tude, though apartheid was a kinder system in practice. The point is that like slavery or apartheid, the doctrine of Muslim

APARTHEID VS. *DHIMMI*TUDE
OR, THE BATTLE OF THE TOLERANT SYSTEMS

Here's a quick look at two systems used to subjugate people defined as "the other" by their ruling elites. We have just taken a detailed look at *dhimmi*tude. In apartheid, the white South Africans, who made up 13 percent of the population, established strict rules to separate each of the country's four main ethnic groups: white, black, colored, and Asian. The nonwhite majority was forced to live under unfair laws in a system of extreme segregation.

In Each System the Subjugated People . . .	Apartheid	*Dhimmi*tude
1. Endured an institutionalized system that reduced them to second-class citizens.	Yes	Yes
2. Had limited or nonexistent property rights.	Yes	Yes
3. Were forced to live in designated areas.	Yes	Yes
4. Had severe limits placed on career opportunities.	Yes	Yes

supremacy and the inferiority of the infidel led to widespread abuse, debasing both the masters and the *dhimmis* by dehumanizing both.

Okay, okay, the history sounds pretty bad, but that all was a long time ago. Certainly things have changed in the Muslim world since then, right?

The answer is a big, um ... *not really.* The genocide waged

	Apartheid	*Dhimmitude*
5. Faced the death penalty for raping a member of the ruling elite, while there was little or no penalty for the reverse.	Yes	Yes
6. Were forced to use separate public facilities such as hospitals and schools.	Yes	Yes
7. Were forbidden to address the ruling elite, though they were allowed to respond if spoken to first.	Yes	Yes
8. Faced death penalty for insulting the beliefs of the ruling elite.	No	Yes
9. Endured ruinous taxes that only they had to pay.	No	Yes
10. Were forced to give up one or more of their children to fill the ruling elite's harems, brothels, civil service positions, and fanatical armies of conquest.	No	Yes

against the Armenian Christians by the Turks happened in the twentieth century, and the genocide practiced against the Sudanese Christians started less than twenty years ago—to say nothing of the continued "intolerance" being waged against black Muslims in the Sudan by the Arab Muslims, or in Egypt against the Coptic Christians.

The fact is that Islamic intolerance is alive in many places around the globe. We've already touched on how many of the rules of *dhimmi*tude mentioned previously are still in force in theocratic states like Saudi Arabia, Iran, Yemen, and other places. Until just recently, the US State Department has been extremely quiet about the state of human rights and "tolerance" in Saudi Arabia—the homeland of Osama bin Laden and fifteen of the nineteen 9/11 hijackers.

In 1998, Congress passed the International Religious Freedom Act, which required the State Department to "put out an annual report on the state of religious freedom around the world." Remarkably, the State Department managed to keep Saudi Arabia off the list until 2004 when it was forced to cede the obvious point: in Saudi Arabia "freedom of religion does not exist."[143]

It's worth pointing out that it is not only Christians who face intolerance in Saudi Arabia. The Sunni majority also harasses and persecutes the minority Shiites who have to smuggle in their religious texts, which are regularly "confiscated and burned," according to Stephen Schwartz, author of *The Two Faces of Islam* and an expert on the Wahhabist sect of Sunni Islam that rules Saudi Arabia. Schwartz says that Shiites, or Shi'a, face "brutal repression" in the desert kingdom. "Shi'a works are smuggled into the country or circulated only in manuscript, and their possession is a criminal offense."[144]

There are over two hundred religious prisoners in Saudi Arabia, seventeen of whom are looking at life sentences. According to Schwartz, "They were arrested on no charge other than the heresy of being Shi'a and as an example to others. Shi'a Muslims are also forced to accept state-dictated names (as were Jews in Nazi Germany, Koreans under Japanese imperialism, and Albanians ruled by the Serbs). Further, thousands of Shi'a Muslims are barred from leaving the Kingdom."[145]

We've already talked about the human rights abuses that are rampant in Iran. There are many, many more examples but there's no need to beat a dead camel.

Okay, but Saudi Arabia and Iran are well known as tyrannical religious states. You don't mean to say that all Muslims are as intolerant as the worst offenders, do you?

Not at all. I do subscribe to the idea that the vast majority of all human beings are decent people who don't want to hurt or persecute anyone. However, we can't ignore either the facts of life in contemporary Muslim communities from Pakistan, to India, to Southeast Asia or the Qur'anic and historical basis for their intolerance.

ON BEING GAY IN THE ISLAMIC WORLD

There is one more group that I want to talk about that suffers severe persecution in the Muslim world: homosexuals. There's an interesting comparison to be made between the treatment of gays in the West and in the Islamic world.

In the 2004 US presidential election, gay marriage was an issue. Though neither party was for it, there was a lively public debate on the subject. Now, whatever side of the discussion you are on, it's hard to argue with the notion that a discussion of what constitutes full rights for all citizens is healthy in a liberal democracy.

In the radical Muslim world there is a similar debate going on. There, the camps are divided on whether it is better to kill homosexuals summarily by beheading, as in Saudi Arabia and Iran, or to subject them to brutal torture first and then to kill them, as in the Palestinian territories. According to the *Chicago Free Press*, the Palestinians have particularly creative tortures for gays, including forcing them to stand in sewage up to their necks, cutting their skin with glass, and pouring toilet cleaner in the wounds. Their methods of execution include stoning and burning.[146] (A side note: even as we speak, Palestinian thinkers are working round the clock to come up with a reason why these human rights abuses are really the fault of the Israelis. So far they've come up dry, though the most promising avenues of thought all begin with declaring that Israelis are the "real terrorists.")

Ironically, the only way for many homosexual Palestinians to escape the danger from their own families, various Islamic groups, and the Palestinian Authority or Hamas themselves is to escape to, of all places, Israel—which is, according to one gay advocacy group, "the one country in the region in which gays have legal rights as citizens and live in safety and freedom."

It's worth pointing out that the West's immoral "tolerance" of gays is one of the things Muslim leaders and communities use to "prove" the superiority of Islam.

FEELING THE LOVE: MODERN EUROPE EXPERIENCES MUSLIM TOLERANCE

We have one more stop in our survey of Islamic tolerance: Europe, which, with its large and growing Muslim population, provides us with an ideal place to study modern Muslim tolerance at work. Western Europe was the birthplace of the Enlightenment and modern human rights. In the post–World War II world, European society has prided itself on its pacifism and genuine tolerance as it invested its wealth in social services instead of military might.

Europe's relatively open immigration policies have led to a large influx of Muslims from all over the Middle East and North Africa. Believe it or not, the Muslim immigrants have not brought a greater degree of tolerance to their new homes. Instead, there have been some very disturbing trends within Europe's growing Muslim communities.

In England, radical clerics spew hate from mosques in the middle of London. "Honor killings," which, as we discussed, is the murder of Muslim women by fathers, husbands, and brothers over minor infractions, has become a serious problem for British police. People who convert from Islam to Christianity are routinely harassed and threatened. Muslims also try to impose their standards on the outside community by supporting and perpetrating widespread vandalism of public ads that upset their delicate religious sensibilities. "Advertisements for perfume, hair dye, bras and television programmes are among those that have been attacked. Photographs of semi-dressed women are the most frequently targeted, with the offending body parts painted over or ripped off," according to the *London Times*.[147]

Much of the vandalism is the work of a group called Muslims Against Advertising, which uses the acronym MAAD (once again showing that radicals have absolutely no sense of irony if they can't see why calling themselves MAAD is funny). Their Web site gives instructions on vandalizing billboards and recommends specific targets.

They would seem like harmless crackpots—an example of MAAD-ness, if you will—but taken with the honor killings and religious persecution of converts, they show an alarming trend in European countries: namely the effort to enforce a form of Islamic values and holy law both within and without the Muslim community. A number of European countries are already finding that whatever the actual law says, Muslims are not afraid to impose their version of holy law on their adopted and secular lands.

There are signs all over Europe of this kind of de facto Shariah taking root. Take the early 2005 case of Hatin Surucu, a twenty-nine-year-old woman murdered in an apparent "honor killing" that was most likely committed by one or more of her three brothers. Hatin was raised in Berlin and then forced into an arranged marriage with a first cousin in Turkey. A few years later, fed up with life in Turkey and, presumably, with her cousin/husband as well, she returned to the German capital with her young son, moved into a home for single mothers, completed school, and began to train as an electrician. "She stopped wearing a headscarf and was said to be outgoing and vivacious," says one press report. Hatin was determined to live like a German. For that she was killed, one of six known honor killings in Berlin within only four months.

The reaction by nearby Muslim middle-school children to her

murder was illuminating. "She only had herself to blame," said one thirteen-year-old. "She deserved what she got—the whore lives like a German," said another. And these were not isolated views.[148]

Got that? Living like a German is considered to be a killing offense by young Muslims living *in Germany*. Suddenly, the contemptuous attitude of the historical minority Muslim ruling class toward the infidels under their "protection" starts to look pretty relevant.

In Sweden, a museum dedicated to world culture had to remove an erotic painting covered with verses from the Qur'an because of complaints—some of which were "aggressive"—from the Muslim community.[149]

The Netherlands was in the news in 2005 after the Islamic ritual murder of Theo van Gogh, the Dutch filmmaker who had made a film called *Submission*, which criticized the treatment of women in Islam. He was attacked on the street in broad daylight, shot multiple times, and then had his throat cut. The assailant remained on the scene long enough to make sure the filmmaker was dead and left a note on van Gogh's chest citing his Islamic motive for the murder.

One could argue that the murder was the work of a single extremist who was a member of a small like-minded group. However, in the summer of 2005, Muslim youths of Moroccan descent twice attacked van Gogh's fourteen-year-old son, Liewe. In one instance, a group of Muslim teenagers recognized him on the street and beat him on the spot. Liewe was also regularly bullied by Moroccans in his school, who taunted him by saying things like, "Good thing they killed your dad."[150]

A full examination of the pathologies of the kind of people who would do that and the kind of school authorities who would allow it would require another book at least. Suffice it to say that things look pretty grim in the Netherlands.

Van Gogh's collaborator on the film, a woman and a former Muslim named Ayaan Hirsi Ali, has had to be housed on an army base because of the death threats against her made by members of the Dutch Islamic community. Ayaan is a member of the Dutch parliament.

Still another Dutch MP, Geert Wilders, has received so many death threats from Islamic militants living in the Netherlands that he has been housed for months in a Dutch prison camp for his own safety.[151]

A number of Dutch artists responded to the murder of Theo van Gogh by creating pieces with themes like "suicide bombers and 'hate imams,' evil-looking preachers, vomiting excrement or spitting bombs." At least one of these artists had to be accompanied by a number of bodyguards to an opening of his work protesting intolerance. Another artist has had to go into hiding. According to the *New York Times*, in Amsterdam, "local people say threats to painters have not been heard since the occupation by the Nazis during World War II."

The situation is so bad that the *New York Times* found itself asking, "Can angry young Muslims dictate what is and is not acceptable in the traditionally open-minded world of Dutch arts? In the last few weeks, it appears, the answer has been yes."[152] When the *New York Times* starts noticing Islamic intolerance, you know things are very bad indeed.

The fact is that the larger the Islamic population, the bigger the problem seems to be. The Netherlands, which is 10 percent Muslim, seems to be faring the worst. Half the people in Dutch jails are foreign born and the vast majority of those are Muslim. When you factor in that most of these criminals are men, you see that an incredibly small percentage of the community is committing nearly half of all crime. The increased crime, fear of Muslim gangs, and what's seen as the rising tide of Muslim intolerance has caused a dramatic increase in Dutch people looking to emigrate to other countries—seeking, as one soon-to-move parent said, "a safer, more peaceful place."[153]

There is no denying that the murder of van Gogh had an immediate effect on the Dutch people. A man who runs an agency for Dutch who want to emigrate said that after the murder "there was a big panic, a flood of people saying they wanted to leave the country." Another telling thing is the fact that whereas in the past most potential émigrés were farmers looking for more land, these new refugees are highly paid professionals and the wealthy.[154]

You know things are bad for the Dutch when one of their most cherished cultural traditions is threatened by Islamic intolerance: legal prostitution—which was the target in a 2005 plot by a Moroccan Muslim pizza delivery boy to attack Amsterdam's red-light district. According to press reports, he and his coconspirators—who had ties to the group that killed Theo van Gogh—were "furious at the lack of morals in the prostitution zone."[155] We don't have time to go into all the pathologies at work here, but it's clear that when your pizza boys start attacking your prostitutes, you are looking at a fundamental societal breakdown.

What's amazing is that these abuses are being perpetrated by Muslims who *choose* to live in the West, presumably because they were somewhat dissatisfied with the situation back in their home countries. This begs the question: just how radical are the folks in the old country who like it there just fine?

THE CARTOON JIHAD

One of the greatest challenges posed to the believers in the notion of Muslim tolerance occurred in early 2006 when the Muslim world reacted, um, negatively to the publication in a Danish newspaper of a dozen political cartoons that dealt with the Prophet Muhammad. The most famous was one depicting Muhammad with a bomb-shaped turban.

In addition to a widespread Muslim boycott of Danish goods, there were a number of violent protests throughout the Muslim world, with a final death toll exceeding fifty people. Angry crowds in Syria attacked the Danish and Norwegian embassies in Damascus. (Though the protestors burned the Danish embassy, no one was hurt because it was closed at the time.) Indonesian Muslims followed suit and broke windows at the Danish consulate. In India, riot police had to use tear gas and water cannons to disperse students protesting the cartoons, while a general strike was called by Muslims in Kashmir. In Thailand, protestors shouted, "God is great," while they stamped on the Danish flag outside the Danish embassy. In Somalia, a fourteen-year-old boy was killed and a number of others were injured when protestors attacked police.

Outside the US consulate in Indonesia, police had to fire warning shots at protestors who were unaware that Denmark and the United States are different countries. Another group of geographically impaired protestors in Afghanistan got into a gunfight with police who stopped them from entering a US base. Two protestors were killed and six policemen were injured in the incident.[156]

Passions ran high in Europe as well as Muslims staged large, angry protests. One of the protestors carried a sign that summed up the spirit of a London protest: "Massacre those who insult Islam."[157]

A protestor in Afghanistan named Mawli Abdul Qahar told the BBC that the publication of the cartoons was a test for the Muslim world. "They want to know whether Muslims are extremists or not." That being the case, Qahar concluded that there was only one way to handle the situation, "Death to them and to their newspapers."[158]

THE FINAL WORD ON TOLERANCE

In conclusion, on the subject of tolerance the Qur'an is ambivalent at best. Muhammad himself supported the death penalty for apostasy and was a harsh critic of poetry. However you slice it, I think we have to put another big check in the *intolerant* column in the entry for "Freedom of religion, free speech, and dissent" in the time of Muhammad.

The Prophet also personally established the basic rules for subjugating non-Muslims. The Arab and Ottoman Muslim empires learned those lessons well and added a few twists like the institutionalized forced conversions and the Qur'an-inspired humiliation of the infidel. All told, from a historical point of view, it's hard to defend the notion that Islam is a "religion of tolerance." So, we have to put still another big check in the *intolerance* column.

How can you slam an entire people and their history?

Well, that is not my intention. I'm simply relaying the truths of history based on overwhelming evidence. The success of the jihad as a means of conquest and the political nature of Islam as a faith combined to make the *dhimmi*tude system without a doubt the most advanced and extensive system of extortion as well as the largest and most successful effort of religious persecution, subjugation, and humiliation in world history. Calling it anything else, in today's climate, is actually dangerous. The fact is that Muslims cannot deal effectively with radicalism within their own ranks, and the West cannot combat it effectively, if we all collectively ignore its religious roots and history. Germany did not become a pluralistic and liberal society post–World War II by pretending that the persecution of the Jews and the Holocaust were really a renaissance of tolerance. Similarly, we can't combat some of the pathologies we are seeing in radical thought by ignoring the terrible human cost of the institution of *dhimmi*tude.

Thus, I'm coining a new term to go with *Holocaust denial* and *jihad denial*: *dhimmitude denial*. Denying so much of actual Muslim history takes away an important weapon in the War on Radical Islam and denies Muslims an important tool for antiradical reform: the truth. The ability to see the truth in the face of propaganda and spin is an important part of developing a working Radical Eye.

A strong dose of the truth and a clear eye for radicals will be needed in Europe if Europeans are going to fight the wave of Muslim intolerance that is literally killing their artists and politicians and vandalizing innocent ads that show women in their underwear.

This brings us back to the question that began this chapter: Is Islam a religion of tolerance?

What do I think? I say, sure, fine, it's a religion of tolerance.

Look, I'm not in the business of defining people's personal faith for them. However, I am what Dennis Miller calls "minimally observant." And using that skill, I can evaluate whether or not real-world Muslims show tolerance *in practice* in their history, their politics, and in their contemporary communities. Given the overwhelming amount of evidence in those arenas, I'm forced to exercise my firm grip on the obvious and say that it's not looking good for tolerance.

The fact is that the more Islamic the society and its leadership, the more intolerant that society is. Saudi Arabia and Iran are the worst examples now that the Taliban are out of power in Afghanistan, but the basis of Islamic intolerance—the religious chauvinism, hatred of the infidel, and so forth—are radiating out from the radical center of the Middle East and reaching Muslim communities even in Europe. Given current trends in both the Middle East and Europe, I can't see much hope for change or "reform" in the near future.

Chapter Six

WAR PART III

Or, How to Lose an Empire and Invent Modern Terrorism

Those who know nothing of Islam pretend that Islam counsels against war. Those [who say this] are witless. Islam says: Kill all the unbelievers just as they would kill you all! Does this mean that Muslims should sit back until they are devoured by [the unbelievers]? Islam says: Kill them, put them to the sword and scatter [their armies]. . . . Islam says: Whatever good there is exists thanks to the sword and in the shadow of the sword! People cannot be made obedient except with the sword! The sword is the key to Paradise, which can be opened only for the Holy Warriors! There are hundreds of other [Qur'anic] psalms and *Hadiths* urging Muslims to value war and to fight. Does all this mean that Islam is a religion that prevents men from waging war? I spit upon those foolish souls who make such a claim.[159]

—Ayatollah Ruhollah Khomeini,
late cleric and revolutionary leader of Iran

IRAN: CHEERLEADER FOR THE JIHAD

In his above comment, the ayatollah seems pretty extreme, but he was revered throughout the Shiite world while he ruled Iran before his death in 1989.

Come on, he represented a minority extremist view, and even the Iranians are ready to throw off the oppression of his revolution.

Well, there has been some coverage of the youth protests in Iran, but there is no clear indication that the majority of Iranians support reform. They may, of course, but in a country as oppressive as Iran, where journalists are routinely jailed for simply telling the truth, and where speaking out against Iran's brand of radical theocracy is a crime punishable by long prison terms, it's hard to get an accurate reading of public opinion. So we're left with anecdotal evidence.

There was a documentary made in 2003 called *Iran: Veiled Appearances*. It showed very reasonable-looking college students discussing a desire for more freedom that I'm sure is sincere and certainly plays well to a Western audience. The film also, however, showed thousands of people crowding around the ayatollah's tomb and wailing at the grave of the man who brought so much misery to his nation. Which group is bigger? Who knows?

Okay, but that's smack dab in the center of the Middle East. No one disputes that there are fairly large numbers of radicals there. Certainly there's no indication that the ayatollah still has influence outside of Iran.

Au contraire, Kemo Sabe. In 2004, a "moderate" Islamic group called the Metroplex Organization of Muslims in North Texas held a daylong seminar that we will call Ayatollah-Palooza. According to press reports, the theme Ayatollah-Palooza was one of a tribute to Khomeini, "the great Islamic visionary,"[160] who popularized the nickname "Great Satan" for the United States.

Okay, but you're quoting the ayatollah out of context. He couldn't have been that bad, if they openly held a day of celebration for him in Texas.

Wrong again, I'm afraid. Just how crazy and/or radical was Khomeini? Turns out he was quite a bit of both. Here's a quote as it appeared on worldnetdaily.com: "Islam makes it incumbent on all adult males . . . to prepare themselves for the conquest of countries so that the writ of Islam is obeyed in every country in the world."[161] Astute readers will note that he does not seem to be advocating the nice, quiet, spiritual kind of jihad. Here's more of the ayatollah on world conquest and other topics from *Frontpage* magazine: "Those who study Islamic Holy War will understand why Islam wants to conquer the whole world."[162]

The ayatollah on family: "Do your best to ensure that your daughters do not see their first blood in your house." (My radical to English translation: Marry them off before they menstruate.) It's worth noting here that Khomeini didn't just talk the talk on this one; he married a ten-year-old when he was twenty-eight and called marriage to a premenstrual girl a "divine blessing."

Khomeini also spoke out strongly against his predecessor: the secular ruler, the shah of Iran. The ayatollah believed that one of the shah's "most despicable sins" was the fact that under the shah, Iran was among the original group of nations that drafted and approved the Universal Declaration of Human Rights.

It's hard to imagine any context that would soften these beliefs and remarks, which fall under that category of things that sound bad no matter how you say them. Continued support for the ayatollah and "his vision" show that the radical spirit is alive and well in places as near and as unlikely as Texas.

By now, our Radical Eye is developed enough to recognize some of the themes of radical Islam (violent jihad, disdain for the laws of man over the laws of Allah, marriage to prepubescent girls, etc.). However, we can also trace much of the ayatollah's fervor (or that of the current leaders in Iran, or al Qaeda, or the Taliban, or the clerics running the show today in Saudi Arabia, or even to Osama bin Laden) to the events that followed the battle of Vienna in 1683.

THE OTTOMAN EMPIRE'S GREATEST BLUNDERS, DEFEATS, AND HUMILIATIONS

1685—Greece: The Venetians take back a portion of Greece's southern peninsula. However, the great Parthenon in Athens is a casualty of the fighting. Used by the Ottomans to store gunpowder, the Parthenon is hit by Venetian fire and largely blown to smithereens.

1688—Hungary: The Austrians permanently take Budapest from the Ottomans, who had occupied it since 1541. As Paul Fregosi puts it, "The Jihad was becoming a loser."

1690—Hungary: At the Battle of Salankeman, the Ottomans face the Hapsburgs again. As they enter the battle, the Ottoman military leader shouts, "Courage my heroes . . . the Houris are waiting for you!"[163] But virgins do not save them this time. The Muslims lose the battle and most of Hungary.

1695—Hungary: The Hapsburgs defeat the Ottomans at Mohacs, the scene of the fateful Battle of Mohacs in 1526, which was the first step in the fall of Hungary to the empire.

1696—Black Sea: The Ottomans lose the port of Azoph to Peter the Great of Russia.

1697—Serbia: On September 11, according to Paul Fregosi, the Hapsburgs defeat the Ottomans in the Battle of Zenta, "eight miles northwest of Belgrade. . . . By nightfall, twenty thousand Turks were lying dead on the battlefield, and the drowned corpses of ten thousand others, who had tried to flee by swimming across, were floating in the river."[164]

1699—Croatia: The Ottoman Empire sues the Hapsburgs for peace and has to seek out the western European countries England and Holland to help them in the mediation. This negotiation leads to the Treaty of Carlowitz, signed in Croatia. Though the Ottomans had negotiated peace before, it was always as equals. Now, as Bernard Lewis says, they were forced to "sign a peace in a war which they had unmistakably lost in the field, and on terms which were basically determined by their victorious enemies." Lewis adds, "The defeat that was suffered at Vienna and sealed at Carlowitz inaugurated a long period of almost unrelieved Muslim retreat before Christian power."[165]

The Treaty of Carlowitz is a turning point because, as Edward Creasy says in *History of the Ottoman Turks*, "From that time forth all serious dread of the military power of Turkey has ceased in Europe." Now, "her importance has become diplomatic."[166] This is an important point because, from this moment forward, the Ottomans owe their existence to the fact that the major European powers (Britain, France, Russia, and the Austrian Hapsburgs) would from time to time prop up the Turks because they did not want any single nation to control all of the Ottoman territory.

Ding dong, the witch was dead.

1715—Hungary: The Ottomans try to strike back against the Hapsburgs and head for Austria with both a ground force and a large fleet of ships. In 1716, the great Muslim Empire clashes with the Hapsburgs who crush them. The Ottomans lose twenty thousand men to the five thousand Hapsburg casualties. The victorious Hapsburg forces continue their push and retake Belgrade, finally freeing the last of Hungary from Ottoman toleration—I mean rule.

1737—Crimea: After a few years of fighting over the Crimea and then trying to hammer out a peace agreement, the Russian and Ottoman forces meet in the field. Sixty-eight thousand Russians defeat a force of ninety thousand Ottomans.

1768–1774—Mediterranean/Crimea: According to Lewis, "Russia began a new offensive against the Ottoman Empire, this time with overwhelming superiority. The Russian armies carried all before them. This was the beginning of the first round of Russo-Turkish wars. This offensive culminates in 1774 when the Ottomans sign the humiliating Treaty of Kairnarji, which expanded Russia's territory and influence in the region."[167] Or as Creasy put it, "consummating the glory of Russia and the degradation of the House of Othman."[168] The salt in the wound for the Ottomans is that the leader of Russia at the time is a woman, Catherine the Great.

1770—Greece and the Aegean Sea: While the Greeks begin what would be an unsuccessful revolt against Ottoman rule, the Russians send a fleet to assist them. The Russian ships defeat an Ottoman force off the island of Chios. The surviving Ottoman ships run and head into the narrow harbor of Chesme. There, the Russians, according to Paul Fregosi, "burned nearly every one of the [Ottoman] vessels at anchor." A single Ottoman ship does survive, but it is captured.[169]

1787–1792—Ukraine: After rising tensions with Russia, the Ottoman sultan declares a holy war, and the second Russo-Ottoman war begins. It is fought in what is now southern Ukraine. American naval hero John Paul Jones ("Don't fire until you see the whites of their eyes!") makes a cameo appearance in the conflict, commanding a Russian Black Sea fleet. He sinks fifteen Ottoman ships and loses only one of his own.

The war ends with the Treaty of Jassy in 1792, which allows Russia to expand its border south.

1798—Egypt: Napoleon Bonaparte invades and quickly takes the country. The French stay for three years and are only forced out when Great Britain assists the Egyptians.

1816—North Africa: A fed up Europe demands an immediate end to the practice of Christian slavery and the ongoing piracy and slave raids conducted by the North African Muslims. Tunis and Tripoli immediately acquiesce to Great Britain's demands, but Algiers refuses.

A joint British-Dutch fleet of twenty-four ships sails to Algiers harbor and attacks the town. The Europeans suffer minimal losses and obliterate the Algerian navy. The Algerians reconsider their position on slavery, and 1,642 European slaves, mostly Italians, are freed.

1821–1827—Greece: The Greeks fight and win their war of independence, finally freeing themselves from Muslim rule. The fighting is brutal, with many atrocities committed on both sides. One of the most famous is the Chios Island massacre, where Ottoman forces kill thousands of Christians and take forty-one thousand slaves, mostly women and children. Greeks retaliate and kill ten thousand Turks in the Turkish town of Morea, in the southern peninsula of Greece.

Greek independence becomes a popular cause in Europe, and many Christians join the fight, including the poet Lord Byron. When the Ottomans refuse to sign a ceasefire in 1827, a joint British, French, and Russian fleet sails into the Bay of Navarino in southern Greece and soundly defeats the Ottoman force, sinking sixty ships and disabling most of the others. The Ottoman Empire is now left with virtually no navy. This is the last major battle of the war, and Greece receives its formal independence in 1829.

1828—Romania: Russians declare war on the Turks and take what is now Romania.

1830—Algeria: The French invade and quickly take northern Algeria, beginning 130 years of French rule of the formerly Ottoman territory.

1839—Yemen: The British take a Red Sea town called Aden, establishing the British Empire's first foothold in the Middle East.

1847—Algeria: The French put down an Algerian rebellion and take the rest of the country.

1878—Berlin: The Berlin Congress is held. Led by Prince Otto von Bismarck, the meeting includes Russia, Austria, Britain, France, Italy, and Turkey. At the congress, Bulgaria, Romania, Serbia, Bosnia, and Herzegovina are all taken from the Ottoman Empire. The British walk away with control of Cyprus. This will be a sore point for the Turks until 1974 when they send in troops to take back about half of this island—which they control to this day.

1881—Tunisia: France takes Tunisia, making it a "protectorate."

1894–1896—Ottoman Empire: In the Anatolia region, which is between the Black and Mediterranean seas, the Ottomans massacre as many as two hundred fifty thousand Christian Armenians. According to Bat Ye'or, this led to "a large number of conversions to Islam. Converted couples were obliged to divorce and remarry, each with a new Muslim spouse. If they reverted to Christianity, they were killed."[170] Over this two-year period, the Ottomans managed the largest massacre in history, up until that time.

1909—Ottoman Empire: In the city of Adana, which is in southern Turkey, near Syria, "about 25,000 Armenian men, women, and children were butchered and burned alive." [171]

1914—Bosnia: After years of internecine fighting in the Balkans, a Serbian from the terrorist organization the Black Hand shoots and kills Archduke Francis Ferdinand of Austria, signaling the start of World War I. Turkey bets on the wrong horse and enters the war on the side of Germany.

1918—Turkey: At the end of the war, a number of western European powers occupy Turkey until 1922.

1923—Turkey: The Ottoman Empire is formally abolished, and the Republic of Turkey is established. The jihad in Europe that began in the time of the Prophet appears to be over.[172]

FAST TRACK TO THE BOTTOM:
THE JIHAD TAKES A NOSEDIVE

From the beginning, Muslims believed that it was incumbent upon them to spread Islam across the globe. They had the ideology of jihad and a promise from Allah that he would give them victory. And for a thousand years, it seemed like Allah was more or less keeping his word.

Then came Vienna and the beginning of a long decline for the Ottoman Empire. I could dwell on each of the humiliating defeats, but

I don't want to take up too much time on that—actually I would love to, but I feel an obligation to keep the discussion moving along and relevant to our situation today. Thus, I will hit the high points and focus on how the Ottoman values we saw at work in the last chapter revealed themselves in the disintegration of the empire.

DEATH MATCH: ISLAMISM VS. THE FREE MARKET

There have been a number of theories about the reason for the decline of the Ottoman Empire. Most of them have to do with Ottoman—and Muslim—resistance to change and innovation. Edward Creasy attributes their defeats on the battlefield to their failure to adopt "the improvements that had been made in the weapons of war," most notably the bayonet.[173] Bernard Lewis concurs: "The decline of the Ottomans was due not so much to internal changes as to their inability to keep pace with the rapid advance of the West in science and technology, in the arts of both war and peace, and in government and commerce."[174]

This is not surprising given the fact that throughout history, Muslims were taught about the superiority of Islam to all other faiths and about Allah's promise that he would never give victory to the infidels over the *Umma*. When you are convinced of your intrinsic superiority, there's no reason to change, particularly if it means adopting the ways of your inferiors. Even after countless defeats year after year, it was a hard lesson for the Ottomans to learn, and in the end, they could not adapt.

Military historian Victor Davis Hanson also makes a strong case for the superiority of Western "civic militarism," which produced free-thinking soldiers who were often landowners or "free persons and not the property of an Imperial autocrat."[175] Of course, Ottoman soldiers were most often slaves and conscripts.

Western Europe also had a secret weapon even more effective than the jihadist's seventy-two virgins: capitalism. According to Lewis, the Ottoman Empire was "a predominantly consumer-oriented society."[176] And in this case, "consumer" seems like a good euphemism for

THE ECONOMICS OF RADICALISM
Or, How to Make Nothing but War

As we have discussed, Islam is much more than a religion. As CAIR describes it, "Islam is both a religion and a *complete way of life.*" The Qur'an even provides guidance on matters of economic policy, laying out—among other things—inheritance law and the tax that non-Muslims must pay to be tolerated in Muslim lands. The most significant economic rule is the absolute prohibition against the charging or paying of interest, or *riba.*

Though this may have seemed like a good idea at the time of the Prophet, it makes the development of a modern, functioning economy in a strict, religiously ruled Islamic land impossible. In addition, this is a significant inconvenience to observant Muslims living in Western countries, making it nearly impossible, for instance, for them to buy a home. In recent years, there have been efforts to bring Qur'an-friendly banking to Great Britain and the United States, but they involve silly schemes that allow Muslim borrowers to pay interest but call it something else.

For many millions of Muslims, seventh-century economic policies are more than an inconvenience; they are a life sentence of poverty. In 2002, the United Nations Development Program released the Arab Human Development Report, which was compiled by a "group of distinguished Arab intellectuals" and "written by Arabs for Arabs." The group included thirty economists, sociologists, and various scholars of Arab culture who performed a comprehensive survey of the state of Arab society in the twenty-two nations that make up the Arab League. The group took pains to include women at every stage of the report.

The study on the state of the economies in Arab countries is particularly bleak. Among the report's findings:

- The GDP (Gross Domestic Product) in all Arab countries, which have a combined population of 280 million, was $531.2 billion in 1999. Thus, though these nations have a population roughly equivalent to that of the United States, they have a combined economy that is significantly smaller than Spain's ($595.5 billion).
- The total of nonfossil fuel exports of all goods for these twenty-two nations is less than the total exports of Finland, a nation of 5.2 million people.
- Twenty-five percent of Arabs live below the poverty line, and one in five lives on less than two dollars a day.
- Over the last twenty years, income growth per person was .5 percent, which makes it lower than anywhere else in the world except for sub-Saharan Africa. This means that it would take the average Arab 140 years to double his income, something that many people in the world will see in about ten years.
- As of 2002, unemployment stood at 15 percent, or twelve million people, and was projected to reach twenty-five million unemployed by 2010.[177]

If the picture looks bleak, that's only because it is. There is very little hopeful data on the horizon. The sad fact is that, economically speaking, Muslim countries produce astonishingly little of value outside of oil. When the hidden costs of the Muslim world's disproportionately high involvement in ethnic conflicts is factored in, the picture gets even more dismal as scant resources are allocated to war.

The only reason Middle Eastern societies and economies work as well as they do is because of the largess from oil revenue. Thus, perhaps the greatest danger to the status quo in the Muslim world would be a cheap, plentiful alternative to fossil fuels. Oil wealth gives the autocratic governments in places like Saudi Arabia and

Iran the resources to stay in power, even if it doesn't trickle down very much to the general population.

The only nation with an economy that performs at a pace comparable to the West is Turkey, which is, not coincidentally, the most secular Muslim country. As a rule, the more Islamic a nation, the worst it fares economically. There are a few apparent exceptions to this rule, most notably Indonesia and Malaysia, which have significant manufacturing sectors and have seen growth in recent years. However, both of these countries were under European rule until World War II and owe much of their industrial infrastructure to the West. Not surprisingly, each of these nations has seen a recent rise in Islamic fundamentalism, as well as a decline in economic performance.

Of course, some nations like Saudi Arabia and Iran have great oil reserves, but this natural wealth has allowed the governments to sustain two of the most strict and repressive Islamic regimes in the world. As long as the oil money keeps coming in, there is no real pressure for either nation to develop real, sustainable economies.

To apply what comedian Dennis Miller said about the reason for the fall of communism to Islamic radicalism, "It turns out, there's no money in it."

"plunder," which, as we know, was one of the driving forces of the jihad and an important part of the Ottoman economy. The Ottomans were also dependent on the heavy, often ruinous, taxes of the Christian and Jewish populations under their rule. However you slice it, that kind of taxation tends to put a drag on an economy. Finally, since they produced very little on their own, the Ottomans depended heavily on their control and taxation of trade routes to the Orient, but this business dried up when sixteenth-century developments in Western shipbuilding allowed European powers to travel to the East by going around the horn of Africa. Then the advent of trans-Atlantic trade with the New World gave Europeans even more options.

In writing about the pivotal Battle of Lepanto in 1571, Hanson credits European victory, in part, to the Western ability "to create capital, and thereby to fabricate excellent vessels, mass-produce advanced firearms, and hire skilled crews. Although Europe was represented in force by only three real Mediterranean powers at Lepanto—the pope, Spain, and Venice—their aggregate economies were far larger than the national product of the entire Ottoman Empire."[178]

THE OTTOMAN EMPIRE'S PARTING SHOT

Though the once great Muslim Empire was no longer a world power, it still had the capacity and the will to do a fair amount of damage, and it did. In their waning days, the Ottomans made a final contribution to world history: the first use of an organized effort to perpetrate what the UN now calls "acts committed with intent to destroy, in whole or in part, a national, ethnic, racial or religious group."[179] In other words, they invented genocide, proving that they were capable of innovation after all.

The Armenians had lived for many years as part of the Ottoman Empire. As Christians, they were oppressed, as were all non-Muslims (as we saw in chapter 5, "Tolerance and Diversity"), with Ottoman abuse of the Armenian population significantly increasing at the close of the nineteenth century, when, as we saw in our timeline, the Ottomans started massacring large numbers of Armenians.

After the Ottomans suffered some early losses in World War I and some Armenians came under Russian control, there was increasing unrest among the Armenians living under Ottoman rule. This unrest was just the beginning of a process that would end with the "Armenian genocide," a term used to describe the effort during World War I to completely eliminate the Armenian people from Ottoman territory. According to Armenian-Genocide.org and supported firmly by the historical record, from the years 1915–1923, "The great bulk of the Armenian population was forcibly removed from Armenia and Anatolia (parts of Turkey) to Syria, where the vast majority was sent into the desert to die of thirst and hunger. Large numbers of Armenians were methodically massacred throughout the Ottoman Empire. Women and children were abducted and horribly abused. The entire wealth of the Armenian people was expropriated."[180]

The Turks killed many Armenians outright and subjected the rest to deportations under harsh conditions. In June of 1915, eighteen thousand Armenians were marched out of Ottoman territory. According to a contemporary US State Department report, they were escorted by Turkish police who raced ahead to inform "the half-savage tribes of the mountains that several thousand Armenian women and girls were approaching. The Arabs and Kurds began to carry off the girls, the mountaineers fell upon them repeatedly, killing and violating the women, and the gendarmes (police) joined the orgy."[181]

Survivors were then marched naked in the hot sun without food or water for five days. When the group reached a fountain, the police kept them from it. After seventy days, there were one hundred and fifty women and children left of the eighteen thousand who had set out. Scenes like this were repeated all over the Ottoman-controlled Armenian territories.

There was a year or so of calm at the end of World War I, and then genocide began again in earnest in 1920 and continued until 1923. By the end, the Ottomans had killed over half a million Armenians (some estimates run to over a million). And, as per Armenian-Genocide.org, "By 1923 the entire landmass of Asia Minor and historic West Armenia had been expunged of its Armenian population. The destruction of the Armenian communities in this part of the world was total."[182]

To this day, Turkey denies that the genocide took place and dismisses the overwhelming evidence as "mere allegations." Maybe the Turkish government will join O. J. Simpson in his search for the "real killers."

AL-WAHHAB: MODERN RADICALISM'S FOUNDING FATHER

Even as the Ottomans were beginning their decline early in the eighteenth century, the beginnings of the next major movement in Muslim life were starting in the birthplace of Islam, the Arabian Peninsula. In 1703, a man named Muhammad Ibn Abd al-Wahhab was born. He would found Wahhabism, the Islamic sect that rules Saudi Arabia today and that is the personal creed of Osama bin Laden and the remaining Taliban.

Al-Wahhab wanted to return to his own version of "true Islam," what was believed to be a purer form of the religion, closer to what had been practiced by the Prophet. He also wanted to bring down the Ottoman Empire, which he saw as being based on a corrupted (read: too liberal) form of his religion.

His personal philosophy was extremely conservative, even by Islamic standards. Al-Wahhab called anyone who did not observe all five prayer times an "unbeliever." He also distrusted reverence for the Prophet or prayers to or on behalf of Muhammad (or any honored Muslim dead) because that came too close to polytheism. He even forbade Muslims who were making their pilgrimage to Mecca to also visit the Prophet's tomb in Medina.

As expert on Islam Stephen Schwartz says in *Two Faces of Islam*, al-Wahhab "ordered that graves of Muslim saints be dug up and scattered, or turned into latrines. He also burned many books, arguing that [the] Qur'an alone would suffice for humanity's needs. Above all, Ibn Abd al-Wahhab and his followers despised music, which they viewed as an incitement to forgetfulness of God and to sin."[183]

Al-Wahhab and his followers formed an alliance with a man named Muhammad ibn Saud, an accomplished bandit.[184] Together, the Wahhabists and the House of Saud conquered most of the Arabian Peninsula by 1788, though the weakened Ottoman Empire easily repelled them.

Not much for tolerance, al-Wahhab would frequently label Muslims from other sects unbelievers or polytheists. He called for a number of jihads against various Muslims groups, and his campaigns of conquest "saw mass murder and rape of Shi'a Muslims as well as adherents of the Hanafi and other legal schools [read: other non-Wahhabist sects] rejected by Ibn Abd al-Wahhab."[185]

Stephen Schwartz makes an interesting case that al-Wahhab is "the first known example of totalitarianism, which may be defined as the merging of an extremist ideology with an absolute state."[186]

When al-Wahhab's forces were working their way west toward Mecca from central Arabia, they stopped to take the town of Ta'if. As a Muslim historian wrote, "They killed everyone in sight, slaughtering both child and adult, the ruler and the ruled, the lowly and the well-born. They began with a suckling child nursing at his mother's breast and moved on to a group studying Qur'an, slaying them, down to the last man. And when they wiped out the people they found in the houses, they went out into the streets, the shops, and the mosques, killing whoever happened to be there. They killed even men bowed in prayer until they had exterminated every Muslim who dwelt in Ta'if and only a remnant, some twenty or more, remained."[187]

THEY'RE BAD, THEY'RE NATIONWIDE: THE BIRTH OF SAUDI ARABIA

In the early nineteenth century, the Wahhabi-Saud alliance received some encouragement from the British because they were enemies of the Ottomans. Ultimately, a Saud named ibn Saud took full control of the Arabian Peninsula in the 1920s and proclaimed himself ruler of the new nation of Saudi Arabia in 1932.

The terms of the Wahhabi-Saud alliance were clear and remain in force today. The House of Saud maintains political and economic control, while the Wahhabists run the Islamic religious and social sphere, which includes education, media, and the courts. Wahhabists also run the infamous "Society for the Encouragement of Virtue and Elimination of Vice." These are the black-robed religious police who roam the streets of Saudi Arabia in packs, ferreting out violations of religious rules, such as a woman showing too much skin (say, an ankle, for instance). They have the power to make arrests, or mete out punishment on the spot with the sticks they carry.

According to Stephen Schwartz, "The Wahhabis established a system of governance based on a monopoly of wealth by the elite, backed by extreme repression and a taste for bloodshed. Their subsidiary methods included a brutal secret police, censorship, rigid control of education, and incitement to genocide against minorities (mainly, the Shi'as, but by extension, all non-Wahhabi Muslims, as well as Christians and Jews)." Also, "Wahhabi doctrine called on the people to read only Qu'ran and Wahhabi texts and to refrain from composing literary works, including poetry."[188]

Ultimately, the Wahhabist creed seemed destined to be another crackpot ideology that would be short-lived, narrow in scope, or both. Then oil was discovered in Saudi Arabia, and serious development of the Saudi oil industry began in 1933. As a result, today Wahhabists have access to virtually unlimited funds and are building more mosques throughout the world than any other branch of Islam—and probably more new houses of worship than any other religious group. They provide funds to numerous Muslim "charities," some of which have proven ties to terrorism. They even help fund self-styled "moderate" Islamic organizations like CAIR. Of course, it was Saudi oil money amassed by the bin Laden family that allowed Osama to fund, plan, and execute the 9/11 attacks.

Today, the Wahhabists have helped make Saudi Arabia one of the most repressive regimes in the world. It was Wahhabist enforcers in 2002 who chased a group of young women back into their burning school because they were not veiled from head to toe. And because of their control of the Saudi educational system, the Wahhabists have been able to use educational propaganda and indoctrination to channel the inevitable discontent of the Saudi people toward the West and Israel, helping to create modern Islamic radicalism. For radicals, the current state of the Muslim world and their own sense of discontent can easily be explained as the fault of the West. As Bat Ye'or said, "Humiliations and frustrations were channeled into an anti-Western mold, whereas the glorification of Islamic superiority filled the gap between narcissistic nostalgia and intolerable realities."[189]

ISLAMIC TOLERANCE IN ACTION:
THE ARAB WORLD AND ISRAEL

This takes us to today's terrorism, which is often linked to the ongoing tension and fighting between Israel and the Palestinian people. Before we get into modern terrorism, I want to talk briefly about the 1948, 1956, 1967, 1973, and 1982 wars between Israel and various Muslim nations, which provided a number of "humiliations" and "intolerable realities" for the Muslim world.

In the late nineteenth century, Jews from around the world began to immigrate to the land known then as "Palestine," adding their numbers to the indigenous Jews in the area. During World War I, Great Britain took Palestine from the Ottomans and issued the Balfour Declaration, which supported the creation of a national Jewish homeland. In the 1930s, Jews from Germany began to emigrate in large numbers to escape the Nazis. In 1947, the UN agreed to split the territory into one Jewish nation and one Arab nation and to put Jerusalem under international control.

Despite their grave concerns over not having control of Jerusalem, their holiest city, the Jews in Palestine accepted this situation. However, the neighboring Muslim countries did not. The Palestinians, who are mostly descendants of ethnic Jordanians and Syrians, were told by their Arab leaders to leave their homes in 1947 so that Arab armies could wipe out Israel.

On May 14, 1948, Israel declared its independence. On May 15, 1948, the armies of Egypt, Syria, Lebanon, Iraq, and Jordan invaded Israel on three fronts. Despite their overwhelming superiority of men and weapons, the Muslim armies were soundly defeated. This gave birth to one of the first Muslim myths/conspiracy theories about the United States—that America had aided the Jews with air power. It wasn't true, of course. America remained neutral, sending no help to Israel. However, for the Arabs, there was no other way to explain the crushing defeat.

From the beginning, Israel had numerous border clashes with its neighbors, and in the 1950s, Egypt started to fund militant groups in the Gaza Strip (which it controlled) that then staged attacks on Israel. The final straw came in 1956 when Egypt closed the Suez Canal to Israeli ships and "nationalized" (read: "stole") the canal, which was mostly owned by England and France at the time. In response, Israel invaded Egyptian territory, and England joined the fight against Egypt shortly thereafter. The Israelis quickly took both Gaza and the Sinai Peninsula. The UN stopped the fighting, persuaded Israel to leave, and established a peacekeeping force in Gaza and the Sinai.

Egypt pressured the UN to leave in 1967 and started a military buildup in the Sinai in preparation for an attack on Israel. The final straw came when it blockaded an Israeli port. Israel launched a pre-emptive attack and destroyed virtually the entire Egyptian air force while it was still on the ground, suffering very few losses of its own, thus beginning the Six-Day War.

Muslim pride quickly made the disastrous situation even worse. Despite the fact that the Egyptians had suffered a serious setback, the general in charge issued the following statement: "Israeli planes have started to bomb air bases of the U.A.R. [United Arab Republic, aka Egypt], and approximately 75 percent of the enemy's aircraft have been destroyed or put out of action."[190]

The author of *The Arab Mind*, Raphael Patai, chalks up this, um, exaggeration to the traditional Arab value placed on saving face, called *wajh*. In this case, it was a costly tradition. Immediately, Syria, Jordan, and Iraq joined the fighting—thinking they were joining the winning side—and Israel promptly smashed their air forces as well.

The next day, when it became impossible to hide the truth, Egyptian leader Gamal Abdel Nasser was still spinning tales. Talking with King Hussein of Jordan, Nasser was so concerned about saving face that he suggested that Jordan and Syria issue a statement that "American and British aircraft were collaborating with Israel and attacking Egypt from their aircraft carriers."[191]

Israel once again took the Sinai and Gaza, and this time it decided—not unreasonably, given the history—to hang on to them to act as a buffer between itself and its enemies.

MYTH ABOUT ISLAM #4: JERUSALEM IS A RELIGIOUS SITE OF GREAT HISTORICAL SIGNIFICANCE FOR MUSLIMS

Jerusalem is never mentioned in the Qur'an. The basis of this myth is in the lore that developed around the Prophet's "Night Journey" in which he ascended to Paradise to pay a short visit to the afterlife.

Apparently, twelve years after the Archangel Gabriel's first revelation to Muhammad, Gabriel cut the Prophet's chest open, removed his heart, and washed it. With his newly clean heart, the Prophet commenced his journey to Paradise on a beast called a *buraq*, a one-of-a-kind mythical creature that had, as Paul Fregosi describes it, "the head of a woman, the body of a mule, the tail of a peacock, and two wings."[192] Interestingly, some historical and religious scholars have posited the notion that the Night Journey may not have happened at all because, and I'm paraphrasing here, the story is so flipping silly. Currently, there's an ongoing debate in some scholarly circles about which is funnier, the Night Journey or the bit about the seventy-two virgins in Paradise.

At any rate, the journey is mentioned briefly in the Qur'an (sura 17) and "included a stopover in Jerusalem," which was the only time Muhammad visited the city. Again, according to lore, the Muslim holy shrine, the Dome of the Rock, stands on the spot where the winged woman/mule/peacock took off and carried the Prophet and Gabriel to Paradise.

Even if you might be skeptical about the Night Journey itself, it would seem that the mythology that has developed around it does give Jerusalem at least some religious status. However, the city was not granted any special significance early in Islamic history. And as Bernard Lewis points out, "Even the name 'Jerusalem' does not figure in early Muslim writings."[193]

Yet in 691, Jerusalem was chosen for the building site of the Dome of the Rock, the first great shrine in Islam. Coincidentally, the site was the Temple Mount, a sacred site for both Christians and Jews. According to Judeo-Christian lore, "The actual spot was the rock on which, according to rabbinic tradition, Abraham had prepared to sacrifice his son, and on which in later times the Ark of the Temple had rested." Of course, it is also the site of King Solomon's temple, of which only the Wailing Wall remains today.

The more cynical among you might think that the choice of that place to build a Great Mosque could have been a political move by a new religion that was trying to establish itself as the successor to Judaism and Christianity. This speculation is supported by the choice of Qur'anic inscriptions that decorate the inside of the shrine, including direct challenges to the Christian notion of God's trinity. The walls of the mosque read, "Praise be to God, who begets no son, and has no partner in [His] dominion." (My radical to English translation: "In your face, Christians.") Then, there are the specific warnings for Jews and Christians: "God's religion is Islam. . . . Let whoever disbelieves in the signs of God beware, for God is swift in reckoning."[194] There are plenty more examples of verses that are clear challenges to the "People of the Book," but you get the idea.

For many years, a large number of Muslims believed that only Mecca and Medina qualified as "holy" places and specifically "denied the sanctity of Jerusalem." There was a dispute over this idea for centuries, one that, according to Lewis, "was only settled in favor of sanctity in comparatively modern times."[195] Of course, when it was clear that the Israelis wanted Jerusalem as an important part of their new nation, the Muslim world settled any remaining difference of opinion and declared Jerusalem absolutely, positively, and without a doubt a very holy city.

RADICALS GET INNOVATIVE:
A BRIEF HISTORY OF MODERN TERRORISM

Genocide was not the only innovation that radical Muslims gave the world in the twentieth century. The second, um, contribution to history was the invention of modern terrorism, which combined murderous impulses, frustration at humiliating military defeats, and an inability to match the economic development of prosperous Western nations or even of their hated enemy Israel, a nation of just over six million people that, according to Victor Davis Hanson, has a larger gross national product than the "aggregate economic output of all Islamic nations along the northern coast of Africa."[196]

Ironically, though the Ottoman Empire collapsed because it could not match or even keep pace with western Europe's innovations, radical Muslims developed their own inventive spirit and applied it to terrorism, the history of which is full of dubious "firsts."

June 5, 1968—United States: A Palestinian named Sirhan Sirhan assassinates presidential candidate Robert F. Kennedy. Sirhan was upset by Kennedy's personal support for Israel during the Six-Day War.

September 5, 1972—Germany: Palestinians from the "Black September" terrorist group (who were connected to Arafat's PLO) take eleven Israeli Olympic athletes hostage in their hotel in Munich. Nine of the hostages die in the eventual shootout with the German police. This marks the first and only time in history that terrorists attack Olympic athletes. There is no indication that Black September sees the irony of a violent attack during the Olympics, which are based on the spirit of peaceful competition between nations.

March 2, 1973—Saudi Arabia: Black September assassinates US diplomats at the Saudi embassy in Khartoum. This is the first attack on US diplomats by Islamic radicals. It will not be the last. Again, there is no indication that the terrorists are aware of the irony of staging a violent attack against diplomats, who are in the business of insuring peace and friendly relations between nations.

May 1974—Israel: Members of the Palestinian Liberation Organization, acting on orders from Yasser Arafat, invent the politically motivated school massacre. Three terrorists from the PLO slip into northern Israel from

Lebanon, murder a family in their home, and then take more than a hundred children hostage in a school. When Israeli troops stage a rescue, the terrorists lob hand grenades at the children and open fire on them. Twenty-one boys and girls die.

June 27, 1976—Uganda: In the first case of the radical Islamic–based hijacking of an airliner to an African nation ruled by a crazy cannibal (Idi Amin), members of the groups Baader-Meinhof and the Popular Front for the Liberation of Palestine force an Air France jet and 258 passengers to land in Uganda. From the point of view of the terrorists, the operation is a complete failure when Israeli soldiers launch an assault on the plane on the runway and successfully rescue almost all of the passengers, except for three who were killed in the raid and one who had been taken previously to a hospital in Kampala and was later murdered on orders from Idi Amin.

November 4, 1979—Iran: Inaugurating a new era in Islamic terrorist hostage-taking, radicals in Iran operating under the authority of an extremist group called the Iranian government take sixty-six American diplomats hostage. This is done by the Ayatollah Khomeini's new revolutionary Islamic regime in response to President Carter's agreement to allow the deposed shah of Iran to enter the United States.

Though thirteen of the hostages are quickly released, fifty-three more are held for more than a year, until January 20, 1981.

September 14, 1982—Lebanon: Popular Christian Lebanese Prime Minister Bashir Gemayel of Lebanon is assassinated by Palestinian terrorists who are from a Palestinian refugee camp on Lebanese soil. The terrorists do not like Gemayel's good relationship with Israel, which is occupying Lebanon at the time. Angry Lebanese Christians enter the Palestinian refugee camps that were the homes of the terrorists and massacre hundreds. Naturally, the Palestinians blame local Israeli military commander Ariel Sharon for the incident.

April 18, 1983—Lebanon: The terrorist group Islamic Jihad introduces an important innovation to the business of terrorism: the suicide bombing. Through the use of a truck bomb, terrorists kill sixty-three people at the US embassy in Beirut.

October 23, 1983—Lebanon: Not ones to rest on their laurels, Islamic Jihad brings the world the first "simultaneous truck-bomb" attack, targeting a US Marine barracks and a French compound in Beirut. Two hundred and forty-two Marines die in the blast.

March 16, 1984—Lebanon: Islamic Jihad kidnaps CIA agent William Buckley in Beirut. Buckley is tortured over several months and then murdered.

June 14, 1985—The Mediterranean Sea near Egypt: Members of the Palestinian Liberation Front commit the first hijacking of a cruise ship, the Italian liner *Achille Lauro*. When they murder sixty-nine-year-old Leon Klinghoffer, the terrorists distinguish themselves by becoming the first Islamic radicals in history to shoot an unarmed, elderly, disabled man in a wheelchair and throw his body into the ocean. There is no proof the terrorists shouted "Allah Akbar!" while they were coming up with this particular innovation, but it's a safe bet.

April 5, 1986—Germany: Libyan radicals invent a new terrorist tactic: the nightclub bombing. They blow up a hotspot in West Berlin, Germany, killing two American soldiers and injuring another seventy-nine. President Reagan orders an air strike on targets in Libya, including the home of Libyan leader Muammar Khadafi. After that, Khadafi ceases open support of terrorism and is, generally speaking, very quiet. In 2003, Khadafi volunteers to cease his nuclear weapons program after watching CNN footage of the war in Iraq, which—according to reliable sources—shocked, awed, and scared the pants off him.

February 17, 1988—Lebanon: A US Marine named Lt. Col. W. Higgins is kidnapped and murdered while serving as a UN *peace*keeper (irony alert!). The terrorist group Hezbollah, which is supported by Iran, is responsible. To this day, most European countries refuse to categorize Hezbollah as a terrorist organization and continue to allow it to raise money on European soil.

December 21, 1988—Scotland: Libyan terrorists blow up Pan American Airlines Flight 103 over Lockerbie, Scotland, killing all 259 passengers. For years, Libyan leader Muammar Khadafi denies involvement in the bombing but, in 2004, he finally admits Libyan responsibility as part of an effort to end international sanctions against his country.

February 26, 1993—New York: Islamic terrorists attempt another first—the complete destruction of an iconographic American skyscraper—when they detonate a bomb in the parking garage of the World Trade Center. Damage to the buildings is minimal, but six people are killed and one thousand injured. In a widely reported statement one of the terrorists writes, "The obligation of Allah is upon us to wage jihad for the sake of Allah. We have to thoroughly demoralize the enemies of God . . . by means of destroying and blowing up their towers that constitute the pillars of their civilization . . . the high buildings of which they are so proud."[197]

November 13, 1995—Saudi Arabia: Terrorists from the Islamic Movement of Change bomb a military facility in Riyadh, Saudi Arabia, killing one US citizen and nearly fifty other people.

June 25, 1996—Saudi Arabia: Terrorists attack the Khobar Towers, US military housing in Saudi Arabia. Nineteen US military personnel are killed, 240 wounded, and another 275 non-US citizens are wounded. A number of terrorist groups fall over themselves to claim responsibility for the attack.

February 23, 1997—New York: In the first murder/suicide by a crazed gunman atop the Empire State Building, a Palestinian terrorist on the observation deck opens fire on tourists, killing a Dutch citizen and wounding an American, as well as people from Argentina, Switzerland, and France. The Palestinian then turns the gun on himself.

August 7, 1998—Africa: Osama bin Laden and al Qaeda bring the world another innovation—the simultaneous attack on multiple diplomatic centers—when they detonate a bomb at the US embassy in Nairobi, Kenya, and kill twelve US citizens, thirty-two Foreign Service nationals, and 247 Kenyans. More than five thousand people are injured, including six US citizens. At about the same time, another bomb explodes outside the US embassy in Tanzania, killing three Tanzanians and seven Foreign Service nationals and injuring one US citizen.

October 12, 2000—Yemen: Acting on orders from Osama bin Laden and al Qaeda, terrorists invent the water-borne suicide-bombing attack when they strike the US Navy vessel, the USS *Cole*, killing seventeen servicemen and injuring thirty-nine others.

September 11, 2001—United States: Nineteen hijackers under orders from Osama bin Laden and al Qaeda offer the world their deadliest innovation yet and use hijacked jetliners as both guided bombs and weapons of mass destruction, leveling the twin towers of the World Trade Center in New York and damaging the Pentagon in Washington, DC. Passengers in a fourth airliner overpower the terrorists and Flight 93 crashes in a Pennsylvania field. In all, 2,986 people are murdered.

July 7, 2005—Great Britain: Al Qaeda loyalists bring the world the first coordinated attack on innocent civilians taking mass transit when they simultaneously detonate bombs during London's morning rush hour on three subway trains and a double-decker bus, killing fifty-two people (not including the bombers) and injuring more than one hundred.

July 21, 2005—Great Britain: Four radical Muslims attempt to engineer the first *midday* attack on innocent civilians taking mass transit when they try to simultaneously detonate bombs in the London subway system. Technically, there was no innovation here, unless you count the staggering incompetence of the terrorists or the mind-boggling cowardice of one of the would-be bombers, who, moments before surrendering in his underwear to waiting British police, told them, "I'm scared."[198]

October 1, 2005—Indonesia: In the first simultaneous-triple-restaurant-suicide-bombing, terrorists kill twenty-five and wound more than one hundred in Bali.[199]

August 2006—Great Britain: More than twenty Muslim extremists are arrested for plotting to destroy as many as ten jetliners in flight, which would have been the first radical Islamic mass murder using simultaneous detonations in multiple transatlantic aircraft. These two dozen terrorists get credit for a second innovation, the baby suicide bomber, since two of the radicals intended to bring their infant onto one of the doomed planes as "cover."

January 1, 2007—New Delhi, India: Two jihadists from the Kashmir region were arrested in New Delhi before they could execute their plan to become the first terrorist toy bombers. They had planted bombs in two boxes of toys containing a toy duck and a toy bus, intending to use the bombs to blow up a busy market in New Delhi.[200]

The Palestinian Liberation Organization (PLO) grew as an effort to use terrorism to free the occupied lands from Israeli control. From the beginning, it was a pan-Muslim group. In fact, it's a little-known fact that Yasser Arafat was actually Egyptian and was not from the Palestinian territories. He was also far from the popular (and most often inaccurate) image of terrorists as poor, oppressed people. Arafat was from an upper-middle-class Egyptian family and had a degree in civil engineering from Cairo University.

In 1973, Egypt and Syria launched an attack on Israel on Yom Kippur, the holiest day of the year for the Jews. As in 1967, the Israelis knew the attack was coming, but they were concerned about international opinion and waited until the attack began to launch a counter-strike. Their restraint nearly cost them their country, and Muslim forces came the closest they ever did to overrunning Israel.

While the plight of the Palestinians is a rallying point for radical and "moderate" Muslims alike, it's pretty clear that they have been exploited by various Muslim nations who wish to wage a proxy war on Israel and win through terrorism what they could not win through military means. Thus, a number of Muslim countries, most notably Saudi Arabia, made it illegal for decades for Palestinian refugees to immigrate to their lands.

This takes us to the 1982 Israeli invasion of Lebanon, which would become another sore point with the Muslim world. The seeds for this invasion were planted in the mid-1970s, when the PLO operated out of Lebanon and used it as a base from which to strike at Israel. They also teamed up with the Lebanese Muslims, who they joined in the 1975–1976 civil war against the Lebanese Christians. At the time, the Christians were nearly half the Lebanese population, the country had a functioning economy, and it was a popular tourist destination. The civil war killed tens of thousands, wrecked the economy, and turned rubble into the Lebanese national symbol.

Although the full-scale fighting ended in 1976, the PLO-Muslim alliance continued to skirmish with Christian Lebanese forces for more than a decade. During this time, the PLO also continued to plan and stage terrorist attacks on Israel. The Israelis finally got fed up and in 1982 invaded southern Lebanon, occupying much of the country until they pulled out as part of a UN-brokered agreement in 1985.

Of course the UN agreement was a limited success, and fighting flared up again in 2006 when Israel decided it had had enough of the regular rocket attacks from the terrorist group Hezbollah and went in with full force, determined to knock out the terrorist organization's ability to strike inside Israel.

MYTH ABOUT OSAMA BIN LADEN #1:
The United States "Created" bin Laden in the 1980s

London mayor Ken Livingstone resurrected this one shortly after the July 7, 2005, attacks in London, saying, "In the 1980s, Americans recruited and trained Osama bin Laden, taught him how to kill, to make bombs, and set him off to kill the Russians and drive them out of Afghanistan." Thus, on 9/11, Americans were simply reaping what they had sown because "they didn't give any thought to the fact that, once he'd done that, [bin Laden] might turn on his creators."[201]

This makes a compelling story, tying into one of the fundamental anxieties of modern man—that he has the capacity to create machines/bombs/supercomputers/devices that will turn on him and destroy him. It has been a staple of literature and film beginning with Mary Shelley's *Frankenstein* up until the *Terminator* movies, *Jurassic Park*, and half of the science-fiction films and television series in recent memory. The tale resonates deeply with the psychosexual realm as it plays out adolescent fears about maturity and the acceptance of adult power and responsibility. In this sort of narrative, man's creation is a dark mirror, reflecting his worst traits combined with great power and the potential to do evil—a combination that makes the Toxic Avenger saga both possible and psychologically satisfying.

THE WILD-EYED FACE OF ISLAMIC EXTREMISM:
OSAMA BIN LADEN

Osama bin Laden's chief grievance against the United States is the presence of American troops on "holy" Saudi Arabian soil. Of course, American soldiers arrived en force when the Saudi government requested (or begged and pleaded, to put it more accurately) that the United States protect its nation from Iraqi forces after Saddam Hus-

There is a problem, however, with the *Toxic Avenger-esque* Osama bin Laden narrative as expressed by Mr. Livingstone: it isn't true. While the United States and other Western powers did support the Afghani resistance to Soviet rule, they never gave any aid or training to Osama bin Laden and his group. The fact is that during the Afghani war against the Soviet Union there were always two distinctly different groups in the fight. The first were the native Afghani people, supported by the United States through the CIA. The second were the so-called Afghan Arabs, which included Osama bin Laden. As one news report put it, the Afghan Arabs group was "financed by Saudi Arabia and the Gulf states and was composed of Islamic extremists who migrated from across the Muslim world"—not unlike the "insurgents" currently fighting coalition forces in Iraq.

With all due respect to Mr. Livingstone, bin Laden himself disputed any connection between himself and the United States. "Personally neither I nor my brothers saw any evidence of American help," bin Laden told British journalist Robert Fisk in 1993. Then in another interview in 1996, bin Laden made it very clear to Fisk that "we were never, at any time, friends of the Americans. We knew that the Americans supported the Jews in Palestine and that they are our enemies."[202]

BIN LADENISM VS. SATANISM: THE MORAL DIVIDE

After 9/11, Americans saw chilling scenes of Palestinians cele-
brating in the streets and literally jumping for joy at news of the
attacks. What was going on here? Americans have fought and won
many wars and battles in the past, but we never publicly celebrated
the deaths of innocents. It seemed like a tremendous moral divide
had revealed itself between Western and radical Islamist thinking.

In mid-November 2001, Osama bin Laden talked to a group of
lieutenants and supporters in Afghanistan. A video camera captured the event, and in between discussing their joy at the successful mass murder of thousands of men, women, and children,
bin Laden and his associates say "Praise be to Allah!" over and
over again.

More than one observer noted that if you substituted the word
Satan for Allah, the conversation made much more sense. However, as it turns out, Satanists would object to the comparison
because they reject violence except as direct retribution against
someone who has harmed them personally. Also, the Church of
Satan has strong and clear rules against harming children.

On the other hand, according to the Wahhabist religious doctrine of Osama bin Laden, children are innocent as per Islamic

sein's invasion of Kuwait. It's also worth pointing out that most of the
combat deployments of US forces in the 1990s were to save Muslim
lives, including the first Gulf War, the interventions in the Balkans,
and the effort to feed people starved by the warlords in Somalia.

ISLAM: WHERE'S THE PEACE?

After three chapters on war and Islam, we've studied relevant passages of the Qur'an, the life of Muhammad, and the history of the var-

holy law. Therefore, Jewish children killed by homicide bombers or American children killed on 9/11 are classified as "involuntary martyrs" and are guaranteed entry into Paradise.[203] So, according to this thinking, murdering a child in the course of committing terrorism is an act of piety and a gift to the child, a lot like the psychotic mother who kills her children to "save" them.

So there you have it. Before radical jihadists and bin Ladenists can close the moral divide between themselves and the West, they will have to close the divide between themselves and Satanists.

Of course, some will point out that bin Laden and other radicals have argued that, in a democracy, everyone is responsible for the actions of the government and therefore everyone is a target. But those arguments are clearly stupid. I would remind everyone that Charles Manson and Adolf Hitler each sought world domination and each had their own evil, ridiculous, and/or crazy justifications for their acts of murder and genocide. But we don't waste much time wondering if maybe they had a point.

Am I really equating militant Islam with Satanism? Absolutely not. From any rational, humanist perspective, Islamic terrorists fall way below the Church of Satan's moral and ethical standards.

ious Muslim empires and nations from the seventh century until today. The question before us remains: Is Islam a religion of peace?

What do I say? Sure, fine, it's a religion of peace. However, if that's the case, I have a few questions:

1. Why are Muslim *clerics* often involved in terrorist actions, like the first attempt to blow up the World Trade Center, which its organizers hoped would kill as many as 250,000 people?
2. Why do so many terrorist cells and radical recruiting centers operate within mosques throughout the Middle East as well as

in countries like the United States, England, France, Holland, Germany, and Russia?

3. If 9/11 was such a perversion of Islamic values, why do so many Muslims around the world consider Osama bin Laden a great hero?

4. During the Afghani war, why did Muslims in places like Indonesia—which had no ties to the Taliban other than a shared religion—protest against the United States and in support of the Taliban, who by any reasonable standard was one of the most corrupt and violently repressive regimes in history?

5. Since jihad-based slavery is looked upon favorably by Allah, is the taking of slaves through religious warfare an obligation or simply an option for Muslims? To paraphrase Bill Murray from *Ghostbusters*, is the taking of slaves more of a guideline or a rule?

6. How is it that after his conversion to the "religion of peace," Cat Stevens went from being a harmless hippie who wrote the song "Peace Train" to one of millions of Muslims calling for the murder of Salman Rushdie for his thought crimes?[204]

7. Further, why is all of Cat Stevens's postconversion music so lame, and what does this say about the effect of radical Islam on musical ability?

8. If they are not practicing "true Islam," why do suicide bombers and other Islamic terrorists and murderers of innocents cry out "Allah Akbar!" before they blow up eighteen-month-olds and their grandmothers on buses?

9. If terrorists and radicals are practicing a perverted/hijacked/untrue form of Islam, why doesn't the rest of the "moderate" Muslim world mention this to them? As in, "Come on guys, enough already. If you keep this up, you'll start to give us a bad name!"

10. Tell me again why Muslims in recent years have been involved in "half of the world's ethnopolitical conflicts," despite the fact that they make up only one-fifth of the world's population?

Chapter Seven

PEACE

Or, How to Find Creative New Ways to Make War

War is deception.

—Muhammad

IN SEARCH OF PEACE IN THE RELIGION OF PEACE

The astute reader may notice that this is the shortest chapter so far. The more cynical among you may be thinking this represents a subtle swipe at the Religion of Peace, but that is not so. The fact is that this chapter functions as an addendum to the earlier chapters on jihad.

You recall, in the first chapter, we established that the very concept of jihad involves a perpetual state of war between the House of Islam and the House of War. You may be wondering quite reasonably how big a role peacemaking could possibly have in that context. The answer is: not a very big one.

I had hoped to use this chapter as a counterpoint to the three chapters on war, but after extensive research, I discovered that it worked mostly as a *point*—in that the peace process allows Muslim powers to either regroup before another attack or to try to win concessions without actual battle. Thus, efforts at making peace are often thinly disguised efforts at making war (see the quote from the Prophet that opens the chapter).

There is an Arabic term for this sort of deception: *al-Taqiyya* or simply *taqiyya*. According to the encyclopedia available at Al-Islam.org, *taqiyya* means "Concealing or disguising one's beliefs, convictions, ideas, feelings, opinions, and/or strategies at a time of eminent danger, whether now or later in time, to save oneself from physical and/or mental injury. A one-word translation would be 'Dissimulation.'"[205] The same encyclopedia maintains that the concept of *taqiyya* is an "integral part of Islam."

There are a number of Hadith and verses in the Qur'an that stipulate that it is permissible, under duress, to do the unthinkable and utter words of disbelief. "Anyone who, after accepting faith in Allah, utters unbelief, *except under compulsion* [emphasis mine] . . . upon them is Wrath from Allah, and theirs will be a dreadful Chastisement" (16:106). Most verses say that the concealment of one's belief is allowed when a Muslim is under threat of life and limb. However, in a world where attacks on Spain, Rome, France, and eastern Europe were waged "in the defense of Islam," it's easy to see how a concept like *taqiyya* can be interpreted fairly broadly. A recent example would have been the kind of compromises of their beliefs that Muhammad Atta and the rest of the 9/11 hijackers would have had to make to gain entry into the United States and interact with the infidel while they were there to plan and execute the attacks. They even made the ultimate sacrifice for radical Muslim men and, according to numerous press reports, visited a strip club to drink alcohol and treat themselves to lap dances—all as part of their undercover terrorist operation.

THE PROPHET WAGES PEACE

Looking at history, it's hard to find examples of peacemaking from the Prophet's own life because though he waged jihad against his neighbors and managed to overrun half the Arabian Peninsula in his ten-year career of conquest, there aren't many examples of peaceful nego-tiations to settle differences.

But what about Muhammad's agreement with the Jews of Khaybar? Didn't he make peace with them?

Good question. The Jews of Khaybar lived in an oasis that Muhammad and his forces attacked and laid siege to for six weeks or so. At the end of the siege, the Jews surrendered, and the terms of the surrender were a peace agreement of sorts. The Jews agreed to give up their land, submit to Muhammad's rule, and pay exorbitant taxes for the Prophet's "protection." So it was a peace agreement in the sense that it ended the fighting, but it also ended the Jews' autonomy.

In his jihad career, Muhammad made a number of similar agree-ments—which we already talked about in chapter 5, the one on toler-ance and diversity—but he didn't make any agreements with other nations in which both sides agreed to leave the other alone. For that sort of peace agreement, we have to look a bit later in Islamic history to the agreements made with Muslim rulers and the rulers of Constan-tinople, which provide a perfect example of the Islamic peacemaking mind-set. Muhammad himself demanded that the ruler of Constan-tinople, Emperor Heraclius, and his people submit to Islam. When the emperor refused, the Prophet started making plans to take the city by force and decreed that "all who took part in the attack on the Christian capital would be forgiven their sins, and those who died in the cam-paign would go straight to Paradise."[206]

But I thought that Muhammad and the Qur'an said that Muslims must make war only in defense?

Yes, they did.

Was Constantinople a threat to Muhammad's empire?

Well, no.

But that doesn't seem very defensive then.

No, it doesn't, but as we have said, Muhammad—as well as many radicals through history and living today—defined the "defense of Islam" very, um, broadly.

The first Muslim attack on Constantinople was launched in 668, *thirty-six* years after Muhammad's death. As per chapter 1, after seven years and an overwhelming defeat, the Muslim invaders had to ask the Byzantine emperor for peace and paid handsomely for the right to return home unmolested.

So the Muslim Empire attacked the capital of a sovereign land and then sued for peace when the attack failed. Given that Islam is a religion of peace, that should have been the end of it, right?

Well, not quite. The next attack (and failure) came in 717, forty-two years after the first. Muslim armies attacked the city another five times that century and a number of more times in the next several centuries until the city fell in 1453.[207] The point is that the Muslim rulers made the first peace agreement as a matter of practical necessity. Remembering Muhammad's maxim, "War is deception," they and their successors simply tried again and again until they brought Constantinople under the heel of the religion of peace.

THE IRONICALLY NAMED
MIDDLE EASTERN PEACE PROCESS

This story and the concept of *taqiyya* is very relevant today when we look at the current efforts to bring peace to the Middle East. We've already talked about the terrible affront to the radical psyche that the success and military supremacy of a nation of infidels (Israel) in the center of the House of Islam represents. As we learned in our discussion of *dhimmi*tude, the subjugation and humiliation of non-Muslims was essential proof of the supremacy of Islam to all other religions and of the superiority of the *Umma* itself.

The existence and supremacy of the West in all matters economic and military is bad enough—and the West is reasonably far away—but Israel is much too close for comfort. It's harder to look away and impossible to forget that the combined military might of the Muslim world was unable to defeat the small nation of infidels in a series of wars. The fact that Israelis now have dominion over the Palestinian "refugees" is the straw that constantly flogs the camel's back.

In any sane universe that a radical Muslim understands, infidels having power over Muslims should be impossible. As we have seen, the Qur'an quite clearly promises that Allah will grant Muslims victory over the infidel. Thus, Israel creates a very real psychological and theological problem. The success of Israel as a nation not only harms the self-esteem of the Muslim world, but it also calls into question the very ideas of the supremacy of Islam and the inimitability of the Qur'an. In this context, the well of anti-Semitism in the Muslim world and the attack on Israeli citizens by Islamic terrorists are the result of a paradigm shifting without a clutch.

For many in the Muslim world, there has been a great deal of emphasis on the "suffering" of the Palestinians, which has also elicited much sympathy in Europe, but the fact is that the Palestinians who came under the dominion of Israel after the 1967 war saw an immediate and marked improvement to the treatment they had seen under their former Egyptian masters. Today, according to a widely reported demographic study released in early 2005, Palestinians enjoy among the highest standards of living in the Middle East.[208]

For all the discussion about Palestinian suffering at the hands of the Israelis, there was not a peep of protest from the Muslim community—or the UN or Europe for that matter—when in the early 1990s Kuwait deported more than 350,000 Palestinian refuges who had been living within its borders. As a thought experiment, try to imagine what would happen if Israel did the same thing and you'll see what I'm getting at. That sound you hear in your mind is the outraged shrieking wails of the Muslim "street."

PEACE IN OUR TIME: OSLO AND CAMP DAVID

The Palestinian situation and the peace process is a complex situation that has been endlessly and heatedly debated, and I won't try to recap it all here. For our purposes, the conflict is worth discussing in terms of *taqiyya* to reveal some of the radical trademarks and illustrate the principles established by early Islamic rulers to use a "peace process" to further the aims of the jihad.

The best-known examples are the Oslo and Camp David accords. In Oslo, Norway, in 1993, Palestinians and Israelis agreed to some broad terms that would eventually pave the way for a new peace agreement, including the eventual transfer of the overwhelming majority of Gaza and the West Bank to Palestinian control. This would have occurred after a five-year interim period of shared control over the area.

Escalating violence cost the Oslo Accords credibility. President Clinton tried to continue the process with the Camp David talks of 2000, but those talks fell apart over disputes about territory, control of Jerusalem, and the "Right of Return"—the right of Palestinian refugees to return to their "homes" or, in most cases, to the areas in Israel where their ancestors lived. During the talks, Israel made historic concessions, but there are strong indications that Yasser Arafat and the Palestinian representatives at Oslo never intended to make peace.

First, Hamas—the largest terrorist and political organization in the Palestinian territories—has made it clear time and again that it will never accept Israel's right to exist. Arafat and his negotiators knew this and made no attempt to bring Hamas on board, even though violence from Hamas would certainly doom any peace plan. According to HamasOnline.com, "Hamas was formed in 1987 with the objective of destroying the Zionist entity that occupies Palestine, and establishing Palestine *from the sea to the river* [italics mine] based on Islamic principles."[209] Hamas has made numerous public statements to the effect that any Palestinian who even enters into peace talks with Israel is guilty of "treason."[210] Even if the late Arafat (or any subsequent Palestinian leader) were sincere in his acceptance of a peace proposal, enforcing it within Gaza and the West Bank would mean an inevitable civil war with Hamas.

Second, after the Israelis made historic concessions at Camp David and there was a real danger of peace, Arafat walked away from the negotiations without making a counterproposal. In a rare moment of honesty, he commented that if he made the agreement, he would soon be "drinking tea with Rabin." Or, in other words, he would quickly meet the same fate as the late Israeli prime minister who had been assassinated by an Israeli rightwing activist angered by the concessions Rabin was offering the Palestinians.

Given that they were doomed from the start, why did Arafat even enter the negotiations? Well, it would fit into the model of using peace talks to regroup and prepare for more conflict. Certainly, that explanation fits the fact that a new wave of suicide bombings began shortly after Arafat signed the agreement at Oslo. There is ample evidence that Arafat was planning the so-called Second Intifada before the Camp David peace negotiations.

Thus, the Oslo and Camp David process allowed the Palestinians to play at being sincere about peace, even as they planned more attacks on Israeli citizens. In that respect, they achieved an important international public relations victory, which acted as cover for their terrorist activities.

SAUDI ARABIA JOINS THE PARTY

Another illuminating peace initiative was started in 2002 by Crown Prince Abdullah, leader of the Saudi Arabian government, which was reeling from the fallout from the 9/11 attacks and the news that fifteen of the nineteen hijackers were Saudis, a fact which, despite all efforts, the Saudis were not able to spin as a statistical anomaly. The Saudi plan was released first to the *New York Times* and was basically a reiteration of the principles of UN Resolution 242, as well as the terms of the failed Oslo peace accords. The proposal called for Israel to return to its 1967 borders and allow for the formation of a Palestinian state. In return for these concessions, the Saudis were offering something new: full normalization of relations between Israel and the Arab world.

However, there can be little doubt that the peace plan, as presented, was a cynical public and international relations ploy, since it included an important nonstarter: a *full withdrawal* to the 1967 borders, something that every Israeli government since 1967 has rejected.[211] At Camp David in 2000, the Israelis came close to offering this when they agreed to give up 95 percent of the territory the Palestinians were asking for to form their new state. The problem is that, as Israelis see it, a full withdrawal would not leave them with borders they could easily defend. As we have seen, the 1967 Six-Day War and the 1973 Yom Kippur War threatened Israel's very existence.

The Saudi plan also left out one of the most important demands that have been made by Palestinians and Muslims worldwide: the "Right of Return." For Israel, the right of return would mean they would be immediately overwhelmed by Palestinian immigrants. Apparently, there is some anecdotal evidence that Israelis would be in danger if they suddenly became a minority in a Muslim-dominated nation.

The right of return and control of Jerusalem (which as we have discussed is the Jews' holiest city) have been major sticking points for both sides. Both the Oslo accords and the Bush administration's "Roadmap" had to defer resolution on these issues to get even as far as they did—which careful followers of recent events will note has not been very far. In fact, the Roadmap is not even a real peace plan; it's just some general principles that might eventually lead to a discussion that could—if things go very, very well—lead to some sort of a plan.

Interestingly, an eminent Palestinian political scientist named Dr. Khalil Shikaki did a study in 2003 in which he asked Palestinians if they would actually exercise their right of return if they had the option to do so. Remarkably, though 95 percent of the Palestinians polled insisted that Israel recognize the right of return, only 10 percent indicated that they would actually want to return to their "homes." According to the *New York Times*, this was "a proportion that decreased if the refugees were told that they would have to take Israeli citizenship or that their old homes were gone."

You might be thinking that this study could have been revolutionary, showing that, from a statistical point of view, the right of return that has been an unsolvable problem in the peace process was, in fact, a small issue in the real world. Well, many Palestinians did not see it that way. Instead, a group of them got very angry and rioted, wrecking Dr. Shikaki's office and roughing him up as they pelted him with eggs.[212]

Another Palestinian, Sair Nusseibeh, president of Al-Quds University in Jerusalem, came under pressure when he tried to bring sanity to the peace process. According to the *San Francisco Chronicle*, "Nusseibeh was beaten up at Bir Zeit University for promoting dialogue with Israelis. Last year (2002), he was dismissed as the PLO's representative in Jerusalem after he publicly questioned whether demanding the right of return was either logical or feasible."

Given that any peace proposal that doesn't deal with the right of return and Jerusalem is doomed, what did this one gain the Saudis? Well, it took some of the 9/11 heat off them, particularly in the Western press. It allowed them to float a plan that was in no danger of succeeding. Thus, when the proposal failed or went nowhere—which it did—the Saudis could blame Israeli intransigence, which they did.

Thus, the plan, which was offered first to the press and never formally presented in any detailed way in a real international forum, became a victory in the ongoing anti-Israeli propaganda war—the only war with Israel in which the Muslim world has seen any success. Think of it as Muslim *taqiyya* dollars at work.

The situation also perfectly illustrates Muhammad's quote that opened this chapter. The full quote from the Hadith is: "Lying is wrong, except in three things: the lie of a man to his wife to make her content with him [I include this one because, though it is not relevant to our discussion of peace, it's pretty funny]; a lie to an enemy, for war is deception; or a lie to settle trouble between people."

MASTERING THE LANGUAGE OF PEACE

SPOT THE *TAQIYYA*

CAIR is the Council on American-Islamic Relations, a self-styled moderate Muslim advocacy group. Their Web site boasts the following: "CAIR's mission is to enhance understanding of Islam, encourage dialogue, protect civil liberties, empower American Muslims, and build coalitions that promote justice and mutual understanding."

Would this kind of organization practice *taqiyya*, using active deception to conceal radical beliefs? Let's find out. Use your new Radical Eye to interpret the following, seemingly innocuous, statements made by CAIR leadership, and see if you can *Spot the* Taqiyya.

1. "Our goal, insha'Allah [if Allah wills], is to register more than 100,000 new Muslim voters over the next eight months," says CAIR in 2002.
2. "We have an obligation, because of the Islamic duty of 'enjoining good and prohibiting evil,' to make our voices heard on a number of important issues. Voting, at both the local and national level, is the best way to accomplish that goal," said CAIR Executive Director Nihad Awad about the 2002 voter drive.
3. "What we fight for here and in the remainder of the world is to practice our beliefs," says spokesman Ibrahim Hooper in a 1993 interview.
4. "I wouldn't want to create the impression that I wouldn't like the government of the United States to be Islamic sometime in the future, but I'm not going to do anything violent to promote that. I'm going to do it through education," said Hooper in a 1993 interview.[213]

Okay, lets use our Radical Eye to analyze these four comments. First, voter registration seems like a good thing, the kind of effort that an immigrant community would make as they were embracing the American dream.

The second quote actually seems exemplary. Fighting evil is something that everyone can get behind, right? Well, that depends on whether you think evil is personified by men who shoot children in the back, or by women who wear shorts. The CAIR spokesman doesn't say which side of that question he is on, but we'll start to get a fuller picture soon.

The third comment is a clear statement of CAIR's commitment to religious freedom, which is as American as apple pie. The problem is that America already has freedom of religion. Why does CAIR feel the need to "fight" for a basic right their members already possess? The answer may lie in the difference between the Muslim "beliefs" CAIR wants to promote and religion as Americans and other Westerners understand the term.

In the final comment, our CAIR spokesman is clearly expressing his desire for the US government to be Islamic in the future. This also doesn't sound so bad until we remember our earlier discussions on Islam as a religious, political, legal, and economic system that is irreconcilably at odds with Western-style democracy, human rights, equality between the sexes, and our distaste for slavery.

But CAIR represents the good, moderate Muslim majority, don't they?

I will accept that they represent the moderate Muslim majority if CAIR says so. Of course, as far as I'm concerned, this just makes them scarier. I will explain . . .

We get a glimpse of CAIR's real beliefs on its Web site, which provides the following description of the Qur'an: "The Quran is the record of the exact words revealed by God through the Angel Gabriel to the Prophet Muhammad. It was memorized by Muhammad and then dictated to his companions. The text of the Quran was cross-checked during the life of the Prophet. The 114 chapters of the Quran have remained unchanged through the centuries."[214]

In other words, CAIR is clearly identifying itself with the widely held belief that the Qur'an is the exact and unchanging word of Allah. (And you thought I was exaggerating when I said that the term *Islamic fundamentalist* is redundant.)

In answer to the question "What is Islam?" CAIR responds that "Islam is both a religion and a complete way of life. . . ." Suddenly, we see what CAIR means when it says that its members want to fight for the right to practice their beliefs. They are not just talking about being allowed to possess a Qur'an, or to go to mosque, or to pray five times a day.

With this additional information and the careful application of our Radical Eye, I offer the following *taqiyya*-adjusted possible radical to English translation of the above quotes from CAIR: "We at CAIR are committed to using the American democratic system to create an Islamic theocracy consistent with the principles of the Qur'an that will completely eliminate human rights as you know them so we can institute a system of Islamic law that will include such Qur'an and Shariah-mandated punishments as stoning, flogging, and amputations. In addition, women may want to spend a little less time going to school and pursuing careers and a little more time guarding their honor and shopping for headscarves, or better yet, formless, full-body black robes."

Of course, this translation is not precise. Some radical Muslims prefer to spell Qur'an as *Quran*.

PEACE SQUARED: MUSLIM VS. MUSLIM

So far, we've focused on Muslim peace efforts with non-Muslim countries. As we've seen, the insincerity and outright deceit in peace negotiations have their basis in Islamic tradition and make perfect sense given Muhammad's words and actions, particularly the perpetual state of war he established between believer and infidel.

However, it's much harder to explain the tendency for Muslims to fight one another when the Qur'an and the Hadith provide numerous prohibitions against conflict within the *Umma*. Yet Muslim nations were involved in more than 50 percent of the ethnic conflicts in the 1990s, and they didn't achieve that by limiting their efforts to non-Muslims.

In *The Arab Mind*, author Raphael Patai quotes Egyptian Foreign Affairs Minister Boutros Boutrous-Ghali, who said in 1982, "In the last three decades alone, more than thirty conflicts between Arab states have erupted, in the Magreb as well as in the Mashrek, between revolutionary regimes as well as between conservative governments. Some of these conflicts have turned into full-scale wars and others have caused tensions and diplomatic confrontations."[215]

Of course, there have been many more inter-Muslim conflicts before that time and since then. There's the Iran-Iraq War that lasted from 1980 to 1988, the Iraqi invasion of Kuwait, and let's not forget the ongoing violence between Arabs and black Muslims in the Sudan. There has also been a civil war between Jordan and Palestinian refugees, problems between Syria and Lebanon, a civil war in Lebanon (fomented largely by Palestinian refugees), strife between Kuwaitis and Palestinian refugees, another civil war in Yemen—the list is nearly endless.

The point is that all of this conflict has given Muslims plenty of opportunity to sharpen their peacemaking skills, with the added incentive that Muhammad himself said that the *Umma* was one community and that there should be no fighting within the "House of Islam," which is also known as the "House of Peace."

One example of the inter-Muslim principle of peacemaking can be found in the Iran-Iraq War. The roots of this conflict go back to the earliest days of Islam and the Sunni/Shi'a split in the religion. The war lasted eight years and cost as many as 1 million dead and 1.7 million wounded on both sides.

All efforts by Muslim nations to mediate and end the dispute were less than completely successful. Finally, the fighting stopped when the UN imposed a ceasefire on the two exhausted, war-torn countries.

Incidentally, the only hope the black Muslims in the Sudan have for protection from the Arab Muslims who are persecuting and killing them is the UN. There's a thought.

Again, Muslim nations are very good at following Qur'anic rules about waging war against unbelievers but much less comfortable following Islamic teachings about keeping peace with other Muslims. If Muslims cannot make peace with each other, what does this say about the potential for peace in the Middle East or the long-term outlook for the problem of worldwide terrorism?

Good question.

Chapter Eight

EDUCATION

Or, What's That about Allah Turning Jews and Christians into Pigs and Monkeys?

Beware matters newly begun, because every innovation is misguidance.

—Qur'an

KNOWLEDGE IS GOOD

To understand the state of education in the Islamic world you need to understand two key concepts:

1. The overwhelming majority of a Muslim's education is centered around Islam.
2. No new thinking, study, or scholarship about Islamic tradition or the Qur'an is permitted, and in some cases such innovation is even punishable by death.

This is actually perfectly logical given the Muslim tradition and the belief in the Qur'an as the exact word and will of Allah.

The Prophet set the tone for the Muslim educational system (to say nothing of the state of science and industry in the Islamic world) when he revealed this chapter's opening quote in the Qur'an. As we have discussed, in all Muslim cultures, and particularly the Arab ones, it is impossible to overstate the reverence that the faithful have for the early, golden days of Islam. This thinking seems absurd to Westerners because, to us, this period seems like a brutal time of conflict, torture, and death—after all, three of the first four caliphs were murdered.

However, you have to remember that for Muslims these early times were when they practiced the purest form of the faith. Since Islamic devotion to Allah is not simply a spiritual matter but a legal, cultural, social, and economic one, the farther Muslims get from the norms and standards of seventh-century Arabia, the farther they fall from grace.

As Raphael Patai put it in his book *The Arab Mind*, "It is believed that the age in which the revelation [of the Qur'an] took place was the greatest and noblest period in its history, followed by gradual decay as the distance between the new generations and the original revelation increased. Every innovation is a sin because it increased this distance. If change is sought, it is only in the direction of return to the original, pure, perfect state of religion."[216]

On the other hand, Westerners believe that the journey to the future is a journey forward toward a better tomorrow. We expect to reach higher and higher standards of social and scientific progress year after year. Computers will get faster, cars more efficient, and people will hold themselves and their leaders to higher and higher standards of civility.

New products—from iPODs to cars to financial services—are marketed as "innovative." We revere the past and call the people who won World War II the "greatest generation," but we wince at the pre–civil rights segregation in their society and resolve to do better in the future.

We fully expect new advances in medicine, and we get them every year: from new gene therapies to AIDS drugs that have turned what used to be a death sentence into a chronic disease with a reasonably good prognosis. Even absurdities of political correctness come from a desire to treat minorities better than we have in the past.

Progress is the engine that drives Western society. To us, "backward" is an insult, as is "medieval." Not so for Muslims. In Islamic thought, the journey into the future is a long fall from the glorious past. The greatest calling is not new invention but the strictest return to the values and practices of the seventh century and the religious and political system as practiced by Muhammad.

In this world, the term *backward* is a compliment; *medieval* is the highest form of praise. If you believe that Muhammad was indeed the Prophet and the Qur'an the word and will of Allah, then this makes perfect sense. Even for skeptics who believe that Muhammad was simply an Arab patriot who wanted to preserve and export Arabian culture and values, we must admit that it was a remarkably successful venture.

The past took on an even more powerful appeal after the crumbling of the Ottoman Empire. Today, the combined strength of the entire Muslim world represents a negligible military power. After the Afghani and Iraqi wars, the Islamic ruling elites throughout the globe know that at any moment, they could be overrun by the immoral, decadent infidels from the United States. Given their vulnerable present and uncertain future, it's no surprise that Muslim culture is even more stuck in its "glorious" past.

Now, some people, confronted by this state of affairs, might conclude there is something to this gender equality, human rights, and progress thing. And they might start to rethink their medieval values. Unfortunately for the Muslim world, there is little sign of this sort of introspection. As Jerry Seinfeld said about the Chinese, "They're hanging in there with those chopsticks. . . . You know they've seen the fork. Oh, they're well aware that we have the fork—and the spoon."[217]

YOU KNOW YOU'RE IN TROUBLE WHEN
EVEN THE UN IS WORRIED ABOUT YOU

The impact of this, um, "conservative" thinking on Muslims around the world is profound. In our discussion of economics in the previous chapter, we talked about the 2002 UN Arab Human Development Report, which was a survey of Arab societies put together by a group of Arab scholars. Their findings were pretty dismal across the board, but the results regarding education and intellectual life were among the most shocking. Despite the fact that Arab countries typically spend more on education than the rest of the developing world, the actual educational performance is dismal.

Among the findings:

- Half of Arab women cannot read or write.
- Internet use is very low.
- A remarkably small number of books are translated into Arabic. "The whole Arab world [of 280 million people] translates about 330 books annually, one-fifth the number that Greece translates," says the report. To put it in even starker terms, it has taken a thousand years for Arabs to translate into Arabic the same number of books that Spain translates in a typical year.[218]

Though thorough in their findings, the authors of the report only make thin connections between Islam and these problems, but because of our studies so far, it is not hard to draw some conclusions. There's the Qur'anic prohibitions against innovation. Information is controlled by the mullahs for the same reason that it was controlled by the Soviet Union in the days of communism. New ideas are not only frowned upon because of cultural bias, they are actively discouraged because they are a direct threat to Islam's seventh-century religious, legal, and social thinking.

Western democracies have been pounded into existence through an adversarial system that has lasted thousands of years, in which new concepts and thoughts enter into the marketplace of ideas and are endlessly debated, tested, and revised. Through this process of reasoned argument, trial and error, and constant reevaluation, we create the progress that defines Western life.

But things have historically worked differently in the Islamic world. As preeminent scholar of Turkish history Halil Inalcik says in *The Ottoman Empire*, "Ottoman scholarship was bounded by traditional Islamic concepts which saw religious learning as the only true science, whose sole aim was the understanding of God's word. The Qur'an and the traditions of the Prophet [the Hadith] formed the basis of this learning; reason was only an auxiliary in the service of religion. The method of the religious science was to seek proof for an argument first in the Qur'an, then in the traditions of the Prophet, then in recorded precedent, and only as a last resort in personal reasoning."[219]

THE THREE R'S: *READIN', RIGHTIN', AND RADICALISM*

There's a saying: *How do you keep them on the farm after they've seen the big city?*

Well, the same thinking applies here. How do you keep them beholden to sexist, brutal, medieval norms once they get their library cards and their MTV? The fact is that the West's liberal intellectual traditions are a direct threat to the seventh-century values and traditions that define radical Islam. This ties directly to the role of women in radical Islamic societies like Saudi Arabia and Iran. Women don't need to read or write or to know anything about the outside world to fulfill their role in traditional Islamic society—which is to cook, clean, bear children (preferably sons), and take care of the home. In fact, education for women doesn't just threaten long-held beliefs, it threatens the very social fabric of many Islamic societies.

If women learned to read and write, they might start to read dangerous Western literature that would cause them to question their place in the culture. In her book, *Reading Lolita in Tehran*, female author

Azar Nafisi writes movingly about a small, secret reading circle that she belonged to in Iran. Members of the Circle read great works of Western literature including *Lolita*, *Daisy Miller*, and *Pride and Prejudice*. This was and is, of course, a very subversive act in a country where a woman who doesn't wear her headscarf in public takes a great risk. The last thing the clerics running Iran want is for women to see how American and Western women live and think.

Even aside from the issue of women's literacy, how do we explain the poor state of general education in the Arab world despite the fact that they spend more than most developing nations on schooling? The reason is simple: the overwhelming emphasis on Islamic education. Again, from the point of view of the ruling religious elites, this makes perfect sense. If the Qur'an and the Hadith are the word and will of Allah, there is little need to muddle heads with other nonsense, particularly Western thought, which goes against many Qur'anic teachings and is therefore immoral and silly besides.

Yet the paradox for many Muslims is that despite the fact that infidels are clearly inferior, the West has outperformed the Islamic world in virtually all areas, from literacy, to standard of living, and to scientific as well as technological and medical advancements. As a rule, the more Islamic a nation, the worse it fares educationally. It's not an accident that the most secular Muslim country, Turkey, has the best-educated populace and among the highest rate of literacy in the Muslim world.

However, many Muslims, particularly religious leaders, have decided that their problems are not due to Islam (since that is patently impossible) but because the people are *not Islamic enough*. A similar kind of thinking emerged after the tsunami in Indonesia where many Islamic clerics around the world (at least the ones who didn't blame the Jews and the Christians) concluded that the disaster was Allah's punishment because the Muslim people who had suffered were *not pious enough*. According to press reports, Mohammed Faizeen, the manager of the Centre for Islamic Studies in Colombo, Sri Lanka, said, "He sent it as a punishment. This comes from ignoring His laws." And it's not like Allah didn't warn them, because Faizeen added,

"Allah first sends small punishments—like loss of business. If we ignore the warning, He sends bigger ones—loss of life. If we still ignore the warnings, the big punishments, like earthquakes and tsunamis will come."[220] This is a world where every problem can be solved by a greater, purer adherence to Islamic faith—in spite of all evidence that the faith is causing the difficulty, or, at best, has nothing to do with the problem.

Of course, there is still the troubling problem of the success of the West. Thus, much of the educational system is geared toward pointing up the West's moral inferiority. Much of the propaganda coming out of the Islamic world (that isn't directed against the Jews) is about the immorality and decadence of the West. Thus, if radicals can claim no other superiority to America, they can claim moral authority because of their pious devotion to punitive amputations and the stoning of rape victims.

THE BELLY OF THE BEAST:
INSIDE THE RADICAL CLASSROOM

So what exactly do they teach in Muslim classrooms? The answer is both depressing and unsurprising. In his book *The Two Faces of Islam*, Stephen Schwartz quotes a ninth-and-tenth-grade Saudi textbook that reads, "Jews and Christians are the enemies of believers. . . . They will never approve of Muslims, beware of them." Another textbook for the same age group says, "It's allowed to demolish, burn, or destroy the bastions of the *kufar*—and all that constitutes their shield from Muslims—if that was for the sake of victory for the Muslims and the defeat for the *kufar [infidel]*." My radical to English translation: go ahead and destroy everything connected with infidels, it's okay as long as it's in the service of the ultimate victory of Islam over unbelievers. Other schoolbooks in Saudi Arabia repeat the ever-popular refrain that "Allah has turned Jews and Christians into pigs and monkeys,"[221] which has its origin in the Qur'an itself.

The tone of the religious education is often so dark that in conservative Saudi Arabia, according to the Middle East research group at memri.org, the public is starting to complain about the culture of death taught in the schools. One parent complained to a Saudi magazine that his daughter was subjected to an Islamic instructional video in class that showed how a dead body was washed and wrapped in a shroud. As the terrified schoolgirls watched images of these tasks being performed, they were treated to a voice-over of Qur'anic readings and poems.

In 2003, the Saudi daily newspaper *Al-Watan* reported about an educational exhibit that took young students through a tent divided into two parts: one that showed the good path of religious observance and the other the evil path of deviation from Islamic practice, drug use, and the like. In the evil section, students were treated to "a model of a dead man wrapped in a shroud and a pit that looked like a grave. This was accompanied by a film about washing the dead, and a wailing sermon weeping about the [physical] state of the dead person and the horrors of the grave."[222]

Remember, *medieval* is a compliment in Saudi Arabia.

Of course, jihad—either in its concrete form or under the banner of "defense of Islam"—is taught in virtually every Muslim country. This sort of instruction is not limited to religious classes. According to the Saudi English daily *Arab News*, after a terrorist bombing at a housing complex for Westerners in Riyadh in 2004, a home economics teacher told her young teenage charges "that the terrorists responsible for the deaths of dozens of Saudis and non-Saudis in the Kingdom since May, were '*mujahideen*'—fighting a holy war—and not terrorists. . . . The teacher went even further by distributing leaflets and tapes from religious extremists . . . calling people Infidels and saying it is permissible to wage war against them." In the same report, there was an account of classroom discussion of Saudi college students who were asked to name people they would like to be, if they could. One of the students responded that she wanted to be a suicide bomber like the ones who had recently murdered a number of foreigners in the Saudi capital of Riyadh because "they are doing so much for the country."[223]

According to the British press, a recent study performed by the Saudi government showed that "pupils in Saudi Arabia are obliged to spend half of the school timetable studying a rigid interpretation of Islam. A recent review of the curriculum by the Saudi government concluded that almost a fifth of lesson plans contained tracts preaching anti-Western and anti-Semitic views."[224] Much has been made of the Saudi educational system post-9/11 because people have seen a direct tie between its anti-infidel propaganda and an incitement to violence. Remember, Saudi schools produced Osama bin Laden and fifteen of the nineteen 9/11 hijackers. Certainly, there's much to criticize in the Saudi educational system, but jihad ideology is taught in overt and covert forms throughout the Muslim world.

In the Palestinian territories, page 208 of an eleventh-grade textbook called *Islamic Culture* talks openly about jihad: "Islam is Allah's religion for all human beings. It should be proclaimed and invite [people] to join it wisely and through appropriate preaching and friendly discussions. However, such methods may encounter resistance and the preachers may be prevented from accomplishing their duty. . . . Then, *Jihad* and the use of physical force against the enemies becomes inevitable."

This is actually a fairly good explanation of jihad. One of the arguments apologists and jihad-deniers make is that jihad is everything from a spiritual struggle to armed combat. This is true, at least theoretically. However, as this textbook shows, the peaceful spread of Islam supported by radicals is recommended, unless it doesn't work. Then, if against all sense and reason, the infidels resist the clear superiority of Islam, "physical force against the enemies becomes inevitable."

The same textbook makes it clear that though jihad is technically a state of war and thus involves killing and whatnot, that's okay because "*Jihad* has noble goals and lofty aims, and is carried out only for the sake of Allah and for His glory. . . . [By contrast] wars by other nations are mainly waged because of wickedness, aggression, love of domination, expanding influence, looting properties, murder, and the fulfillment of ambitions and desires, such as the war that the Western

countries waged to exploit Islamic countries for imperialistic purposes, to control their Muslim citizens and to rob their resources and
richness."[225] Of course, once again, the irony of the endless accusa-
tions of "imperialism" from the point of view of the religion that was
the most successful *imperial* power in world history is lost on the
authors of the schoolbook.

What follows in this textbook is a complex discussion of the various
types of jihad, a discussion of the responsibilities of Muslims to wage
jihad, its role in propagating Islam, and the risks of ignoring jihad and
the various punishments for abandoning Islam—the final punishment
for those stubborn souls who fail to join the jihad is, of course, death.

It's worth noting that the same Palestinian book carries a detailed
discussion of the dangers and problems associated with *Christian* mis-
sionary activity, revealing once again the desperate need for irony education and awareness in Islamic schools.

MILITANTS IN THE CLASSROOM
ARE CLOSER THAN THEY APPEAR

Much of this anti-Christian and anti-Jewish indoctrination has happened under the radar of Westerners because texts and lessons are in
Arabic and for years were read only in the Middle East. However, after
9/11, there has been increased scrutiny of these materials. With
growing Muslim populations in Europe and America, there has been a
greater awareness of militancy in the classrooms in Islamic religious
schools in Western countries. According to a news report on
Expatica.com, "A Koran school in the German city of Bonn has come
under renewed official pressure with the revelation that a staff
member's son-in-law supported al-Qaeda and was planning to blow
himself up in a terrorist attack in Iraq." Moreover, "The infants-to-
teens King Fahd Academy narrowly escaped closure last year after
education officials discovered teachers were calling for a holy war
against Christendom at school assemblies."[226]

HOLY WAR 101

The need for battle between Muslim and infidel is a common theme in Islamic school curriculum, as is the eventual annihilation of the Christians and Jews by Muslims. One of the best-known Hadith is the "Promise of the Stone and the Tree." The story is recounted in a ninth-grade Saudi schoolbook called *Al-Hadith* and tells the story of how the natural world will help the Muslims in this struggle: "The hour [Judgment Day] will not come until the Muslims fight the Jews and kill them. A Jew will [then] hide behind a rock or a tree, and the rock or tree will call upon the Muslim: 'O Muslim, O slave of Allah! There is a Jew behind me, come and kill him!'"

The Saudi textbook provides the following helpful study points and then questions to test the radicals'—I mean students'—mastery of the material. For the record, I am not making this up. The following comes directly from the schoolbook:

Study Points:

1. *It is Allah's wisdom that the struggle between Muslims and Jews shall continue until the Day of Judgment.*
2. *The Hadith brings forth the glad tidings about the ultimate victory, with Allah's help, of Muslims over Jews.*
3. *The Jews and the Christians are the enemies of the believers. They will not be favorably disposed toward Muslims, and it is necessary to be cautious [in dealing with them].*

Questions:

1. *Who will be victorious on the Day of Judgment?*
2. *With what types of weapons should Muslims arm themselves against the Jews?*
3. *Name four factors leading to the victory of Muslims over their enemies.*[227]

Ladies and gentlemen, I give you the Curriculum of Peace.

Right in the United States there's a Saudi-backed school called the Islamic Saudi Academy in Virginia that teaches first-graders through high-school students. As per a 2004 article in the *Washington Times*, "One page in the manual for the first-grade textbook instructs teachers to tell students that any religion other than Islam is false." School officials referred reporters to the Saudi embassy, which dismissed the criticism by saying, "They are making a big thing out of nothing. If that's the only thing they have to bring up, how pathetic the argument is. Judaism does not recognize Christ as the Messiah. Christians say the only way to salvation is accepting Christ in your heart."[228] However, those comments lost some of their credibility in 2005 when an Islamic Saudi Academy valedictorian from the class of 1999 confessed to his part in an al Qaeda plot to kill President Bush.

In Europe, people are seeing the incompatibility of traditional Islam with quaint Western traditions like equality between the sexes. Very recently, the British have discovered that the Saudi religious schools on their soil have brought some awkward traditions from home. Boys and girls at one London school are strictly segregated. The girls receive little or no physical education while, according to a press report, their classes are geared to "comply with Saudi education policy," which states that a girl's education should "enable her to be a successful housewife, an exemplary wife, and a good mother" or prepare her for work that is "suitable to her disposition as a woman."

Moreover, "the books they taught the girls from kept going on about idolatry and sin and how to avoid it. It was about the fires of hell, torture in the grave, and how to make sure that your ways are not those of the Infidel." These are for children living in England where, presumably, they will have to deal with the infidel every day.

The overall thrust of the school's curriculum is "didactic, with a lot of rote learning and factual stuff. There is not much in the way of understanding and applied learning."[229] This is very telling because the Qur'an is often called the most memorized book on Earth. This is not an accident. Remember, Islam is not designed to be a philosophical religion. Muslims are encouraged to memorize the Qur'an, the rules, and follow them without question. After all, the word "Islam" means "submission."

This kind of rigid thinking explains why so few discoveries of any kind come out of the Islamic world. The powerful taboos against innovation and creativity take a toll.

ADVANCED RADICAL STUDIES

In higher education, Islamic studies is by far the most popular major—especially in Saudi Arabia where it attracts more students than any other three university majors combined. Given the focus on Islam in higher education, you might think that all this study and thought would drive some amazing scholarship on the subject.

Guess again.

The fact is that almost all genuine study and real scholarship on the Qur'an and Islamic tradition happens outside the mainstream of Islamic higher education. Why? Partly because of the taboos against innovation and because the death penalty is meted out for apostasy, which creates strong disincentives to learn new things about core Muslim beliefs. Given that the Qur'an is the eternal and uncreated word of Allah, no one is going to become an academic star by uncovering a new verse of the Qur'an or challenging traditional interpretations of existing ones.

Case in point: in Egypt, a scholar named Abu Zaid said, "The Koran is a text, a literary text, and the only way to understand, explain, and analyze it is through a literary approach." For challenging the notion that the Qur'an is the unchanging word of Allah, Zaid was branded an apostate by the Egyptian courts in 1995, a ruling that was upheld by the country's highest court in 1996. Then, because Islamic holy law forbids a Muslim woman from marrying an unbeliever, the court ordered Zaid to divorce his wife. After numerous credible threats, Zaid fled to Holland with his wife.

According to the book, *What the Koran Really Says*, "Abu Zaid seems to have been justified in fearing for his life: in 1992 the Egyptian journalist Farag Foda was assassinated by Islamists for his critical writings about Egypt's Muslim Brotherhood, and in 1994 the Nobel Prize–winning novelist Naguib Mahfouz was stabbed for writing, among other works, the allegorical *Children of Gabalawi* (1959)—a novel, structured like the Koran, that presents 'heretical' conceptions of God and the Prophet Muhammad."[230]

Qur'anic scholar Toby Lester relays a telling event that happened in 1972 when the renovation of a very old mosque in Yemen turned up twenty potato sacks full of ancient documents that dated back to the first two centuries of Islam. The parchment sat for years until someone from the Yemeni Antiquities Authority sought out the help of a German scholar who organized a German restoration project.

What they found was remarkable: The documents were likely the oldest Qur'ans in existence. The scholars found "small but intriguing aberrations from the standard Qur'anic text" as well as variations in the ordering of some of the verses. Now, you might think that Islamic scholars would be thrilled to find, perhaps, a more authentic version of the Qur'an. After all, this was a potential opportunity to know the word and will of Allah even better. Not so much, as it turned out. Apparently, the slight differences were troubling and "at odds with the orthodox Muslim belief that the Koran as it has reached us today is quite simply the perfect, timeless, and unchanging word of God."

More than fifteen thousand sheets of the Yemeni Qur'ans were preserved, yet they waited for years for detailed examination, which the Yemeni government was reluctant to permit. As one of the two German scholars from Germany's Saarland University who had extensive access to the documents observed, "They want to keep this thing low-profile. . . . They don't want it made public that the work is being done at all, since the Muslim position is that everything that needs to be said about the Koran's history was said a thousand years ago."[231]

It is worth pointing out that radical Islamic indoctrination, I mean education, does not stop when a Muslim leaves school. Anti-Western and anti-Semitic propaganda represents an adult outreach program that can be found everywhere in Muslim societies, particularly in mosques. Much of the propaganda is a simple defense mechanism. Demonizing the West minimizes its appeal to Muslims and helps maintain Islamic social order. Thus, it has the same function as anti-Western propaganda did in the communist era. (My wife is from the Soviet Union, and she recounts that in addition to the typical "Western decadence" propaganda, she was taught in her school that Americans often faced shark attacks. I guess even long lines, frequent shortages, and a low standard of living looked good compared to being eaten by a shark.)

The Saudis are particularly vicious in their efforts to teach hatred at all levels of their society. For years, this was a useful tool. They built one of the most repressive regimes on Earth and then directed their people's inevitable discontent by teaching them that all of their problems were caused by the West—mostly the Jews and Americans, of course.

In a journal for Saudi soldiers called *Al-Jundi Al-Muslim* (*The Muslim Soldier*), the Religious Affairs Department of the Saudi armed forces published an article in 2004 in the *Know Your Enemy* section titled "The Jews in the Modern Era." Some highlights include:

- The majority of revolutions, coups d'état, and wars that have occurred in the world, those that are occurring, and those that will occur are almost entirely the handiwork of the Jews.
- World Jewry has established a shadow government run by three hundred satans who call themselves "Elders."
- The Jews caused the outbreak of both World War I and World War II.
- The Jew [Rene] Cassin drew up the program for human rights.[232] (To radicals, this is one of the greatest crimes in history since it is one of the greatest threats to seventh-century radical values.)

GETTING A SOLID RADICAL EDUCATION
RIGHT HERE IN THE UNITED STATES

Despite the fact that Wahhabism is Osama bin Laden's brand of Islam and was the ideology behind the 9/11 attacks, people tend to disregard it as a relatively small part of the Islamic world. After all, the overwhelming majority of Wahhabists live in Saudi Arabia itself, which has a population of only about twenty-four million people.

However, Saudi oil wealth has allowed Saudis to become the leading builders of mosques around the world. In fact, the Indian public affairs magazine *NewsInsight* revealed in 2005 that the Saudi royal family planned to build 4,500 mosques in countries like India, Bangladesh, Nepal, and Sri Lanka. These mosques will be run by Wahhabists in order to promote "modern and liberal education with Islamic values." The program, according to the Saudis, is to correct the *distorted* worldwide image of Islam in these post-9/11 times.[233]

Coincidentally, a few months after this announcement, the human rights group Freedom House released a report based on an extensive yearlong study of publications created by the Saudi government and distributed throughout the United States. The report, titled "Saudi Publications on Hate Ideology Fill American Mosques,"[234] shows pretty conclusively what the Saudis mean when they talk about "modern and liberal education with Islamic values." The research determined that "Saudi-connected resources and publications on extremist ideology remain common reading and educational material in some of America's main mosques."

How extreme is the material? One of the publications studied told American Muslims to be "dissociated from the Infidels, hate them for their religions, leave them, never rely on them for support, do not admire them, and always oppose them in every way according to Islamic law."

Not surprisingly, there is the boilerplate anti-Semitism and support for the underpinnings of a jihad ideology that includes the notion that the House of Islam and the House of War are two "antagonistic realms that can never be reconciled." There were numerous publications that taught jihad outright, including a book for high-school students that was created by the Saudi Ministry of Education that said, "To be true Muslims, we must prepare and be ready for Jihad in Allah's way. It is the duty of the citizen and the government. The military education is glued to faith and its meaning, and the duty to follow it." Astute readers will note that there is a possibility that this doesn't refer to the inner, spiritual sort of jihad.

The study also found publications on Muslim tolerance that say those who convert from Islam to any other religion "should be killed." With regard to homosexuals, one publication said that for a Muslim who engages in homosexual activity, "it would be lawful for Muslims to spill his blood and take his money."[235]

It doesn't take a highly developed Radical Eye to see that these materials represent radical Islamic thought. Remember, these publications aren't being shared among a tiny minority of wild-eyed militants or radicals in a cave somewhere in the tribal badlands of Pakistan. These are "educational" materials available in the United States and are created, funded, and distributed by the Saudi government.

The question I have is that if we believe the experts from organizations like CAIR who tell us that most Muslims are peaceful and tolerant, then how is it possible that these kinds of materials can be found in any mosque anywhere, let alone in Brooklyn or Los Angeles?

Why wasn't this kind of thinking forced out of American mosques long ago? Why hasn't the "tolerant majority" cried bloody murder that these kinds of un-Islamic rantings are found in its houses of worship? How long would this have had to continue before the Muslims themselves mentioned the problem to anyone?

Either Muslims living in the United States are less tolerant than we have been led to believe, or they are a *silent* majority, sitting on the sidelines while rabid radicals set the tone in Islamic houses of worship. Either way, there is a serious problem here. Most people accept that the majority of all races and religions are decent, hardworking folks who are happy to leave others alone. You could make the case that this was true even for Germans in the 1930s. Yet, World War II and the Holocaust still happened. Both of those events were possible because a group of monsters rose to power, with either the support or the silence of the German people.

It's hard to argue that the aggressive, intolerant ideology of radical Islam is any better than fascism. The only question is how much support do radicals have among everyday Muslims? And even if they don't have broad support, what hope is there when radicals set the religious agenda even within the borders of the United States?

THE FINAL EXAM

In the spirit of our education theme, we will close this chapter with a quiz:

NAME THE CONSPIRATOR QUIZ

According to many top Islamic scholars, clerics, political leaders, journalists, and scientists, the Muslim people have been the target of a number of conspiracies over the years. Below are ten such recent plots identified by these Islamic thinkers. Now is your chance to match wits with the greatest minds in the Islamic world to *Name the Conspirator*.

Read the description of each conspiracy. Then, using your understanding of Islamic history, culture, and religious thinking, try to identify the party determined to be behind each plot. Finally, make a selection from the provided list.

Bear in mind that not all of the answers will be obvious. Arab and Muslim intellectuals use complex mental and investigative tools to discern the conspirators' often shadowy methods and work. Be sure to use similarly subtle gradations in modalities of thought, and don't be afraid to apply counterintuitive thinking when cross-inferring with various sociocultural imperatives.

Good luck!

1. According to Muslim clerics from Saudi Arabia to the Palestinian territories, the tsunami that killed hundreds of thousands of people (the vast majority of whom were *Muslims*) was really sent by Allah to punish *This Group*. According to Saudi cleric Muhammad Al-Munajiid, *This Group*'s holidays "are accompanied by forbidden things, by immorality, abomination, adultery, alcohol, drunken dancing, and revelry. . . . Allah struck them with an earthquake."[236] The guilty party is:
    a. The Solid Gold Dancers
    b. The Nazgul
    c. The Thundercats
    d. The Christians

2. Quite a few learned Islamic clerics have identified *This Group* as secretly being behind the Beslan school massacre where Muslim terrorists killed hundreds of children, shooting some of them in the back as they ran for their lives. Bahraini religious *scholar* Ali Abdullah discerned the work of *This Group* in the attack to "tarnish the image of Muslims."[237] Name the conspirators:
    a. The Cylons
    b. The Starland Vocal Band
    c. The Mutant Brotherhood
    d. The Jews

3. Ayatollah Ali Khamenei is the supreme religious and political leader of Iran and is considered by millions of Shiites to be the greatest Islamic mind in the world. The ayatollah himself determined that *This Group* was really responsible for a series of car bombs in Iraq in December of 2004—including one that killed fifty-two people during a funeral procession. This was done to keep "the Iraqi people busy so that they miss the chance [to participate in] elections."[238] Name the conspirators:

a. The original cast of *Cats*
b. The Movementitarians
c. The Decepticons
d. The Americans

4. According to Abd Al-Wahhab 'Adas, the deputy editor of the Egyptian government daily newspaper *Al-Gumhouriyya*, *This Group* is behind "all the violent and terror operations that have occurred everywhere in the world."[239] Among this group's crimes were the Madrid train bombings. Name the conspirators:
   a. The Children of the Corn
   b. SkyNet
   c. The World Crime League
   d. The Jews

5. After the terrorist attacks in Sinai, Egypt, which killed dozens of vacationing Jews, Palestinian Security Chief Jibril Rajoub concluded that *This Group* was really behind the attacks.[240] Name the conspirators:
   a. The Not Ready for Prime-Time Players
   b. The Man
   c. The Fresno Elks Club
   d. The Jews

6. The major government-controlled newspaper in Saudi Arabia, *Al-Watan*, broke the story that soldiers working for *This Group* were killing Iraqis for their organs, which were then sold to hospitals. According to the report, the value of a kidney was forty dollars and the value of an eye was twenty-five dollars.[241] Name the conspirators/organ salesmen:
   a. The cast of *Friends*
   b. Vandelay Enterprises
   c. Famous Ray's Pizza, weekend crew
   d. The Americans

7. Hisham Sharabi, a *professor* of Arab Culture at Georgetown University in Washington, DC, said that these *Two Groups* are waging war against the Arab world and intend to colonize the region.[242] Name the conspirators:
   a. The Professor and Maryann
   b. Spinal Tap and the Silver Platters
   c. The Blue Meanies and the Camp Fire Girls
   d. The Americans and the Jews

8. According to Ibrahim Al-Fayoumi—identified as a member of Egypt's Al-Azhar Islamic University—American contractor Nicholas Berg was not in fact beheaded as shown in the widely seen Internet video. Rather, representatives from *This Group* staged the murder to divert attention from the Abu Ghraib prison scandal. Al-Fayoumi came to this conclusion after collaboration with a "forensic expert." Moreover, the murder could not have been committed by Muslims because, as he said with a completely straight face, "the beheading of any person, dead or alive, is forbidden by Islamic law." His conclusions were confirmed by Iranian newspaper and television reports.[243] Name the conspirators and true beheaders:
   a. The Olsen Twins
   b. Various Moles within C.T.U.
   c. The 1919 Chicago White Sox
   d. The Americans

9. According to journalist Hassan Hanizadeh of Iran's *Teheran Times*, the Arabic television network Al-Jazeera was created by agents of these *Two Groups* to "divide Islamic countries and tarnish the image of Islam."[244] Name the conspirators:
   a. Joanie and Chachi
   b. The Sith and the Cardassians
   c. The Bradys and the Partridges
   d. The Americans and the Jews

10. According to Palestinian Supply Minister Abdel Aziz Sha-
heen, *This Group* shipped low-cost strawberry-flavored
chewing gum laden with female sex hormones to the Palestinian Territories. The point of this conspiracy was threefold.
First, to arouse irresistible sexual urges in women. Second, to
sterilize those women. And third, to completely destroy "the
genetic system of young boys." The director of the Palestinian
Health Ministry saw the wrappers of the gum and immediately "suspected there would be something related to hormones or sex" because "we expect many things." His suspi-
cions were confirmed by Egypt's Cairo Food and Technology
Research Institute, whose examination was so rigorous and
thorough that it found evidence of the hormones despite the
fact that a scientific test commissioned by the *Washington
Post* could not.[245] Name the conspirators:
   a. Desperate Housewives
   b. S.P.E.C.T.R.E.
   c. Delta House
   d. The Jews

EXTRA CREDIT:

According to a 2002 article in the government-run Saudi Arabian
newspaper *Al-Riyadh*, as well as a 2004 article in the Egyptian
religious weekly magazine '*Aqidati*, *This Group* uses the blood of
Muslim youth to make their holiday bread:[246]
   a. Cute Fuzzy Bunnies
   b. Men in Black
   c. MENSA.
   d. The Jews

If you answered "d" to all of the above questions, you are a true
radical Islamic scholar.

BACK TO THE FUTURE

Or, Forward to the Seventh Century

The propagation of crazy ideas such as secularism,
liberalism, and humanism are part of our enemies'
plans to sow disunity in [our] society.[247]
—Iranian cleric Ayatollah Nouri-Hamedani

LOOKING AHEAD WITH A RADICAL EYE

In our journey through Islamic society, culture, and history, we have developed and honed our Radical Eye. We've seen militant Islam at work in fourteen hundred years of jihad across the globe, from the Middle East to Africa to Europe. We've seen radicalism in the deep recesses of Middle East theocracies like Saudi Arabia and Iran, as well as on the streets of Amsterdam. Two of the most worrisome examples of radical trends were in the Americas: Shariah in Canada and Ayatollah-Palooza in Texas.

Nevertheless, the notion that Islam is a religion of peace and tolerance persists, and recently, according to Pakistan's leading English newspaper, US diplomat Michael A. Spangler said, "The message of the Holy Prophet has strengthened the ideas of democracy, tolerance, and moderation in my own thinking and action. I beg all of you Muslims to help me understand the message of Islam more clearly. Please condemn acts of terrorism and stand up for the message of peace and justice that the Holy Prophet has taught."[248] With all due respect to Mr. Spangler and what I'm sure is a distinguished record of public service, he's completely full of crap. In this day and age, this kind of politically correct reality-warping talk is not just silly but dangerous, since it empowers our enemies as it undermines our own resolve by denying clear truths.

Certainly, there are worthy passages in the Qur'an and there is much in Islamic tradition that deserves respect, but there is no ignoring the fact that many of the problems we've seen in the Muslim world—from the jihad to Islamic slavery, intolerance, and religious persecution—are firmly rooted in the Qur'an, the Hadith, the example of Muhammad himself, and Islamic tradition. Because of the widely held belief that the Qur'an is the exact word of Allah and the Hadith are given almost as much credence, it's hard to separate the grain from the chaff. Thus, radicals can legitimately argue that they have Islam's holy texts on their side.

There has been much discussion on reforming Islam to make it more compatible with modernity, human rights, and peaceful coexistence with other peoples. Stephen Schwartz, author of *The Two Faces of Islam*, maintains that the Sufist strain of Islam provides hope for a tolerant, liberal future for the religion. I hope he's right. However, there are clear challenges here. For one, there is no central authority in Islam like the Vatican in the Catholic Church that can make changes like the Council of Trent and Vatican II that will affect the lives and beliefs of a large number of the faithful. How can changes be made that contravene the clear teachings of the Qur'an when apostasy leads to the death penalty? Or when even Muslims in Europe are not safe to speak their minds about their own religion? How can a problem be fixed when simply discussing it can be fatal?

If Islam is a religion of peace and tolerance, an increase in Muslim religious feeling would lead to an even more peaceful and more tolerant society. Yet the opposite is true. Both historically and at the present time, there is overwhelming evidence that the more "Islamic" a country is, the worse its record on human rights, the more brutal its criminal justice system, the harder it is on women, the more intolerant it is of other religions, the greater its support of terrorism, the more toxic its educational system, and, if that were not all bad enough, the worse it performs economically.

Again, inconvenient facts.

And even if we were able to get the majority of the world's Muslims to agree that the Qur'an was perhaps not the *exact* word of Allah, there remains the problem of the example of the Prophet. He owned slaves, gave and received women as "gifts," made war against his neighbors, advocated amputation as a punishment for theft, and on and on . . .

Under those circumstances, how does anyone reform Islam?

Good question.

MILITANT ISLAM AND DEMOCRACY: CATS AND DOGS LIVING TOGETHER

As more and more Muslims emigrate to the West, the issue of whether or not Islam is compatible with Western-style democracy becomes more important. Again, there are a few serious obstacles here, including the verse in the Qur'an that says, "He [Allah] maketh none to share in His government (18:26)," which makes it clear that religious rule is the only way to go.

The real question is not whether Western analysts think democracy can work for observant Muslims based on *our* interpretation of the Qur'an, but whether Muslims think it can. I've shown a number of instances in which Muslim culture bucks up against Western norms, and I'll offer two more examples.

First, in the spring of 2005, there was a lecture by Muslim cleric Sheik Faiz Mohamad, who was born in Sydney and teaches at the Global Islamic Youth Centre in Liverpool, England. More than a thousand Muslim faithful in Australia paid fifteen dollars a head to hear Mohamad say, "A victim of rape every minute somewhere in the world. Why? No one to blame but herself. She displayed her beauty to the entire world. . . . Strapless, backless, sleeveless, nothing but satanic skirts, slit skirts, translucent blouses, miniskirts, tight jeans: all this to tease man and appeal to his carnal nature."[249] This was from a man who was born and grew up in a liberal Western culture.

Second, Agence France Presse (AFP) reported that in April of 2005, fifteen Muslim protestors invaded a press conference held by the Muslim Council of Britain, England's largest Muslim group, where an upcoming general election was being discussed. The radicals brought the press conference to a halt shouting, "Voting is an act of apostasy!" and "Allah is the only legislator; there is no law but His!"[250]

Clearly, these radicals don't believe that democracy and Islam are compatible, though, interestingly, they are living in a democratic nation by choice. How big a percentage of England's Muslims do they represent? Who knows? But they are a loud voice and are happy to proclaim their views publicly. They present a definite problem for both their adopted countries and for moderate Muslims who want to live peacefully in the West.

Certainly, we should do everything we can to assist the tolerant Muslim majority. For now, the best way to do that is to completely defeat and discredit the radical minority—militarily, culturally, and in any other way we can think of. The benefits to us in terms of security are clear, and the benefits to the Islamic moderates are equally clear. Remember, the moderate Germans who didn't believe in Nazi ideology were not free to act or even speak out until the Nazis were crushed in battle and discredited in public life.

Thus, the first order of business is to decisively win the War on Terror/radicalism by smashing jihadist movements wherever they operate while we reveal and completely discredit the radical ideology behind jihad. This, we do know how to do. Defeating the Taliban and Saddam Hussein were important first steps. The Taliban were vanguards of extremist ideology and bore direct responsibility for the 9/11 attacks. Whatever your position on the wars in Afghanistan and Iraq, four things are undeniably true:

a. Saddam Hussein's regime was a human rights catastrophe.
b. Saddam controlled the greatest military power in the Muslim world and was considered to be a modern-day "Saladin" for standing up to the United States and the West. The story of this modern-day Saladin being found hiding in a hole in the ground, footage of his humiliating dental exam, pictures of him in his undershorts, and videos of his execution were great blows to militant Islamic pride.
c. Worldwide terrorism lost two important state sponsors.
d. There have been important side benefits to the toppling of those two regimes, namely Libya's voluntary disarmament and Syria's pullout from Lebanon, with probably more to come.

So simply continuing to fight the War on Terror is very important. There are some doubters, of course, and in 2005 there was the news that global terror attacks had tripled in 2004. Today, Iraq is still a danger zone and 2006 saw a new, major terror attack in India, while Hezbollah—with support from Syria and Iran—became even more aggressive in its terror campaign against Israel. From all of that you might conclude that fighting radicals just makes them madder and more dangerous. However, we know that it was the US pullout in Somalia and relative inaction after the bombings of the US embassy in Nairobi and the USS *Cole* that emboldened Osama bin Laden and al Qaeda to plan and execute the 9/11 attacks. The terrorists also believed that, if it was successful, 9/11 would bring down the pillars of American civilization and convince the United States to retreat from the world. Clearly, they were wrong, and they have paid a heavy price for their lack of vision.

The reason terrorist attacks are on the rise is because the West is winning its war, in the same way that much of the bloodiest fighting of World War II happened near the end, when the fascists in Japan and Germany were fighting for their lives and beliefs. The analogy to World War II is a good one. Military historian Victor Davis Hanson has made convincing comparisons between the War on Terror—or as he calls it the War on Islamo-Fascism—and the Second World War, which was "a single conflict that combines the Pacific and European theaters, unified by a common struggle against fascism (an ideology) in its various manifestations in Germany, Italy, and Japan."[251]

In the case of the War on Terror, the enemies are not always as clear as the Axis powers in World War II, but the ideology is just as easy to identify. In many ways, terrorism was invented to give jihadists cover. If they could not be connected to a state, retribution for their acts of terror was less likely or at least much more difficult. The key is to go after state sponsors of terrorism (like Afghanistan and Iraq) and get terrorists where they are hiding (see the Israeli response to Hezbollah in the summer of 2006).

For both fascists and radical Islamists, according to Hanson, "their common ideological enemy is liberal democracy—specifically its global promotion of freedom, individualism, capitalism, gender equity, religious diversity, and secularism that undermines both Islamic fundamentalism in the cultural sense, and politically makes it more difficult for tyrants to rule over complacent and ignorant populations."[252]

The War on Terror has been called World War III or IV (depending on whether or not you count the Cold War). Again, the comparison is a good one, though you could argue that since Muhammad himself declared the jihad against the non-Muslim world, the jihad could be called World War I. Personally, I think the analogy to World War II is most fitting. If we accept the comparison between radicals and Nazis, it suggests a number of other courses of action and fronts for the War on Terror.

THE ANTI-JIHAD'S ULTIMATE WEAPON

First, we need to recognize the nature of the enemy and talk honestly about the roots of his ideology. Thus, truth becomes an important weapon. Telling the truth isn't always popular, however. In the 1930s, at a time when prominent Americans like Joseph Kennedy and Charles Lindbergh expressed their admiration for Hitler's Germany, Winston Churchill never wavered in his criticism of the Nazis. In the beginning of the war—until Germany attacked communist Russia—many antiwar groups called it "England's Imperial War."

It's time to stop calling Islam a religion of peace and tolerance and deal honestly with its history and current state. Then, perhaps, if Muslims are willing, they will be able to enact reforms. Ultimately, however, the primary concern of the United States and the West is not the "reform" of Islam, if that's even possible or necessary. The primary job is to defeat radicalism soundly and completely, just as the first and most important task in the European theater of World War II was the defeat of the Nazis, not the "reform" of German society.

Once we've identified the enemy and his beliefs, the next step is to deny him access to the nations he wishes to destroy. That means closing the borders to illegal immigration and severely limiting immigration and even travel from Middle Eastern countries with a proven history of creating terrorists—at least for the duration of the War on Terror. We have to remember that Muhammad Atta and his fellow 9/11 hijackers entered the United States *legally* and stayed for years planning, training, and going to strip clubs. It's time to close the door.

But that's not fair. Most Muslims and people from those countries are decent, law-abiding citizens.

True, but so were most Germans during World War II. You could argue that the Nazis were also a tiny minority of extremists, but how many German immigrant and travelers do you think were allowed into the United States and Allied nations during World War II? The answer is—not surprisingly—very few. The reason is that the Allied governments thought that there was no "acceptable" number of Nazis bent on their destruction that could be allowed to enter their countries. The same thinking should apply to the War on Terror. Counterterrorism analyst and scholar of Middle Eastern history Daniel Pipes estimates that 10 percent of the world's Muslims are "militants." I'll accept that number, though I recognize that there probably is an even greater number of radical sympathizers in the larger population—just as many Germans supported the Nazis, even if they didn't belong to the party.

Even if we go with the 10 percent figure, it means one in ten Middle Eastern visitors to Western countries is a serious potential threat. Remember, the nineteen 9/11 hijackers exploited the US immigration system to enter the country. While it may annoy countries like Pakistan or other nations known to produce terrorists to have their citizens' student and travel visas denied, the primary responsibility of the US government is to safeguard its citizens. While this sort of action seems extreme, it is standard operating procedure during a real war. The problem is that, as a culture, the West is still wrapping its brain around the notion that the War on Terror is in fact a real war with soldiers on the other side who have made an art of hiding in civilian populations. This denial persists despite the fact that the United States has been fighting the War on Terror for longer than it fought World War II.

We can already see the effect of unrestricted immigration on Europe. The Netherlands has a population that is 10 percent Muslim, and they have paid a heavy price for their open policies. Half of the prison population is foreign-born, and whatever their constitution and laws say, the fact is that the Dutch no longer have free speech as Westerners understand the term. When filmmakers are murdered for speaking their minds, artists have their work suppressed, and politicians who stand up to extremists must live in prisons and military bases for protection, there's no kidding ourselves that it's pluralist business as usual.

Dutch MP Geert Wilders (the one who has to live in a prison) has made a controversial proposal to put an immediate halt on all non-European immigration until the Dutch can figure out how to assimilate the immigrants they have. This is a reasonable course, given that the

Netherlands is the most crowded nation in Europe, and they are seeing a rising and dangerous tide of Islamic extremism.

But the fact is that even if Dutch immigration is halted sometime in the next few years, because of their relative high birth rates, Muslims will make up a majority of the population in a few decades. In fact, if you're under thirty now, it's not only possible but also likely that in your lifetime you will see the Netherlands cease to exist as a distinct ethnic and political entity. We're not just talking about swapping one genetic stock for another while the society lives on; we're talking about the loss of Dutch culture and its centuries-long tradition of liberalism and tolerance.

If you will recall from our chapter on women's rights, in much of the Muslim world women meet the criteria for receiving asylum in the United States. Since the overwhelming majority of Islamic terrorist attacks (and all attacks perpetrated on the United States) have been perpetrated by men, we might consider allowing only women from countries with radical movements to enter. Ultimately, treating the War on Terror like a real war is key, and all reasonable proposals should be considered.

Until Hitler's June 1941 attack on Russia, there was a real and robust antiwar movement in the United States. Charles Lindbergh's America First group was the best known of many such groups. After Pearl Harbor, the country banded together and supported the war effort. Actors, comedians, and musicians all joined the fight, either literally, by joining the service like Jimmy Stewart, or by making a cultural contribution like Dr. Seuss, who wrote antifascist allegories for children during the war.

Now, however, comedians and TV comedy shows tend to ignore radicals despite the fact that wild-eyed extremism, nutty conspiracy theories, and polygamy are pretty funny. Why? Part of it is political correctness. No one wants to disparage all Muslims.

But we have to be able to draw the line between making fun of radicals and slamming all Muslims, just as we differentiate between the Nazis and the German people. Satire has long been a tool of fighting extremism. In the West, we use it to marginalize extremists, and certainly Christians have taken more than their fair share of abuse from stand-up comedians and late-night comedy shows. The value of applying the same scrutiny to radical Muslims would be great. First, it would help mobilize the whole culture against the very real threat of Islamic radicalism. And firmly discrediting radical ideology would make it harder for radicals to recruit in the West. We've done this with the Nazis. Certainly, neo-Nazi groups exist in the West, but they are tiny minorities with zero credibility.

AWARDS AND HONORS

THE NATURAL SELECTION AWARD FOR TERRORISTS WHO CONSPICUOUSLY IMPROVE THE GENE POOL BY ELIMINATING THEMSELVES FROM IT

Most everyone has heard of the Darwin Awards, given to people who through an "astounding misapplication of common sense" remove themselves from the gene pool, usually through some spectacular and astonishingly dim-witted stunt. I offer this new award, completely unaffiliated with the Darwin Awards, to the terrorist who improves the gene pool most by removing him or herself from it in a particularly stupid fashion. Honorable mention for this award goes to all suicide bombers who insure that their own particular brand of wild-eyed lunatic genes make no further inroads into the larger body of humanity.

Suicide bombers form the largest single category of nominees for this award because they reasonably often fail in their original objective (the murder of innocents) yet succeed in committing suicide. Most of these "operational failures" occur because the bomber's explosives go off prematurely, or he or she is identified and shot by an alert Israeli soldier or civilian.

The first award goes to British citizen Omar Sharif, no relation to the actor. According to numerous British press reports, he was a well-liked British man from a wealthy family who was described as "a nice young man" and a "teddy bear of a person" who "loved cricket" and was "very educated." The married twenty-seven-year-old father of two made his way to Tel Aviv with a partner and targeted a seafront bar called Mike's Place.

When Sharif's partner was stopped at the door of the bar, Sharif tried and failed to detonate his own device. After struggling with pedestrians, Sharif dove into the Mediterranean and became the first failed suicide bomber to die of—drowning.

Though Sharif lost points for already fathering two children, he scored well because he was a young married man who presented a clear and present danger of procreating again. Though his partner killed three people and injured fifty, Sharif hurt no one but himself. Finally, he gained irony points for managing to remove himself from the gene pool in a way that was completely nonviolent.[253]

Failure to speak out against extremists gives them a veneer of respectability that we cannot afford—not when the ayatollah is celebrated in Texas. The danger is that if they are unopposed culturally, we could end up in a situation where radicals get a greater and greater voice in public life—as they do in England where advertisers now have to take into account fundamentalist Muslim sensibilities when hanging posters for *Sex and the City*. There's the looming danger that we'll eventually have artists and/or writers killed on the street for speaking out against radical intolerance, as happened to Theodore van Gogh in the Netherlands.

We simply have to get over the political correctness that prevents us from engaging Islamic radicalism in a real culture war simply because we fear offending Muslims. Take for example the 2004 Academy Awards, which included in its tribute to filmmakers and performers who died during the previous year the famous Nazi propagan-

THE RAVENOUS BUGBLATTER BEAST OF TRAAL AWARD FOR SPECTACULAR DENIAL

The Ravenous Bugblatter Beast is an invention of Douglas Adams, author of *The Hitchhiker's Guide to the Galaxy*. When confronting this "mind bogglingly stupid animal," galactic travelers are told to put a towel over their own heads because the creature is a beast so dim-witted it believes, "If you can't see it, it can't see you."[254] In the same spirit, we present this award to people who think if they pretend they don't see terrorists, the terrorists won't be able to see them.

THE 2005 RAVENOUS BUGBLATTER BEAST OF TRAAL AWARD GOES TO:

Charles Rangel, a top Democrat in the United States House of Representatives

We honor Representative Rangel for his comments on the subject of *Islamic terrorists*, a term whose very use, he thinks, is an act of prejudice. When asked for his thoughts on the 2005 refusal of some European powers (okay, the French) to list Hezbollah as a terrorist organization, Rangel said, "To call it Islamic terror is discriminating, it's bigoted, it is not the right thing to say." (Astute

dist Leni Riefenstahl, who made the film *Triumph of the Will*, a celebration of Nazism. The following year, in 2005, the Academy neglected to mention Theodore van Gogh, who literally died for a film he made to defend women's rights. I'm not saying we should never honor the contribution to the arts of the Nazis; I'm just saying that perhaps we could *also* honor the contribution of men and women who fight for liberal values and speak out against, say, the abuse of women—even if it might offend some religious zealots in the audience.

readers will note that Rangel's comments in no way addressed the issue of Hezbollah's status.)

It's worth pointing out that Hezbollah has countless acts of terrorism on its résumé, including the 1983 homicide-bombing attack on the US Marine barracks in Lebanon that killed 241 Americans. Oh yeah, and the offshoot that Hezbollah used to carry out the operation was called the *Islamic* Jihad.

Representative Rangel elaborated on his comments, saying, "When we had the Ku Klux Klan, we didn't call them Baptist terrorists. When Hitler was killing Jews, we didn't call it [*sic*] Christian terrorists."[255] Though this is true, it is also irrelevant because neither group primarily identified itself by its Christian ideology, and the Nazi Party was, of course, famously antireligious. We quite accurately call the Nazis *fascists* because we often identify political groups by their ideology. The fact is that Hezbollah and many other Islamic terrorist groups like the *Islamic* Jihad, the Egyptian *Islamic* Jihad, Armed *Islamic* Jihad, Ansar al *Islam*, and the *Muslim* Brotherhood all identify themselves as primarily Islamic groups that proudly claim their religion as their primary motivation for their acts of murder.

But Congressman Rangel thinks it is discriminating and bigoted to call terrorists by the same name they call themselves. Thus, he is the recipient of the first Ravenous Bugblatter Beast of Traal Award.

Speaking out against radicalism will make it easier for moderate and/or reform-minded Muslims to fight for their beliefs. A real tyranny exists in the mosques, even in Western countries, where extremist propaganda is freely distributed, but Muslims who speak out against it or wish to change their religion face intimidation, threats, and even death. The truth is a potent weapon, and people in public life who actively lie or deny the obvious should be called to account and/or made fun of mercilessly as the situation warrants.

JUST SAYING NO TO EXTREMISM

On the international level, the United States and other liberal democracies should do more to not only oppose dangerous regimes like Saddam Hussein's but also to actively oppose governments that institute Shariah. Trade with the West gives theocracies like Saudi Arabia and Iran much-needed capital. These countries don't need to develop tolerant, pluralist societies with real economies that empower all of their people because oil wealth props up the mullahs in charge.

Remember, there were two major economic factors in the fall of the Ottoman Empire. First, Western military might stopped their expansion and denied them the plunder that was so important to their economy. Second, Western shipbuilding technology broke the empire's financial stranglehold on trade between the West and the Orient. It's time to get serious about bankrupting regimes that support radicals.

The fact is that both the United States and the European Union trade with the Saudis, and though the United States does not trade with Iran, the European Union still does. It's time for the free world to stop supporting oppressive regimes, period. That means we should apply strong economic pressure to nations that don't offer freedom of religion and equality between the sexes, or countries that do not support the other basic tenets of human rights. Most important, we should stop importing oil from theocracies.

This may sound unrealistic and, certainly, instituting this policy would pose a challenge. Western economies depend on oil, and the Saudis and the Iranians do have a big chunk of the world's supply. Even if we cut back or eliminated imports from these nations, rising demand in China and India would offset the loss over time.

The key is to develop a plan for energy that completely eliminates the global need for fossil fuels. This is a huge undertaking that would require a massive sustained effort across diverse groups of people who don't always play well with one another. However, the benefits would cut across ideological lines.

The elimination of the threat from radical theocracies would please both hard-line national security conservatives and traditionally liberal human rights activists. In the same way, staunch conservatives who support energy independence for the West could find common ground with environmentalists who want to promote alternative and eco-friendly forms of energy.

On Long Island, the local utility, the Long Island Power Authority, has a "Green Choice" program that allows consumers, businesses, and municipalities to pay a little extra to buy power created from nonpolluting sources like wind farms in Pennsylvania. It's a great idea, but it has only been marketed for its environmental benefits. Why not sell it as a way to help fight the War on Terror as well?

And of course there is nuclear energy. Though this is a mature technology with the capability of generating enormous amounts of power at prices comparable to fossil fuel-based systems, it has been a political hot potato for many years. As a result, no new nuclear power plants have been built in decades, but consider this:

- The burning of fossil fuels kills over two hundred thousand people a year in the United States and Europe, and four hundred thousand more in China.[256]
- More people were killed in the 2006 coal-mining accidents in the United States than were killed due to nuclear power in the entire history of the American civilian nuclear power industry.

Most alternative energy solutions center around the development of new technology (an expensive and time-consuming process) or large subsidies, as in the case of the solar power and ethanol derived from corn. However, nuclear power already provides cost-effective power around the world. While nuclear waste is an issue, it can be contained and buried deep in the ground whereas the pollution from the burning of fossil fuels harms the environment even as it kills hundreds of thousands each year.

While nuclear energy may not be the only solution, it is a practical one. Nuclear power plants have the capability of not only generating electricity but of powering systems that extract hydrogen fuel from water—which would provide a good replacement for gasoline.

Here, the challenges are not technological or cost-based. Rather, the chief obstacles to nuclear power are political. After 9/11 and five years of the War on Terror, it's time to change our thinking about the cost of business as usual: petrodollars funding worldwide Islamic radicalism, oppression of women, and persecution of gays and minorities, Western economies held hostage to the whims and turbulence of radical regimes, and thousands dead and hundreds of billions spent in two Gulf wars and the war in Afghanistan. The stakes could not be higher, and human rights activists, foreign policy hawks, economic conservatives, and environmentalists can all achieve their goals if they can stand to work together.

AN ANTITERRORISM "TO DO" LIST

That all sounds great as a long-term project, but what can I do today to fight terrorism and radicalism?

Well, there are a few things. First of all, conserve energy—get yourself a home solar energy system or a hybrid car—but understand that any conservation efforts we make in the West will be offset in a few years by increased demand in the developing world. Thus, save a watt, by all means, but do it while bugging your local, state, and federal politicians for an energy plan that doesn't just call for *reduced* emissions and *reduced* dependence on foreign oil, but *zero* emissions and *zero* energy imports. This is a reasonable goal that could be accomplished in a few decades with off-the-shelf technology. The biggest obstacle is political will. Keep the pressure on.

There's also a "Divest from Terror" movement that is based on the divesture model created by antiapartheid activists in the 1980s who were protesting the racial segregation in South Africa. Check out the Web site www.DivestTerror.org. According to its Web site, "Divest-Terror.org is a nationwide campaign aimed at some 400 public companies worldwide that are providing revenues, technology and moral cover to governments that sponsor terrorism. The primary objective of this campaign is to force governments to choose between their sponsorship of terrorism and critical partnerships with publicly traded firms."[257]

Ultimately, the first line of defense against a dangerous ideology is the truth. We've spent quite a bit of time together developing our Radical Eye. During the time it took you to read this book, you probably saw the hidden signs of radicals and radicalism (the water towers we talked about in the beginning of the book) when you read the newspaper or watched the news. Use your Radical Eye, and spread the word. Simply recognizing and speaking the truth is the first step toward progress.

Will the truth make some people, especially Muslims, uncomfortable? Certainly, and we should sympathize, just as we should sympathize with the German schoolchildren as they study their own history and World War II. However, we need to remember that Germany didn't build a liberal, tolerant society by pretending WWII and the Holocaust didn't happen, or that the Nazis were really paragons of tolerance. The truth helped remake Germany and Japan after the war. It can help in the fight against radical Islam as well. It certainly can't hurt.

Chapter Ten

AN ISLAMIC MAKEOVER

Or, Radical Eye for the Infidel Guy

Islam is both a religion and a *complete way of life*.
—CAIR Web site

So far, we have taken a look at Islamic radicalism from a number of different perspectives: from the point of view of war and peace, women's rights, criminal justice, education, tolerance, and even economics. We've developed a Radical Eye that reveals extremism in places as varied as news reports about the latest terrorist attack and seemingly innocuous statements by "moderate" groups.

Based on what we've seen, radical Islam can look pretty dark, but some of you may nonetheless be wondering if it might be for you. In Europe, the radicalization of secular Muslims is a growing concern. Nonreligious Muslim immigrants come to the Continent and get radicalized, and the children of secular or moderate Muslim parents all too often fall under the spell of militancy. Part of the reason may be that the dominion over women that goes with radical Islam is attractive to young Muslim men who don't immediately succeed in European countries.

ARE YOU A RADICAL?

Take the following quiz to determine how radical you really are:

1. Do you want to marry:
   a. A woman just like the one who married dear old dad.
   b. A woman who shares your faith and deeply held values.
   c. A woman who challenges you intellectually and has a good sense of humor.
   d. Seventy-two women with renewable virginities.

2. When you see a diverse group of non-Muslims sitting in a pizza parlor, are you most likely to:
   a. Engage them in a lively interfaith dialogue.
   b. Join them in a delicious snack.
   c. Scope out the babes.
   d. Blow them up using a combination of homebrew explosives and densely packed nails.

3. If a close friend or loved one referred to you as "the bomb," would he most likely be referring to:
   a. Your remarkable and exemplary personal characteristics.
   b. Your infectious and explosive laughter.
   c. Your inability to properly digest some foods, most notably legumes.
   d. The high-explosive belt tied around your waist.

4. When you meet a Christian or Jewish guy on the street, are you most likely to:
   a. Smile and wish him well.
   b. Tell him the one about the priest, the rabbi, and the Presbyterian minister.

    c.   Tolerate him.

    d.   Kill him where you find him.

5. Are you most likely to describe your infidel roommate as:

    a.   A hog with the TV remote.

    b.   A stoner who plays loud music all night long.

    c.   A guy who knows *way* too much about *Buffy the Vampire Slayer*.

    d.   A brother to pigs and apes.

6. If you found your girlfriend kissing another boy, would you:

    a.   Confront her immediately and tell her you think *she* is the one who's being immature.

    b.   Cry like a baby and beg her to come to her senses.

    c.   Wait until later and end the relationship with dignity.

    d.   Bury her in the ground up to her chest and invite the entire community to pelt her with rocks.

7. If you won a slave girl in battle would you most likely:

    a.   Free her immediately because you think slavery is an inhumane institution.

    b.   Get to know her as a person.

    c.   Offer her a chance to win her freedom in a round of Yahtzee.

    d.   Recognize her as a gift from Allah and take her to your bed.

8. Do you think Jessica Simpson is:

    a.   A great talent.

    b.   An amusing and harmless cultural icon.

    c.   Hot.

    d.   A harlot worthy of death because of her revealing clothing.

9. As per the Qur'an, in the afterlife, do you think infidels will:
    a. Suffer an awful doom (2:6, 2:114, 3:176, 14:2, 16.94, 35:7, 41:27–28).
    b. Suffer a *painful* doom (2:104, 3:21, 3:87–88, 3:91, 3:177, 4:18, 4:150–51, 4:160–61, 5:36, 5:73, 6:70, 9:3, 9:34, 9:74, 9:90, 10:4, 17:10, 22:25, 25:37, 26:201, 29:23, 29:23, 37:31–38, 45:7–8, 45:11, 58:4, 64:5, 67:28, 84:22–24).
    c. Have their bellies eaten with fire (2:174).
    d. Have a boiling drink *and* a painful doom (10:4).
    e. Burn forever in the fire (2:217, 2:257).
    f. Have their skin burned off, replaced with new skin, and burned off again (4:56).
    g. Have their faces showered with molten lead (18:29).
    h. Be forced to wear garments of fire as boiling liquid is poured down on their heads (22:19).
    i. Be tortured with iron hooks (22:21).
    j. All of the above.

10. When you heard that thousands of innocent people were killed on 9/11, did you:
    a. Mourn the senseless loss.
    b. Become angry at the cowardly viciousness of the attack.
    c. Pray for the victims and their families.
    d. Celebrate in the streets.

* * *

Scoring

Count up the number of times you chose options "d" or "j." Use the following key to decide where you fall on the radical scale.

10 out of 10:	You are Osama bin Laden.
9 out of 10:	You are the current ayatollah of Iran.
8 out of 10:	You are a raving mad radical.
7 out of 10:	You are a barking mad radical.
1 to 6 out of 10:	Under "radical" in the dictionary, there is a picture of you.
0 out of 10:	You are not a radical.

Often, high unemployment for young European Muslims is blamed for their radicalization. However, despite the persistence of the mythical connection between poverty and Islamic radicalism, there is no evidence of a clear connection between the two. Again, Osama bin Laden, the 9/11 hijackers, and the British subway bombers were middle class or actually wealthy and generally better educated than most Muslims, as are most suicide bombers.

Part of the problem is that radicals can legitimately claim to have Islam's holy texts on their side, so their ideology is appealing to people looking for simple answers to the questions raised by the complexity of modern life in the West.

So let's assume that you want to look into the radical "lifestyle." The first step is to take your newly developed Radical Eye and turn it inward to see where you fall on the radicalization scale.

You may recall in the introduction that I discussed my wife's friend, who wondered if things would go easier in the world "if we all just converted to Islam." Well, let's imagine for a moment what it would be like if you not only converted to Islam but to Osama bin Laden's particular brand of radical Islam.

Let's say that you are an average American man with a wife and two teenage children, one son and one daughter. You're currently very low on the radicalization scale, but you are interested in converting to militant Islam. What you need is a radical makeover. Welcome to *Radical Eye for the Infidel Guy*. We have assembled a team of experts to ease your transition from a member of a decadent Western culture to a radical who has fully embraced the seventh-century values of fundamentalist Islam.

The first step will be to take care of your religious life and get you fully immersed in Islam. Your spiritual makeover expert—we'll call him Ahkmed—will assist you in finding a local radical mosque. Fortunately, since bin Laden's friends, the Wahhabists, build more mosques than any other branch of Islam, this should not be much trouble, particularly if you live near a big city. The mosque will be able to provide you with numerous pamphlets and publications about Islam, many of which will give lots of details on why it's important to hate Jews and Christians and how to live as a pious Muslim among the decadent infidels. Once the women in your family have been made presentable, they will accompany you to the mosque. If you're lucky, you'll find a mosque that completely segregates men and women. However, keeping the women in the very back of the mosque (for "protection") is an acceptable compromise.

Your religious adviser will provide you with a copy of the Qur'an and a collection of the Hadith. You will study both, but it is very important to memorize the Qur'an so you will always have its wisdom available to you. A careful study of the Hadith will help you apply what you have learned in the Qur'an according to the example of the Prophet. This is particularly useful on matters of Islamic holy law, family life, and "slave management."

Your professional and financial counselor, Akeem, will help you manage your work and business. Assuming you're a midlevel executive or manager in a corporation, you can probably keep your job as long as you're able to leave five times a day to go to prayers. As for finance, of course, you'll immediately have to remove any money from banks that pay or charge interest, or *riba*. Naturally, you'll also have to pay off any outstanding loans, including your mortgage.

Now that you are on the road to radical religious enlightenment and have your business in order, it's time to make some changes at home. Your radical interior design expert is Mohammad. He will make sure that your home is fundamentalist Islam-friendly. The first step will be to toss out any family photos or artwork—anything that shows an image of people or any living thing like an animal or a plant. You can replace art and photographs with approved decorative arts—that is, various *nonrepresentative* shapes and patterns.

The television and your DVD and CD collections will have to go, as well as any books that are not specifically Wahhabist approved. Fortunately, from this point forward, the Qur'an and the Hadith will be the only reading material you will really need. Of course, all of these rules apply to the children as well, so that means all posters of movie stars and pop idols will have to come down.

Some teenagers will resist at first as they can be particularly attached to their music, but you will simply explain to them that it's either keeping their music or having their skin burned off, regenerated, and burned off again for eternity while they are fed a boiling drink, poked with iron hooks, and have their faces showered with molten lead.

Next, it's time for your personal appearance and grooming expert—we'll call him Ali—to help get you and your family looking their radical best. You and your son will start growing those nice long beards and will have to wear loose slacks and oversized shirts that properly hide the human form. Fashion guidelines are a bit stricter for your wife and your daughter. They will have to dress very modestly and start wearing a large, black, Saudi-style robe called an *abaya*. On their heads, they will wear the *hijab*, or headscarf that will completely cover the head, hair, and neck. In addition, they will wear a *burqa*, which is basically a tent that completely covers the head and face (be sure to get ones that are extra long). Ideally, they would wear a screen over their eyes, but since you'll be living in the West, you might want to loosen things up a bit and allow them to leave a small uncovered strip over their eyes for improved vision.

By now, the house is free of satanic Western art, music, books, and the family is properly attired. Now it's time to focus on making important changes in the women of the family. For that, we turn to your female management expert, Yusef. Unfortunately, your teenage daughter will probably have to go. If she's so much as kissed a boy, she's already nearly irrevocably damaged your honor. The good news is that you can undo most of the damage by simply killing her. This can be a sticking point for some families as parents are almost inexplicably attached to their female offspring, but you are on the road to enlightenment, and you can't make an omelet without breaking a few eggs.

Once your daughter is sorted out, it's time to turn your attention to your wife. Of course, she'll have to quit her job and give up her driver's license. From this point forward, she won't be able to leave the house unless she's escorted by you or your son. All forms of travel are out for her, as is shopping in areas where she might come into contact with men, such as supermarket and department store clerks. On the plus side, she will get additional satisfaction from focusing on what's most important: cooking and cleaning for you, and making sure that your new radical household runs smoothly. You can make this easier for her by insuring that she never leaves that household.

For women, this transition can be tricky and can take days, or in some cases even weeks. Be prepared to give her this time. Then, when she has adjusted to her new life, you can think seriously about taking another wife. Technically, of course, polygamy is against the law in the United States and all other Western countries, but those are the immoral, secular laws of the infidel. You now answer to a higher authority—and the eternal and uncreated word of Allah says you can have as many as four wives.

The first place to look for a new wife will be right in your own family, particularly cousins on your father's side. Don't worry too much about whether a girl is above the legal age of consent. Remember that the Ayatollah Khomeini said that marriage to a pre-adolescent girl is "a blessing." Again, you might be in violation of one or more state and local laws here, so remember to be discreet and keep any such marriages on the down low.

Now that your spiritual, professional, and family life are all in order, it's time to give something back to the radical faith that has given you so much. I'm talking, of course, about waging jihad and properly defending Islam against the infidel. Your jihad-counselor—we'll call him Osama—can be a great help here. For many new radical converts, the temptation is to jump right into blowing themselves up, killing a bunch of Jews and Christians, and taking the final reward in Paradise with seventy-two virgins. This is fine as a long-term goal, but let's not get ahead of ourselves. First things first.

You have an obligation to tell your infidel neighbors and coworkers about Islam to give them an opportunity to come to the religion of their own free will. If you do so successfully, you will be helping to spread the word and law of Allah on earth peacefully. This method has the advantage of not being as messy as suicide bombing and doesn't give people the ridiculous idea that your new faith isn't peaceful.

However, on the off chance that the infidels don't immediately see the wisdom of the righteous path you are offering them, you are not only within your rights but have an obligation to wage war on them. Some people have a problem with this, but remember that Qur'an 2:216 says: "Warfare is ordained for you, though it is hateful unto you; but it may happen that ye hate a thing which is good for you."

Remember, suicide bombing is only one road to jihad. There are a number of ways you can contribute in the planning and execution of military operations against your neighbors. After all, it took more than just the nineteen hijackers to make 9/11 happen. Get to know the people in your Wahhabist mosque. With luck, you'll be able to find some like-minded spirits, and you'll be well on your way to crushing the infidel.

Ladies and gentlemen, I give you a radical Islamic makeover.

For some of you, the radical lifestyle may simply not work. As an alternative, I suggest we fight and win the war on radicalism on all fronts, including the cultural front line. This is what I'll be doing because, personally, I find my wife much easier to live with if I let her out of the house once in a while.

NOTES

1. Dennis Miller, "Border Disorders," September 7, 2003, http://www.foxnews.com/story/0,2933,96602,00.html (accessed January 9, 2007).

2. Human Rights Watch World Report 1999: Iraq Human Rights Developments, http://www.hrw.org/worldreport99/mideast/iraq.html (accessed January 8, 2007).

3. Abdel Rahman al-Rashed, "Innocent Religion Is Now a Message of Hate," *Daily Telegraph,* September 5, 2004.

4. *Sahih Muslim*, book 19, number 4294.

5. Michael Skube, "Either You Are a Believer or an Infidel," *Washington Post*, October 20, 2001.

6. Paul Fregosi, *Jihad in the West: Muslim Conquests from the 7th to the 21st Centuries* (Amherst, NY: Prometheus Books, 1998), p. 63.

7. Ibn Warraq, *What the Koran Really Says* (Amherst, NY: Prometheus Books, 2002), p. 121.

8. Ibid., p. 120.

9. Bernard Lewis, *The Middle East: A Brief History of the Last 2,000 Years* (New York: Scribner, 1995), p. 53.

10. "About Islam and American Muslims," http://www.cair-net.org, 2005.

11. Fregosi, *Jihad in the West,* p. 59.

12. Adil Salahi, "The Prophet as a Man—29: Perfect Role Model in All Situations," March 25, 2005, http://www.arabnews.com/?page=5&section=0&article=61031&d=29&m=3&y=2005 (accessed January 9, 2007).

13. "London Islamist Dr. Hani Al-Sibaai Justifies Slaughters in Iraq: The Prophet Muhammad Used to Slaughter as Well," February 22, 2005, http://www.memritv.org/search.asp?ACT=S9&P1=576 (accessed January 9, 2007).

14. Fregosi, *Jihad in the West*, p. 46.

15. "Bad Dreams: Exploitation and Abuse of Migrant Workers in Saudi Arabia," July 2004, http://www.hrw.org/reports/2004/saudi0704/ (accessed January 9, 2007).

16. "Saudi Telethon Host Calls for Enslaving Jewish Women," April 26, 2002, http://www.nationalreview.com/document/document042602.asp (accessed January 9, 2007).

17. Bat Ye'or, *Islam and Dhimmitude: Where Civilizations Collide*, trans. Miriam Kochan and David Littman (Madison, NJ: Fairleigh Dickinson University Press, 2002), pp. 40–41. Please note that Bat Ye'or uses Richard Bell's translation of the Qur'an.

18. "Speech Meant to Tell Real Meaning of 'Jihad,'" June 6, 2002, http://archives.cnn.com/2002/US/06/06/american.jihad.cnna/index.html (accessed January 9, 2007).

19. Lewis, *The Middle East*, p. 233.

20. Wolfgang Bruno, "The Stages of Jihad," http://www.faithfreedom.org/oped/WolfgangBruno50318.htm (accessed January 9, 2007).

21. "Britain's Online Imam Declares War as He Calls Young to Jihad," January 17, 2005, http://www.timesonline.co.uk/article/0,,2-1443903,00.html (accessed January 9, 2007).

22. I pulled most of this information from Paul Fregosi's *Jihad in the West*, about which I really can't say enough good things.

23. Lewis, *The Middle East*, p. 233.

24. "Friday Sermons in Saudi Mosques: Review and Analysis," September 26, 2002, http://www.memri.org/bin/articles.cgi?Area=sr&ID=SR01002 (accessed January 9, 2007).

25. Steven Stalinsky and Y. Yehoshua, "Muslim Clerics on the Religious Rulings Regarding Wife-Beating," March 22, 2004, http://www.memri.org/bin/articles.cgi?Area=sr&ID=SR2704 (accessed January 9, 2007).

26. "Death Sought in Pakistan Gang Rape," July 17, 2002, http://www.cbsnews.com/stories/2002/07/02/world/main514039.shtml (accessed January 9, 2007).

27. James Rupert, "Report from Pakistan, Pakistani Women: A Cruel Repression," *New York Newsday,* March 29, 2005.

28. Molly Moore, "In Turkey, 'Honor Killing' Follows Families to Cities," *Washington Post,* August 8, 2001.

29. Rupert, "Report from Pakistan, Pakistani Women."

30. Amir Taheri, "Islamic Headgear Is Not Essential," August 19, 2003, http://www.townhall.com/columnists/GuestColumns/Taheri20030819.shtml (accessed January 27, 2005).

31. Amir Taheri, "Censoring the Olympics," *New York Post*, January 27, 2005.

32. Bruce Bawer, "Tolerating Intolerance: The Challenge of Fundamentalist Islam in Western Europe," *Partisan Review* 69, no. 3 (2002), http://www.bu.edu/partisanreview/archive/2002/3/bawer.html (accessed January 9, 2007), and Daniel Pipes and Lars Hedegaard, "Something Rotten in Denmark?" *New York Post*, August 27, 2002.

33. Bruce Bawer, "Tolerating Intolerance: The Challenge of Fundamentalist Islam in Western Europe," Partisan Review, http://www.partisanreview.org/archive/2002/3/bawer.html (accessed January 7, 2007).

34. Miranda Devine, "Racist Rapes: Finally the Truth Comes Out," July 14, 2002, http://www.smh.com.au/articles/2002/07/13/1026185124700.html (accessed January 9, 2007).

35. Sarah Lyall, "Lost in Sweden: A Kurdish Daughter Is Sacrificed," *New York Times,* July 23, 2002.

36. Ralphael Patai, *The Arab Mind* (New York: Hatherleigh Press, 2002), p. 29.

37. Ibid.

38. "Saudi Court: The Value of One Woman's Life is Equal to That of One Man's Leg," February 4, 2005, http://www.jihadwatch.org/dhimmiwatch/archives/004920.php (accessed January 9, 2007).

39. "Female Genital Mutilation: A Fact Sheet," August 25, 2005, http://www.amnestyusa.org/women/pdf/fgm.pdf (accessed January 9, 2007).

40. "The Egyptian Controversy Over Circumcising Girls," November 7, 2003, http://www.memri.org/bin/articles.cgi?Area=ia&ID=IA15203 (accessed January 9, 2007).

41. Patai, *The Arab Mind*, p. 32.

42. "Arab Development: Self-Doomed to Failure," July 4, 2002, http://www.economist.com/displaystory.cfm?story_id=1213392 (accessed January 9, 2007).

43. Donna Abu-Nasr, "The Veiled Life of Saudi Women," *Washingon Post,* December 8, 2000.

44. "Saudi Arabia: Religious Police Role in School Fire Criticized," March 15, 2002, http://www.hrw.org/english/docs/2002/03/15/saudia3801 .htm (accessed January 9, 2007).

45. "Women and Girls in Afghanistan," March 10, 1998, http://www .state.gov/www/global/women/fs_980310_women_afghan.html (accessed January 9, 2007).

46. Sarah Kershaw, "Saudi Arabia Awakes to the Perils of Inbreeding," *New York Times,* May 1, 2003.

47. Patai, *The Arab Mind*, p. 37.

48. Brian Carnell, "United Nations Highlight Problems of Child Marriage," May 16, 2001, http://www.equityfeminism.com/archives/years/2001/ 000063.html (accessed January 9, 2007).

49. "Refuge," http://www.immihelp.com/misc/glossary.html (accessed January 9, 2007).

50. Eleanor Evans, "Learning about Islam," http://www.edailynews .info/articles/2005/02/18/news/news06.txt (accessed January 9, 2007).

51. Tarkek el-Tablawy, "Woman Leads Muslim Prayer Service in NY," *Newsday*, March 19, 2005, and Robert Polner, "Prayers and Protest," *Newsday*, March 19, 2005.

52. Robert Spencer, "Khomeini in Dearborn," November 17, 2004, http://www.frontpagemag.com/Articles/ReadArticle.asp?ID=15983 (accessed January 9, 2007).

53. Ibid.

54. Lewis, *The Middle East*, p. 138.

55. Dr. Andrew G. Bostom, "The Living Legacy of Jihad Slavery," April 12, 2005, http://www.americanthinker.com/2005/04/the_living_legacy _of_jihad_sla.html (accessed January 9, 2007).

56. Hilary Andersson, "Born to Be a Slave in Niger," February 11, 2005, http://news.bbc.co.uk/1/hi/programmes/from_our_own_correspondent/ 4250709.stm (accessed January 9, 2007).

57. "Death Penalty in Iran 'Vice' Case," December 22, 2004, http:// news.bbc.co.uk/2/hi/middle_east/4118727.stm (accessed January 9, 2007).

58. "Punishment for Non-Marital Sex in Islam," September 18, 2002, http://www.religioustolerance.org/isl_adul1.htm (accessed January 9, 2007). Most of the information in this listing comes from this article, though the

story about the odd history of stoning and the Qur'an comes from Paul Fregosi's *Jihad in the West*, p. 63.

59. "Afghan Christian Convert Flees to Italy," March 29, 2006, http://www.foxnews.com/story/0,2933,189440,00.html (accessed January 9, 2007).

60. "Iran Adamant Over Rushdie Fatwa," February 12, 2005, http://news.bbc.co.uk/2/hi/middle_east/4260599.stm (accessed January 9, 2007).

61. "Muslim Apostates Cast Out and at Risk from Faith and Family," February 5, 2005, http://www.timesonline.co.uk/article/0,,2-1470584,00.html (accessed January 9, 2007).

62. "Indonesia Seeks to Save Kissing for Marriage," February 5, 2005, http://www.int.iol.co.za/index.php?set_id=1&click_id=3&art_id=qw110760 3540334B253 (accessed January 9, 2007).

63. Edward Won, "Leading Shiite Clerics Pushing Islamic Constitution in Iraq," *New York Times*, February 6, 2005.

64. "Canada Weighs Using Muslim Law," September 17, 2004, http://www.foxnews.com/story/0,2933,131715,00.html (accessed December 14, 2006).

65. Ibid.

66. "Ontario Must Say 'No' to Islamic Law," February 2, 2005, http://www.csmonitor.com/2005/0202/p09s01-coop.html (accessed January 9, 2007).

67. Daveed Gartenstein-Ross, "When Muslims Convert," February 18, 2005, http://www.commentarymagazine.com/cm/main/viewArticle.aip?aid =11902068_1 (accessed February 18, 2005).

68. "Ontario Rejects Use of Islamic Law," September 12, 2005, http://www.foxnews.com/story/0,2933,169125,00.html (accessed January 9, 2007).

69. Fregosi, *Jihad in the West*, p. 68.

70. Ibid., pp. 66–68. I used Fregosi for much of this list with additions from the Qur'an and the Hadith.

71. Ibid., p. 75.

72. Ibid., pp. 80–85.

73. Ibid., p. 93.

74. Ibid., p. 124.

75. Ibid., p. 105.

76. Ibid., p. 113.

77. Victor Davis Hanson, *Carnage and Culture: Landmark Battles in the Rise of Western Power* (New York: Anchor Books, 2001), pp. 140–41.

78. Fregosi, *Jihad in the West*, p. 132.

79. Lewis, *The Middle East*, p. 233.

80. Thomas F. Madden, "Crusade Propaganda," November 2, 2001, http://www.nationalreview.com/comment/comment-madden110201.shtml (accessed January 9, 2007).

81. Lewis, *The Middle East*, p. 97.

82. Fregosi, *Jihad in the West*, p. 210.

83. Edward Creasy, *History of the Ottoman Turks* (Beirut: American University of Beirut Press, 1961), p. 15.

84. Fregosi, *Jihad in the West*, p. 210.

85. Ibid., p. 220.

86. Ibid., p. 214.

87. Lewis, *The Middle East*, p. 107.

88. Fregosi, *Jihad in the West*, p. 224.

89. For this piece I used three sources: Paul Fregosi's *Jihad in the West*, Edward Creasy's *History of the Ottoman Turks*, and "The Ottoman Sultans and Caliphs, 1290–1924 AD," http://www.friesian.com/turkia.htm (accessed January 9, 2007).

90. Fregosi, *Jihad in the West*, p. 228.

91. Ibid., p. 242.

92. Creasy, *History of the Ottoman Turks*, p. 166.

93. Fregosi, *Jihad in the West*, pp. 250–59.

94. Ibid., p. 260.

95. Ibid., p. 262.

96. Ibid., p. 283.

97. Hanson, *Carnage and Culture*, p. 246.

98. Ibid., p. 234.

99. Fregosi, *Jihad in the West*, p. 237.

100. Hanson, *Carnage and Culture*, p. 239.

101. Ibid., p. 255.

102. Fregosi, *Jihad in the West*, p. 345.

103. Ibid., p. 346.

104. Ibid., p. 347.

105. Lewis, *The Middle East*, pp. 276 and 115.

106. Creasy, *History of the Ottoman Turks*, p. 294.

107. Lewis, *The Middle East*, p. 277.

108. Most of this material comes from Paul Fregosi's *Jihad in the West* with additional information from Edward Creasy's *History of the Ottoman Turks*. Here are the page references for specific quotes from Fregosi:

"The first major Arab naval enterprise". . . . p. 80
"The dying or rotting corpses of dissidents". . . . p. 127
"Marked by much fighting". . . . p. 132
"Most of the leading citizens". . . . p. 151
"The greatest provider of laborers for the work force". . . . p. 289
"Raped, cowed and abducted". . . . p. 290

109. Fregosi, *Jihad in the West*, p. 151.

110. Lewis, *The Middle East*, p. 274.

111. Ye-or, *Islam and Dhimmitude*, p. 81.

112. "Saudi Publications on Hate Ideology Fill American Mosques," 2005, http://www.freedomhouse.org/religion/publications/Saudi%20Report/FINAL%20FINAL.pdf (accessed January 9, 2007).

113. Sebnem Arsu, "If You Want a Film to Fly, Make Americans the Heavies," *New York Times*, February 14, 2006.

114. Clark Boyd, "The Price Paid for Blogging Iran," February 21, 2005, http://news.bbc.co.uk/1/hi/technology/4283231.stm (accessed January 9, 2007).

115. This material, as well as the accounts of the fates of the writers Abu Afak and Cab, are from Fregosi, *Jihad in the West*, pp. 43–44.

116. Lewis, *The Middle East*, p. 256.

117. Ye-or, *Islam and Dhimmitude*, p. 37.

118. Ibid., pp. 40–41. Again, please note that Bat Ye'or uses Richard Bell's translation of the Qur'an.

119. Ibid., p. 88.

120. Fregosi, *Jihad in the West*, p. 217.

121. Lewis, *The Middle East,*, p. 109.

122. Ye'or, *Islam and Dhimmitude*, p. 60.

123. Fregosi, *Jihad in the West*, p. 218.

124. Creasy, *History of the Ottoman Turks*, p. 13.

125. Ye'or, *Islam and Dhimmitude*, pp. 60–61.

126. Ibid., p. 88.

127. Ibid., p. 65.

128. Ibid., pp. 68–69.

129. Ibid., p. 69.

130. Ibid., p. 72.

131. Ibid., p. 73.

132. Ibid., p. 70.

133. Ibid., pp. 90–91.

134. Most of the rules governing infidels, unless otherwise noted, come from Robert Spencer, "What Jihad?" February 28, 2005, http://www.frontpage mag.com/Articles/ReadArticle.asp?ID=17153 (accessed January 9, 2007).

135. Ye'or, *Islam and Dhimmitude*, p. 91.

136. *Saudi Publications on Hate Ideology Fill American Mosques*, pp. 24–25.

137. Sandro Magister, "Mission Impossible: Building a Church in Turkey," December 28, 2004, http://www.chiesa.espressonline.it/dettaglio .jsp?id=21393&eng=y (accessed January 9, 2007).

138. For this piece, I used *Islam and Dhimmitude: Where Civilizations Collide* by Bat Ye'or, *Jihad in the West* by Paul Fregosi, and the article "What Jihad?" by Robert Spencer.

139. Ye'or, *Islam and Dhimmitude*, p. 95.

140. Bishop Joesph Coutts, "Pakistan: Fear of the Holy," October 12, 2006, http://www.compassdirect.org/en/display.php?page=news&lang=en &length=long&idelement=4580 (accessed January 7, 2007).

141. Ye'or, *Islam and Dhimmitude*, p. 90.

142. Darryn Simmons, "Entertainment Media's Muslims Bear Little Resemblance to Reality," February 18, 2005, http://www.montgomeryadvertiser .com/NEWSV5/storyV5Islam18w.htm (accessed February 22, 2005).

143. Terry Eastland, "Speaking the Truth about Saudi Arabia," October 11, 2004, http://www.foxnews.com/story/0,2933,134992,00.html (accessed January 9, 2007).

144. Stephen Schwartz, *The Two Faces of Islam: The House of Sa'ud from Tradition to Terror* (New York: Doubleday, 2002), p. 266.

145. Ibid., p. 275.

146. All of this information on Palestinian gays comes from Paul Varnell, "Israel, Palestine, and Gays," *Chicago Free Press,* August 28, 2002.

147. "Muslim Group Targets Poster Nudity," January 22, 2005, http:// www.timesonline.co.uk/article/0,,2-1451224,00.html (accessed January 9, 2007).

148. Sonia Phalnikar, "When Freedom Gets the Death Sentence," February 24, 2005, http://www.dw-world.de/dw/article/0,1564,1499191,00.html (accessed January 9, 2007).

149. "Museum Removes Erotic Art after Muslim Anger," February 2, 2005, http://www.uk.yahoo.com/news/notfound.html?uri=%2F050202%2F325%2Ffbmu9.html (accessed March 3. 2005).

150. Roger van Bakel, "Moroccans Beat Up van Gogh's Son, 14," July 28, 2005, http://www.bakelblog.com/nobodys_business/2005/07/moroccans_beat_.html (accessed January 9, 2007).

151. "Wilders in Prison," February 18, 2005, http://www.dutchreport.blogspot.com/2005/02/wilders-in-prison.html (accessed January 9, 2007).

152. Marlise Simons, "Militant Muslims Act to Suppress Dutch Film and Art Show," *New York Times*, January 31, 2005.

153. Marlise Simons, "More Dutch Plan to Emigrate as Muslim Influx Tips Scales,"*New York Times*, February 27, 2005.

154. Ibid.

155. "Pizza Courier 'Targeted' Amsterdam Sex Zone," December 10, 2004, http://www.expatica.com/actual/article.asp?subchannel_id=1&story_id=14924 (accessed January 9, 2007).

156. "Muslim Cartoon Fury Claims Lives," February 6, 2006, http://news.bbc.co.uk/2/hi/south_asia/4684652.stm (acessed January 9, 2007).

157. "Muslims March on Embassy," February 3, 2006, http://news.sky.com/skynews/article/0,,30100-13501917,00.html (accessed January 9, 2007).

158. "Muslim Cartoon Fury Claims Lives."

159. Spencer, "Khomeini in Dearborn."

160. Art Moore, "U.S. Muslim Event Hails Khomeini," December 15, 2004, http://www.worldnetdaily.com/news/article.asp?ARTICLE_ID=41939 (accessed January 9, 2007).

161. Ibid.

162. This quote and the quotes immediately following it are from Robert Spencer's "Khomeini in Dearborn."

163. Creasy, *History of the Ottoman Turks*, p. 310.

164. Fregosi, *Jihad in the West*, p. 351.

165. Lewis, *The Middle East*, p. 277.

166. Creasy, *History of the Ottoman Turks*, p. 321.

167. Lewis, *The Middle East*, p. 279.

168. Creasy, *History of the Ottoman Turks*, p. 415.

169. Fregosi, *Jihad in the West*, p. 364.

170. Ye'or, *Islam and Dhimmitude*, p. 129.

171. Ibid., p. 130.

172. Most of the information for this piece came from Paul Fregosi's *Jihad in the West*, Edward Creasy's *History of the Ottoman Turks*, Bernard Lewis's *The Middle East: A Brief History of the Last 2,000 Years*, as well as various historical references. I note specific quotes and other sources below.

173. Creasy, *History of the Ottoman Turks*, p. 355.

174. Lewis, *The Middle East*, p. 289.

175. Hanson, *Carnage and Culture*, p. 258.

176. Lewis, *The Middle East*, p. 290.

177. "Self-Doomed to Failure," *Economist*, July 4, 2002, and "How the Arabs Compare," *Middle East Quarterly* (Fall 2002).

178. Hanson, *Carnage and Culture*, p. 258.

179. "Frequently Asked Questions About the Armenian Genocide," http://www.Armenian-Genocide.org/genocidefaq.html (accessed April 8, 2005).

180. Ibid.

181. Fregosi, *Jihad in the West*, p. 405.

182. "Frequently Asked Questions About the Armenian Genocide."

183. Schwartz, *The Two Faces of Islam*, p. 71.

184. Ibid., p. 74.

185. Ibid., p. 75.

186. Ibid., pp. 74–75.

187. Ibid., p. 77.

188. Ibid., pp. 105–106.

189. Ye'or, *Islam and Dhimmitude*, p. 214.

190. Patai, *The Arab Mind*, p. 108.

191. Ibid., p. 110.

192. The information on the "Night Journey" is from Paul Fregosi's *Jihad in the West*, p. 67.

193. Lewis, *The Middle East*, pp. 67–70.

194. Ibid.

195. Ibid., p. 71.

196. Hanson, *Carnage and Culture*, p. 270.

197. Mike Evans, "21st Century Terrorism," http://www.eimes.org/21st Century.asp (accessed January 9, 2007).

198. "Police Hold Four 21 July Suspects," July 30, 2005, http://news.bbc.co.uk/2/hi/uk_news/4727975.stm (accessed January 7, 2007).

199. For this piece I used various historical references and two noteworthy articles: "Terrorist Attacks on Americans, 1979–1988," 2001, http://www.pbs.org/wgbh/pages/frontline/shows/target/etc/cron.html (accessed January 9, 2007), and "Why," September 9, 2004, http://www.mudville gazette.com/archives/000327.html (accessed April 8, 2005).

200. "Bombs Found Hidden in Toys—Police," *Australian*, http://www.theaustralian.news.com.au/story/0,20867,20997042-1702,00.html (accessed January 7, 2007).

201. Fraser Nelson, "Outrage as Livingstone Tries to 'Explain' Suicide Bombers," July 21, 2005, http://www.thescotsman.scotsman.com/index.cfm?id=1658982005 (accessed January 9, 2007).

202. Richard Miniter, "Dispelling the CIA-Bin Laden Myth," http://www.foxnews.com/story/0,2933,98115,00.html (accessed January 9, 2007).

203. Schwartz, *The Two Faces of Islam*, p. 247.

204. Craig R. Whitney, "Cat Stevens Gives Support to Call for Death of Rushdie," *New York Times*, May 23, 1989.

205. "al-Taqiyya/Dissimulation," 2005, http://www.al-islam.org/ENCYCLOPEDIA /chapter6b/1.html (accessed January 9, 2007).

206. Fregosi, *Jihad in the West*, p. 84.

207. Ibid., p. 250.

208. Joel Mowbray, "Palestinian Overcount," January 14, 2005, http://www.washtimes.com/op-ed/20050113-091121-5993r.htm (accessed January 9, 2007).

209. "Harakat al-Muqawamah al-Islamiyya," http://www.hamason line.com/ indexx.php?pafe=Hamas/hamas_profile (accessed June 8, 2005).

210. "Palestine Peace Plan Branded Treacherous," December 2, 2003, http://www.asiantribune.com/oldsite/show_news.php?id=8133 (accessed January 9, 2007).

211. "The Saudi Peace Initiative: What Is and Isn't New," March 15, 2002, http://www.theestimate.com/public/031502.html (accessed January 9, 2007).

212. James Bennet, "Palestinian Mob Attacks Pollster Over Study on 'Right of Return,'" *New York Times,* July 14, 2003.

213. Art Moore, "American Islamic Lobby Gets Out the Vote," February 21, 2002, http://www.worldnetdaily.com/news/article.asp?ARTICLE _ID=26545 (accessed January 9, 2007).

214. "About Islam and American Muslims," http://www.cair-net.org/default.asp?Page=aboutIslam (accessed January 9, 2007).

215. Patai, *The Arab Mind*, pp. 358–59.

216. Ibid., p. 297.

217. Jerry Seinfeld, "Chinese People," *I'm Telling You for the Last Time*, Universal Records 1998, ASIN: B00000AFGO (compact disc).

218. Most of the information for this section on the 2002 report came from "How the Arabs Compare: Arab Human Development Report 2002," *Middle East Quarterly* (Fall 2002), and "Self-Doomed to Failure," *Economist*, April 11, 2005.

219. Hanson, *Carnage and Culture*, p. 266.

220. Bryan Pearson, "God Signed the Tsunami," October 1, 2005, http://www.news24.com/News24/World/Tsunami_Disaster/0,,2-10-1777_1645055,00.html (accessed January 9, 2007).

221. Schwartz, *The Two Faces of Islam*, p. 176.

222. "Educators and Parents Protest against the 'Culture of Death' Taught in Saudi Schools," June 11, 2004, http://www.memri.org/bin/articles.cgi?Page=countries&Area=saudiarabia&ID=SP73004 (accessed January 9, 2007).

223. "The Writings of Liberal Saudi Journalist Raid Qusti," February 20, 2004, http://www.memri.org/bin/articles.cgi?Area=saudiarabia&ID=SP66504 (accessed January 9, 2007).

224. Emma Hartley and Julie Henry, "Girls at London Saudi School Are Treated 'As Inferiors,'" May 30, 2004, http://www.telegraph.co.uk/news/main.jhtml?xml=/news/2004/05/30/nsaud30.xml&sSheet=/news/2004/05/30/ixnewstop.html (accessed January 9, 2007).

225. "Trouble in the Holy Land: PA Textbook Calls for Jihad, 'Martyrdom,'" November 15, 2003, http://www.worldnetdaily.com/news/ article.asp?ARTICLE_ID=35632 (accessed January 9, 2007).

226. "Bonn Koran School under Renewed Pressure," February 2, 2005, http://www.expatica.com/actual/article.asp?subchannel_id=26&story_id=16475 (accessed January 9, 2007).

227. Steven Stalinsky, "Preliminary Overview—Saudi Arabia's Education System: Curriculum, Spreading Saudi Education to the World and the Official Saudi Position on Education Policy," December 20, 2002, http://www.memri.org/bin/articles.cgi?Area=sr&ID=SR01202 (January 9, 2007).

228. Christina Bellantoni, "Islamic Groups Hit Curriculum at Saudi School," *Washington Times*, August 2, 2004.

229. Hartley and Henry, "Girls at London Saudi School Are Treated 'As Inferiors.'"

230. Warraq, *What the Koran Really Says*, pp. 115–16.

231. Ibid., p. 109.

232. "Saudi Armed Forces Journal on the Jews: 'The Fabricated Torah, Talmud, and Protocols of the Elders of Zion Command Destruction of All Non-Jews for World Domination,'" August 20, 2004, http://www.memri.org/bin/articles.cgi?Area=sd&ID=SP76804 (accessed January 9, 2007).

233. "Saudis for 4,500 Madrasas in South Asia," September 13, 2004, http://www.indiareacts.com/nati2.asp?recno=2938 (accessed January 9, 2007).

234. "Saudi Publications on Hate Ideology Fill American Mosques," pp. 11–15.

235. "Hate Grows in Brooklyn," February 1, 2005, http://www.nysun.com/article/8565 (accessed January 9, 2007).

236. Arnaud de Borchgrave, "Commentary: Allah Off the Richter Scale," January 4, 2005, http://www.wpherald.com/storyview.php?StoryID=20050104-101947-4978r (accessed January 9, 2007).

237. Susan Sevareid, "Acts Taint Islam Image," *Newsday*, September 5, 2004.

238. Julie Stahl, "Iran Accuses US, Israel of Carrying Out Iraqi Terror Attacks," December 20, 2004, http://www.cnsnews.com/ForeignBureaus/archive/200412/FOR20041220g.html (accessed January 9, 2007).

239. "Leading Egyptian Journalist: The Jews Are Behind Every Disaster or Terrorist Act," April 23, 2004, http://www.memri.org/bin/articles.cgi?Area=sd&ID=SP70004 (accessed January 9, 2007).

240. "Palestinian Security Chief Jibril Rajoub: Israel/Bush May Be Behind Sinai Attacks," October 10, 2005, http://www.memritv.org/Transcript.asp?P1=281 (accessed January 9, 2007).

241. Brit Hume, "Soldiers Stealing Organs," http://www.foxnews.com/story/0,2933,142503,00.html, December 24, 2004 (accessed January 19, 2007).

242. Maha Al-Azar, "US-Based Professor Claims Jews Want to Control Arab World: 'Conspiracy Involves Americans,'" http://www.campus-watch.org/article/id/351 (accessed January 9, 2007).

243. Steven Salinsky, "The Making of a Mid-East Conspiracy: Nicholas Berg Was Not Beheaded," June 11, 2004, http://www.jewishworldreview.com/0604/memri2004_06_11_04.php3?printer_friendly (accessed January 9, 2007).

244. Hassan Hanizadeh, "Al-Jazeera's Psyops," December 2, 2004, http://www.tehrantimes.com/Description.asp?Da=12/2/2004&Cat=14&Num =002 (accessed January 30, 2005).

245. Barton Gellman, "Pop! Went the Tale of the Bubble Gum Spiked with Sex Hormones," *Washington Post*, July 28, 1997.

246. "Saudi Government Daily: Jews Use Teenagers' Blood for 'Purim' Pastries," March 13, 2002, http://www.memri.org/bin/articles.cgi?Area =sd&ID=SP35402 (accessed January 9, 2007), and "Egyptian Government Weekly Magazine on 'The Jews Slaughtering Non-Jews, Draining the Blood, and Using It for Talmudic Religious Rituals,'" August 17, 2004, http://www .memri.org/bin/articles.cgi?Page=archives&Area=sd&ID=SP76304 (accessed January 9, 2007).

247. "Ayatollah Nouri-Hamedani: 'Fight the Jews and Vanquish Them So as to Hasten the Coming of the Hidden Imam,'" April 22, 2005, http:// memri.org/bin/articles.cgi?Page=archives&Area=sd&ID=SP89705 (accessed January 9, 2007).

248. Ashfaq Yusufzai, "Islam Religion of Peace, Justice: Diplomat," April 25, 2005, http://www.dawn.com/2005/04/25/nat22.htm (accessed January 9, 2007).

249. Miranda Devine, "Muslim Cleric: Women Incite Men's Lust with 'Satanic Dress,'" April 24, 2005, http://www.smh.com.au/news/National/ Muslim-cleric-women-incite-mens-lust-with-satanic-dress/2005/04/23/ 1114152362381.html (accessed January 9, 2007).

250. "Protestors Upset British Muslims' Pre-Election Press Conference," http://news.yahoo.com/s/afp/20050419/wl_uk_afp/britainvotemuslim (accessed April 19, 2005).

251. Victor Davis Hanson, "From Manhattan to Baghdad," February 21, 2003, http://www.nationalreview.com/hanson/hanson022103.asp (accessed January 9, 2007).

252. Ibid.

253. Gethin Chamberlain, "Friends Shocked by News of Suicide Bombers," May 2, 2003, http://www.news.scotsman.com/index.cfm?id =498752003 (accessed January 9, 2007), and Anton La Guardia, Said Ghazzali, Ohad Gozani, and Sean O'Neill, "British Bombers Posed as Peace Activists, May 2, 2003, http://www.telegraph.co.uk/news/main.jhtml?xml=/ news/2003/05/02/wbomb02.xml&sSheet=/news/2003/05/02/ixnewstop .html (accessed January 9, 2007).

254. Douglas Adams, *The Hitchhiker's Guide to the Galaxy* (New York: Pocket Books, 1981), p. 28.

255. Steve Malzberg, "Rangel: Don't Call It 'Islamic Terrorism,'" February 22, 2005, http://www.newsmax.com/archives/ic/2005/2/22/102357 .shtml (accessed January 9, 2007).

256. Keith Bradsher and David Barboza, "China's Burning of Coal Casts a Global Cloud," *International Herald Tribune*, June 11, 2006.

257. "Mission Statement," http://www.divestterror.org, August 31, 2006.

FURTHER READING

THE QUR'AN AND THE HADITH:

You can find a Qur'an in most bookstores and there are some excellent online resources including:

www.usc.com, which has multiple translations of the Qur'an as well as a large collection of Hadith.

You can read *The Skeptics Annotated Koran* at www.skepticsannotatedbible.com/quran/.

This is a great way to read the Qur'an because it provides the whole Qur'an in order, as well as breaking it down into some interesting categories like "Women," "Family Values," and "Science and History."

If you're interested in a good book *about* the Qur'an, I strongly recommend Ibn Warraq's *What the Koran Really Says* (Amherst, NY: Prometheus Books, 2002). It's a collection of essays from Qur'anic scholars that examines the Qur'an in its historical, cultural, and literary context.

THE JIHAD

I highly recommend Paul Fregosi's book *Jihad in the West: Muslim Conquests from the 7th to the 21st Centuries* (Amherst, NY: Prometheus Books, 1998). This truly amazing work is an account of the jihad from the earliest days of Islam to today, with a focus on the clash between Islam and the West. Absolutely riveting, it's a comprehensive and very accessible account of the subject.

Jihad Watch, a great Web site run by expert Robert Spencer, can be found at www.jihadwatch.org. It provides articles and links on the state of the jihad and jihadist activity throughout the world. Spencer is the author of a number of excellent books on Islam and is a frequent contributor to FrontPageMag.com. He also runs a sister Web site called www.dhimmiwatch.org that fights "the dhimmi (attitude of chastened subservience [for non-Muslims]," which "has entered into Western academic study of Islam, and from there into journalism, textbooks, and the popular discourse." This site provides some more excellent articles and links to eye-opening news from around the world.

Victor Davis Hanson is an eminent military historian who often brings his considerable knowledge and understanding of military history to bear on the War on Terror. He writes for the *National Review*, and you can find his columns at www.nationalreview.com. I cite his book *Culture and Carnage: Landmark Battles in the Rise of Western Power* (New York: Anchor Books, 2001), which provides some fascinating insight into the clash between the West and the Middle East.

MUSLIM HISTORY AND CULTURE

Bernard Lewis is probably the greatest living Middle Eastern scholar and I found his book *The Middle East: A Brief History of the Last 2,000 Years* (New York: Scribner, 1995) to be a great help. It's a comprehensive look at the pre- and post-Islamic history of the region. He's also written a number of other excellent books, including *What Went Wrong: The Clash Between Islam and Modernity in the Middle East* and *The Crisis of Islam: Holy War and Unholy Terror.*

And finally, I also recommend Raphael Patai's book, *The Arab Mind* (New York: Hatherleigh Press, 2002). The book was originally written in 1972, but the psychological and cultural insights it shares are more relevant than ever. Though most of the world's Muslims are not Arab, the values and norms of seventh-century Arabia as enshrined in some interpretations of Islam are at the heart of the problem with world terrorism.

INDEX

Page numbers in *bold* indicate Qur'anic verses; page numbers in *italic* indicate boxed information